Globalisation and the Rule of Law

Globalisation and the Rule of Law reassesses the idea of the 'rule of law' within the present complex and increasingly internationalised environment. There have been many books studying the phenomenon of globalisation and its economic, social or cultural consequences. This book, however, is the first to relate globalisation exclusively to law. It examines the impact of globalisation upon the rule of law, a fundamental value within liberal democratic sovereign states.

The book opens with three chapters discussing the theory of the rule of law and its necessary reconceptualisation in a global environment. Then, in three parts considering human rights, global trade and security, it proposes new ways of thinking about global law and its application in new and existing institutions of global governance. Its contributors consist of top-flight academics, politicians and judges, making it significant and relevant in both jurisprudential theory and political practice.

Globalisation and the Rule of Law will be of interest to students and researchers of international law and globalisation.

Spencer Zifcak is Associate Professor of Law at La Trobe University, Melbourne, Australia, and Vice-President of the International Commission of Jurists (Australian Section). He has acted as a consultant to the United Nations and a wide range of other parliamentary, governmental and non-governmental organisations.

Routledge/Challenges of globalisation
Edited by Charles Sampford and Haig Patapan
Griffith University, Australia

This series seeks to make systematic contributions to international debates over two intimately related issues:

- The values that should inform the governance of modern states and the globalising world in which they are increasingly enmeshed, in particular whether the liberal democratic values that sought to civilise the sovereign states need to be reconceived as global values.
- The institutions that are needed to realise those values, be they local, national, regional, international, transnational or global.

1 **Globalisation and Equality**
Edited by Keith Horton and Haig Patapan

2 **Globalisation and the Rule of Law**
Edited by Spencer Zifcak

3 **Environmental Values in a Globalising World**
Nature, justice and governance
Edited by Jouni Paavola and Ian Lowe

Globalisation and the Rule of Law

Edited by
Spencer Zifcak

Routledge
Taylor & Francis Group
LONDON AND NEW YORK

First published 2005
by Routledge
2 Park Square, Milton Park, Abingdon, Oxon OX14 4RN

Simultaneously published in the USA and Canada
by Routledge
270 Madison Ave, New York, NY 10016

Transferred to Digital Printing 2005

Routledge is an imprint of the Taylor & Francis Group

Typeset in Baskerville by
Newgen Imaging Systems (P) Ltd, Chennai, India
Printed and bound in Great Britain by
Antony Rowe Ltd, Chippenham, Wiltshire

British Library Cataloguing in Publication Data
A catalogue record for this book is available from the British Library

Library of Congress Cataloging in Publication Data
Globalisation and the Rule of Law / edited by Spencer Zifcak.
p. cm.
Includes bibliographical references and index.
1. Rule of law. 2. Globalisation. I. Title: Globalisation and the Rule of Law. II. Zifcak, Spencer, 1950–

KZ1275.G58 2005
340′.11–dc22 2004009648

ISBN 0–415–32655–9

This book is dedicated to my son, Sam, and all those of his generation, whom I would like to live in a safer world, made more so at least in part by governance under the international rule of law.

Contents

Contributors

Ross P. Buckley is Professor and Executive Director of the Tim Fischer Centre for Global Trade and Finance, Bond University, Queensland, Australia.

Hilary Charlesworth is Professor and Director of the Centre for International and Public Law, Australian National University, Canberra, Australia.

Malcolm Fraser AC, CH was Prime Minister of Australia from 1975–83. He now writes extensively on international and national political affairs.

Michael Kelly is a Lieutenant-Colonel in the Australian Defence Force. He has participated in peacekeeping missions in Kosovo, East Timor, Afghanistan and Iraq.

David Kinley is Professor and Director of the Castan Centre for Human Rights, Monash University, Melbourne, Australia.

Michael Kirby AC, CMG is a Justice of the High Court of Australia. He has held many distinguished international positions including that of UN Special Rapporteur on Cambodia.

Sir Anthony Mason AC, KBE was Chief Justice of the High Court of Australia from 1987–94. Between 1994–99 he was Chancellor of the University of New South Wales, Sydney, Australia.

Charles Sampford is Foundation Dean and Professor of Law, and Foundation Director of the Key Centre for Ethics, Law, Justice and Governance, Griffith University, Brisbane, Australia.

Spencer Zifcak is Associate Professor of Law and Legal Studies at La Trobe University, Melbourne, Australia, and Australian Vice-President of the International Commission of Jurists.

Acknowledgements

In the production of this volume I would like to acknowledge the special contribution of many colleagues and friends.

Professor Charles Sampford had the initial idea for the book and the series of which it forms a part. His collaboration and friendship has been greatly appreciated.

Virginia Berry and Helen Wheatley acted as research associates for the project. Their organisational, editorial and research skills have been remarkable. Without their assistance, the book would not have come to fruition.

Each of the contributors was generous with their time, patience, application and knowledge. Their comments on the volume and individual chapters within it have contributed significantly to its currency and cogency.

The encouragement of my family and friends during the book's writing and editing has been invaluable in providing the emotional support so necessary for its successful completion.

Introduction

Spencer Zifcak

Globalization is the phenomenon of our times. In almost every area of human activity, the international interconnectedness of peoples, institutions, states and systems is increasing exponentially. This applies whether the activities are economic, social, cultural, technological, environmental or political. The issues and problems that arise in each of these spheres are also becoming increasingly global in scale. The huge cross-border flows of peoples, swift and massive movements of capital, the spread of disease, environmental degradation, the widening poverty gap between North and South, the development of terrorist networks, the abuse of human rights and the inter-state arms race are but some of the more notable examples.

These global changes, which we effect and by which we are affected, give pause for thought about whether and how legal values, traditionally held dear within nations, may be preserved and reinstitutionalized in the international arena. If everything is different, so must our thinking be. If everything is more complex and difficult, so too must our knowledge, attitudes and values adapt and progress.

This book is concerned with one of these great values: the rule of law. There is almost no disagreement, anywhere in the world, with the proposition that the rule of law is a good. The problem arises in that value's interpretation and application. This is evident within nations. It is even more apparent globally where its principal institutional manifestation, international law, whether public or private, possesses far less influence and sway. The idea of global law, general in its treatment and equal in its application, is a distant and deeply contested one.

The purpose of this edited collection, then, is to attempt a reconceptualization of the rule of law, as it might apply in the new global context of our times.

The project began as a conference – the Vice-Chancellor's symposium at Griffith University in Brisbane, Australia, 2001. The symposium brought together an extraordinarily distinguished body of speakers and participants – politicians, judges, international lawyers, members of the defence forces and academics. It took place after the events in Kosovo and the disruption of the meeting of the World Trade Organization in Seattle but before the September 11 attacks and the more recent war in Iraq. Each of these events stamped their firm impression on contemporary understandings of international law and justice. As these crises unfolded, the contributors revised and rewrote their contributions to ensure that, as far as possible, the discussions in this volume would continue to be of immediate relevance and interest. As an editor, one could ask no more.

The collection is divided into four parts: three introductory chapters exploring the idea of a globalized rule of law, from theory to practice; and then three further parts discussing the reconceptualization and re-application of this central, legal value in three different, more specialized contexts – human rights, international trade and commerce and international politics and defence.

The first part begins with a chapter by Professor Charles Sampford. Sampford provides a comprehensive, historical and conceptual analysis of the rule of law first at the domestic and then at the international level. He compares and contrasts 'thick' and 'thin' theories of the rule of law and argues that internationally, a thin theory should prevail. In other words, he believes, that a global rule of law should be more formal than substantive. This, he says, is not to deny the importance and relevance of related political ideas and values, such as democracy, equality and human rights. It is simply to say that these should be accorded independent standing and be evaluated separately rather than being rolled into a larger reconception of the rule of law as understood internationally. He then delineates the critical differences between the domestic and global contexts in which the rule of law will be interpreted and applied. Having done so, he concludes his contribution by examining a comprehensive series of arguments that militate against this legal value's materialization in the global arena, providing a persuasive counter-argument to each that paves the way for a sophisticated understanding of how an adapted conception of the 'rule of law' should be made manifest internationally.

In the second chapter, I define the values I believe should underlie the rule of law globally. These are the values of legality, equality, legitimacy, accountability and a commitment to fundamental human rights. This is a somewhat 'thicker' conception than Sampford's in its inclusion of the human rights dimension. This, I suggest, is both historically and conceptually justified. Having delineated these values, I propose a number of important, related, institutional mechanisms in and through which each of these values may be incorporated and implemented. These mechanisms include the creation of relevant constitutions, judicial review, dispute resolution processes, enforcement procedures, and the infusion of human rights principles into the operation of major international regulatory organizations. I then apply this framework by way of example to the governance of the United Nations, the World Trade Organization and the UN Human Rights Treaty Monitoring System.

Justice Michael Kirby brings a wealth of practical knowledge, skill and experience to the problem in the third chapter. He argues that what we in the world are experiencing through internationalization currently is natural to the realities of human and global evolution. Its speed and form may be changing but the process of adaptation is the same. He uses his extensive personal experience of and participation in the development of international law with respect to privacy, self-determination, the fight against AIDS and the resolution of intra-state conflict, among others, to suggest that we ought to be more sanguine than pessimistic about contemporary developments with respect to the international rule of law. The application of international law in the domestic arena, he argues, usually has been for the good. Whether, however, this will remain the case as the international community tackles ever more complex and difficult problems, in particular in relation to economics and trade and the elimination of the abuse of international human rights, remains to be seen.

In the second part of the book, Professors Hilary Charlesworth and David Kinley continue the engagement with the theme of fundamental human rights. Charlesworth accepts that international human rights protection falls properly within the province of the rule of law. This simple acceptance, however, can conceal beneath a formal commitment to observe human rights, a substantive measure of continuing gender inequality. It is critical, then, to include the feminist discourse in any reconceptualization of the rule of law globally. She illustrates her position vividly with examples that concern the implementation, or non-implementation, of the Beijing Declaration and Platform of Action with respect to women's equality; the differential, gendered application and impact of economic and social rights; and the effect of arguments and actions founded upon the cultural relativism of rights. To advance the position of women within a global framework of law, she concludes, requires that acute attention be given to the gendered constitution of international institutions of justice and to enlargement of the category of 'foundational' human rights so as better to accommodate the realities of women's lives and concerns across the globe.

Kinley attacks the enormously complex interaction between global economic development on the one hand and the desire to protect and advance individual human rights on the other. The global liberalization of corporate and commercial endeavors he characterizes broadly in legal terms as 'globalized localism'. In contrast, he describes the universalization of human rights as 'localized globalism'. Sometimes these two trends are complementary. At others, they are clearly in conflict. They are complementary where corporate and commercial progress results in the enhancement of individuals' capacities to meet their needs and make the most of their capabilities. They may conflict where the cost of economic progress is the enlargement of global poverty and inequality with a corresponding reduction in the fulfilment of needs and realization of capabilities in many parts of the globe. Given the complexity, pervasiveness and multiple configurations of these contradictory trends, Kinley concludes that the rule of law, particularly that which embraces a commitment to human rights, may have only a limited role to play in working out the relevant dilemmas. The rule of law alone cannot ensure universal human rights observance. Broader economic, political and social strategies and policies will be of equal if not greater importance.

The book's third part expands our consideration of the rule of law in global economic regulation. Sir Anthony Mason first considers the case for global economic regulation and concludes that it is a strong one. Nevertheless, its implementation in practice is fraught with difficulty, not least because nation states, whether individually or in combination, do not presently possess the power or authority to achieve effective control of international financial transactions and flows. The focus, therefore, must rest upon refining and strengthening the existing international regulatory agencies. Sir Anthony then focuses his attention on the World Trade Organization and North American Free Trade Agreement (NAFTA). He examines their present dispute resolution mechanisms and capabilities and concludes that the primary objective in the achievement of an international rule of law should be to strengthen them and, in the process, to make these organizations, and other international regulatory agencies like them, ever more transparent and accountable.

Professor Ross Buckley tackles the thorny issue of how global capital flows may be regulated legally in the international public interest. He describes the scale of capital flows and observes that capital markets have become integrated and interdependent to an unprecedented degree. Consequently, the task of intervening to regulate these markets, assuming this is thought to be desirable, has become immense. Nevertheless, Buckley proposes four principal options for the regulation of global capital flows, each of which would require significant alteration in the existing international, financial architecture. He explores the merits and demerits of a global bankruptcy court, a global central bank, a global lender of last resort and the imposition of a tax on international financial flows. He then concludes his discussion with a consideration of the measures sovereign nations might take to assist in the regulatory endeavor.

The book's final part is concerned with the rule of law in the context of international peace and security. In his chapter, Australia's former Prime Minister, Malcolm Fraser, provides a sweeping and insightful analysis of the major political crises that have beset the world in the last 5 years. He explores the implications for the international rule of law of NATO's intervention in Kosovo, the September 11 attacks and the recent war in Iraq. He deplores the marginalization of the United Nations in its Charter founded task of securing international peace and security. At the same time, however, he notes that the Security Council has performed less than perfectly in determining whether and when to intervene in circumstances where humanitarian considerations may have required it. He concludes that for all its imperfections, it is to the Security Council that grave international crises should first be referred. The Security Council, in turn, should be reformed and strengthened. Fraser argues further that, in order to entrench the international rule of law, judicial review of Security Council decisions and actions should seriously be considered. Without strengthened accountability, combined with greater international cooperation and support, the entire system for resolving international disputes established since the World War II may well be at risk.

Michael Kelly provides a micro-counterpoint to Fraser's macro-analysis. Kelly draws on his extensive experience in the conduct of international peacekeeping operations to argue that Western military forces, and in this case in particular the Australian Defence Forces, have a critical role to play in the re-establishment of the rule of law in nations fractured by civil war or ruined by political machination. He explores and analyses the military's role in this respect in a number of different contexts: the restoration of the rule of law in the framework of complex peace operations; military support to international criminal tribunals; the protection of human rights; and the fight against international terrorism – a phenomenon that is the very antithesis of the rule of law. He makes a persuasive case that in each of these spheres, military forces that are properly mandated, trained and equipped can provide a critical underpinning for the task of restoring the rule of law in failed states and societies.

This book, in short, provides a comprehensive overview of existing challenges to the rule of law internationally, and provides many pointers to the manner in which law may assume in the future its proper, primary status in the regulation of global activity in the political, social and economic arenas.

Part I

From theory to practice

1 Reconceiving the rule of law for a globalizing world

Charles Sampford

Introduction

Strong sovereign nation states emerged in seventeenth century Europe, sweeping aside the previous untidy patchwork of feudal cities, principalities, and empires that, together with guilds and the church, had governed European life for a millennium. After the Treaty of Westphalia ended the Thirty Years War in 1648, '[a]n international structure composed of a hierarchy of emperor, kings, princes, and cities was replaced with one composed of many formally-independent and formally-equal states'.[1] The nation-state was welcomed as a solution to the chaos that had followed the break-up of the mediaeval order when religious and trade schisms (or religious schisms and trade) had overflowed across traditional boundaries and submerged them.[2] Although these nation states were highly authoritarian, their theoretical champions – writers like Jean Bodin, Jean-Jacques Burlamaqui, Thomas Hobbes, and Samuel Pufendorf – applauded and justified them for that very reason. When life was 'poor, nasty, brutish, and short'[3] due to civil war, banditry or religious zealotry, a rational man [*sic*] would happily choose to submit without complaint to a government strong enough to keep the peace by whatever means necessary. Modest and minimalist as it was, the Westphalian bargain was observed within Europe – both 'horizontally' among different nations' governments and 'vertically' between each government and its citizens – for almost three centuries.[4]

Once life and civil peace were secure, citizens began to expect more from their states. The eighteenth-century North Atlantic Enlightenment[5] sought to civilize these authoritarian states by holding them to a set of more refined and ambitious values – notably liberty, equality, citizenship, human rights, democracy and the rule of law. These values were necessary, not for bare survival, but for comfortable, civilized, and dignified existence.[6] Nineteenth-century thinkers extended the range of rights championed, for example, adding concern for environment and for practical and social equality. By the mid-twentieth century, disputes had moved on to the interpretation and ranking of those rights – especially between civil and political rights and social and economic rights.

Ideals are not self-implementing, especially ideals that aim for a better society. They require institutions to realize them. If the font of new ideas was located in the Atlantic nations of Scotland and France, the centre of gravity for institutional innovation was the eastern seaboard of the United States. Initially, the early European philosophers – apart from a few who wanted to copy English constitutionalism – simply proposed institutions modelled on the monarchical states most familiar to them.[7] Enlightened despotism, of course, requires a despot, so philosophers like Voltaire and Diderot pinned their hopes in turn on Frederick the Great in Prussia, then Peter and Catherine the Great in Russia, and finally Napoleon in France. But these despots and their institutions, too, eventually dissolved into chaos and violence.[8]

While superficially the US Constitution may seem simply to have 'frozen' key elements of the 1776–87 British constitution[9] (as famously misdescribed by Montesquieu),[10] its most distinctive features – federalism, a constitutionally entrenched court, a states' upper house, legislative ratification of treaties, and various other 'checks and balances' – were important innovations, and have often been copied. It was only in the nineteenth century that Europe began generating institutional innovations of its own: responsible parliamentary government, the welfare state, and accountability mechanisms such as the administrative tribunal and the ombudsman.

However, a series of recent trends, popularly labelled 'globalization', have challenged these values, primarily by challenging the power of nation state institutions which are currently the only feasible means for upholding these values. I eschew the two most common responses – (1) abandoning whatever values cannot be realized by global or transnational institutions, (2) clinging to the nation-state as the only possible way of preserving these values. Rather, I advocate a third way, namely reconceiving liberal democratic values, and reinstitutionalizing them for a global world, calls for nothing less than a new enlightenment. Such a global enlightenment should aim to civilize the increasingly harsh global economy, just as the eighteenth-century enlightenment began the process of civilizing the absolutist post-Westphalian states. Of all these values, the rule of law is primary.[11]

So what exactly does the rule of law require within, and among, sovereign states? What are its implications, foreign and domestic? Most writers today agree that the rule of law can be defined widely or narrowly, depending on how many liberal-democratic values are read into the concept. Certainly there are difficulties in applying it to a wider sphere than the nation-state. Indeed, many argue that, therefore, the rule of law cannot meaningfully exist in the international arena, where there is no 'common sovereign power'. But these objections are, at most, only arguments for modifying the concept. Almost all the reasons why we value the domestic rule of law are also reasons for working towards an international rule of law.

The enlightenment and the rule of law

The sovereign nation-state was a response to the chaos of the early seventeenth century. Pre-Elizabethan England and Reformation France caught brief glimpses of that chaos. Germany suffered the full brunt during the Thirty Years War, while England looked into the abyss during its 1640s Civil War almost falling into what Hobbes saw as the ultimate chaos – a state of nature. The only solution was an unquestioned sovereign, a 'Leviathan', powerful enough to impose order on what would otherwise be a factionalized, violent, self-destructive rabble. Hobbes argued that individuals in a state of nature would freely consent to subject themselves unconditionally to such a sovereign power because the alternative was too terrible to contemplate.

The parties to Hobbes' social contract were individuals in the lawless state of nature. The sovereign was established by the social contract, but was not party to it. The sovereign's will would rule and, although it was prudent to express this will in the form of laws proclaimed for the subjects, the law did not bind on the sovereign itself. Hobbes' conception of the law as command left no room for the commander being bound. Locke, however, subsequently insisted that the sovereign was also a party to the contract, and also bound by laws made under it. For him, the supreme ruler was 'bound to govern by established standing laws, promulgated and known to the people'.[12] A sovereign who broke the agreement could be brought to account by his/her subjects, through the people's right to revolt. The enforcement mechanism was much cruder and lacked the sophistication of later means of securing accountability (namely the courts and ballot-box). Nevertheless, it did offer a means of ensuring that government officials, right up to the sovereign itself, obeyed the law (or at least did not flagrantly disregard it).

Late seventeenth-century Europe was governed by many absolute monarchs. Several of them based their legitimacy on having imposed order on chaotic states – none more effectively than Louis XIV. The philosophers of eighteenth-century France were much taken by Locke's analysis, and the rule of law was, arguably, the first enlightenment value they propounded and demanded – looking to England as the model. Official behavior had to conform to rules external to the officials themselves and interpreted by courts not subject to direct sovereign control.

By the end of the eighteenth century, other enlightenment values had been asserted. Some of them demanded that the content of the laws secure individual liberty, equality and the 'Rights of Man'.[13] Enlightenment thinkers also re-examined who should make the laws (namely a democratic assembly) and, most important of all, who comprised the state (all citizens). These largely superseded Locke's right to revolt because it enabled the people to rid themselves of oppressive laws and rulers by lawful, peaceful, and orderly means. It also produced a Feuerbachian reversal of the relationship between the state and its people. Individuals no longer had to justify themselves to the state as loyal and obedient subjects of their sovereigns. Rather, the governments of sovereign states had to justify themselves to their citizens.

This story offers some important parallels and contrasts for contemporary international rule of law. In the late seventeenth century, while modern states were being formed and sovereigns were imposing their will on their subjects, philosophers like Hobbes were devising useful creation myths about social contracts. But externally, states were still in a state of nature with each other.[14] Such international law as existed was a matter of contract and custom rather than binding law. The Treaty of Westphalia was a pact between independent and equal states who recognized themselves as such (and, in one of its most important provisions, recognized the United Dutch Provinces). It also provided one of the key foundations of customary international law.[15]

It is ironic that while Hobbes was telling his tale about individual citizens contracting to create a constitution and laws, their rulers (governments/states) were in fact contracting with each other. International law was almost entirely composed of these contracts – that is, treaties – and it noticeably lacked a constitution. The content of these treaties was limited to the few matters on which trans-state agreement could be reached. They did not set up any sovereign to police them nor did they create enforcement mechanisms to replace self-help (one of the factors Hobbes saw as contributing to the state of nature). Further, the bargaining positions of states were fundamentally different to those of individuals in a state of nature. As H.L.A. Hart emphasized, the conditions that Hume identified for the establishment of laws – relative scarcity of resources, and vulnerability of individual humans – do not exist in international law.[16] However, the relative vulnerability of states and the normal inability of anyone (between Rome and post-Cold War USA) to dominate the rest was a critical factor in the development of such international law. Had one of these states possessed enough power to establish dominion over the others, a different system would have emerged – one of Empire, instead of equal sovereign states subject to weak international law. In Hobbes' day, one power did indeed claim the nominal title of Empire, and an alliance with Spain, enriched by its new colonies, gave the Holy Roman Empire a chance to give the title real power. But the defeat of that alliance (before Italian-inspired fortifications were built by the Dutch) led Spain and the Emperor to accept the Westphalian settlement.[17]

As a result, international law was even more minimalist and incomplete than the minimal states that are today's neo-liberal ideal and were the early enlightenment reality. Many wondered if international law should even be called 'law' – especially as the strength of domestic law of sovereign states increased and became the paradigm for law, and the capacity for enforcement came to be seen as crucial to the definition of law.

International relations and warfare, however, were not subject to the rule of law. Until the twentieth century, their content reflected very few enlightenment values. But that the application of the rule of law, the primary enlightenment value, should extend to international law – it is as urgent now as it was in the new sovereign states of pre-enlightenment Europe. Although it would be highly desirable if the other enlightenment values were also incorporated into international law, the rule of law's inclusion should still be an independent priority to be pursued with utmost vigor. Before making this argument, however, I shall consider the rule of law as a value within sovereign states, that is, the 'domestic rule of law' by way of introduction.

Jurisprudence of the domestic rule of law

Before launching into a reconception of the rule of law for a world largely without strong sovereign states, let us consider the various definitions of the rule of law proposed, in and for, strong sovereign states.

'Rule of laws, not men'

One of the simplest and most enduring versions of the idea of the rule of law centres on an evocative but impossible ideal: 'the rule [or government] of law[s], not the rule of men' (or of women, or indeed of any fallible mortals).[18] Taken literally, this is nonsense. Laws are not and cannot be self-creating or self-enforcing edicts. Unlike the laws of gravity or thermodynamics, they need human beings to create, interpret and enforce them. A more feasible meaning for this ideal is that all humans (especially officials of the state) are subject to law. Sovereign authorities rule through human beings, but the rule of law ensures that the process is, as far as possible, channelled through the means of rule making and attempts at faithful rule implementation. In other words, it ensures that individual citizens have a fair warning before they break a law and a fair hearing afterwards. They are not simply punished without any (or with insufficient) regard to the laws at the time they acted.

Joseph Raz thought that this was crucial to the nature of law itself. He saw law as a two-stage decision-making process, where rules are first made by the legislature and then interpreted by the executive and judiciary. Ideally, the officials applying the law at both stages view themselves as part of an enterprise in which the state has attempted to make rules that guide citizens; therefore, officials conscientiously seek to draw their own reasons for decision from these rules. There are, of course, imperfections in the way rules are made and interpreted, but those who are involved in both stages of the process still endeavor to be true to their ideal function. This does not mean that judges can pretend that the answer is always clearly, unequivocally and uncontroversially found 'in' the rules that have been made at the first stage, nor that there is no creative role. What Raz means is simply this: it is not the judge's role to think, afresh, what the right answer should be, but to find the right answer already determined – or at least bounded – by the rules set down in advance. Judges use these rules as the basis for their decision-making.

This idea is linked to Raz's 'sources' thesis – that all legal rules have sources, and it is at the source of each that the first stage of decision-making occurs. This offers a more realistic revision of the 'rule of laws, not men' formulation: the law comes from a source outside the officials who are applying it. It need not be Divine or natural or otherwise superhuman in origin; it is enough that those who enforce the rules are not the same people that make them.

Another recent reformulation of this enduring ideal is Ronald Cass' idea of 'fidelity' to rules. According to Cass, decision-makers should be faithful both to laws as a whole, and also to the principles and standards contained in them. Indeed, the principles make the rules coherent and allow a judge to act faithfully with law as a whole as opposed to a series of disconnected edicts.[19] Cass' view is very similar to Ronald Dworkin's famous view of 'Law as Integrity', which calls on officials, especially judges, to make every statute and common law rule the 'best it can be'.[20]

Fleshing out the epigram – the 'thin theory' of the rule of law

Despite various attempts to define and elucidate 'rule of law', many prominent theorists – notably Friedrich Hayek, Joseph Raz and Lon Fuller – seem to converge upon the same basic core.

Hayek defines the rule of law as a regime where 'the government in all its actions is bound by rules fixed and announced beforehand – rules which make it possible to foresee with fair certainty how authority will use its coercive powers in given circumstances on the basis of this knowledge'.[21] The problem with this formulation is that quite draconian restrictions would be consistent with this kind of rule of law, as long as fair warning is given ('No-one shall knowingly read, possess or publish The Satanic Verses').[22]

Fuller[23] explains how he arrives at his version the rule of law through the parable of a king ('Rex') whose eight attempts to make laws for his subjects end in such abject failure that they do not even amount to law, because he:

1 tries to make special rules for everyone to suit their particular needs. But this only arouses confusion and anger at differential treatment;
2 fails to publicize them, so nobody knows what laws to follow;
3 makes all his laws retroactive;
4 enacts vague or obscure rules;
5 enacts rules that contradict each other;
6 enacts rules that could not be followed;
7 fails to apply rules consistently;
8 changes his laws so often that his subjects cannot rely on them to plan their decisions.

From this via negativa, Fuller derives eight 'virtues of law'. Ideally, all or most laws should be general, publicized, prospective, clear, non-contradictory, compliable, consistently applied, and reasonably stable. He is not suggesting that a just society can never have any laws that deviate from these virtues, that is, laws that are retroactive, unclear, frequently changed and so on. It is simply that these deviations are the exceptions rather than the rule.

Drawing on Hayek and Fuller, Cass sees the rule of law as involving 'principled predictability'.[24] He emphasizes the importance of:

1 predictability being based on rules;
2 sufficient clarity for predictability;
3 accessibility;
4 reasonableness and cost (clarity and accessibility are not free);
5 generality – so that each law covers many cases (which makes communication easier) and is framed neutrally rather than being directed at particular people.

Unlike some conservative writers on the rule of law (such as Geoffrey de Q Walker),[25] Cass' model neither elevates predictability above every other value, nor suggests that perfect predictability is possible. The point is that unpredictability in laws is resolved through resort to principled reasoning from legal rules – reflecting Raz's conception of law as a two-stage decision-making process and Dworkin's idea of law as integrity.

One of the most influential authors on the rule of law since Fuller is Raz. His 'thin theory' of the rule of law involved eight desiderata. The first three reflect most of Fuller's virtues:[26]

1 laws should be prospective, open, and clear;
2 laws should be relatively stable;
3 law making should be guided by open, stable, clear, and general rules.

The next five prevent enforcement machinery being distorted:

4 independence of the judiciary must be guaranteed;
5 principles of natural justice should be observed;
6 courts should have review powers;
7 courts should be easily accessible;
8 discretion of crime-policing agencies should not be perverted.

Raz emphasized that this is a limited concept of the rule of law. For him, it is essentially a negative value insofar as it is directed at preventing some of the harms that could be done by those wielding power. It does not, however, eliminate all harms and might exacerbate others.

The rule of law, so conceived, made law a more effective tool. Officials would enforce rules uniformly and those subject to it would modify their behavior in the light of those rules (to realize the benefits it provided or avoid the harm it could do to them). This made the law more effective and, for most people, self-enforcing. In his famous analogy, the rule of law is good law in the same sense as a knife is good. Whether harm results depends on what the law, like the knife, is used for.

This limited concept of the rule of law does not seek to incorporate the other enlightenment values of democracy, citizenship, and human rights. It does not eschew these values but allows them to be defined more independently and their presence or absence to be determined more reliably. This does not mean that the other values cannot be embraced wholeheartedly. Rather, it means that there are a number of values for assessing the worth of a legal order of which the rule of law is one. The lack of one or more of the other values might well justify us in overthrowing a legal order that had the one virtue of exhibiting the rule of law. The lack of democracy, for example, will generally justify the replacing of that order with a democratic one – although a democracy with no rule of law may generate at least as much misery as an autocracy with the rule of law.

A good legal order needs more than one virtue. As Raz argues, it is better to identify separately the various virtues we would wish legal orders to demonstrate rather than to roll them all into a single virtue. Theories that do not seek to incorporate other enlightenment values, I call 'thin theories' of the rule of law.

In contrast, theories that add other enlightenment values I call 'thick theories' of the rule of law.

Broader definitions – 'thick theories' of the rule of law

Fuller's listing of rule of law virtues has tempted many to add other desiderata to the list. (The International Commission of Jurists added 'social, economic, educational, and cultural conditions'.[27] Others have included legitimacy, accountability and respect for human rights.) Herein we see a tendency to add many of the later enlightenment values (particularly democracy and rights) as well as some of the institutional mechanisms thought to be most effective in realizing those values, to the minimalist early-enlightenment value of the rule of law.[28]

It seems prima facie hard to argue with these broader definitions, the 'extra' values being widely shared. If we can secure their acceptance from everyone who claims to believe in the rule of law by showing that they are necessarily inherent within the rule of law, then why not do so? Surely this would spare us the need to expend political capital fighting these battles later to secure values we thought we had already won. I think, however, that we should restrain ourselves from this temptation and opt for a narrower conception of the rule of law – a 'thin theory' of the rule of law'.[29]

There are various reasons for preferring a thin theory of the rule of law:

1 One must be cautious about the 'imperialism of values'. If we view democracy, liberty, or the rule of law as good things, we are tempted to include most of the (political) things that the author considers to be good within the relevant concept.
2 The different values lose their focus with a number of undesirable ideological consequences. Different, potentially conflicting values are incorporated into the one value. The most common conflation over the last 50 years is that of human rights and democracy. Political liberty is a prerequisite for democracy.[30] However, the entrenchment of rights against democratic legislatures is a restriction of democracy. Some such entrenchment is, in this author's view, justified. But it is justified as a restriction of democracy rather than as a part of over-expansive concept of democracy.[31]
3 As some of the values added become controversial, it will weaken support for the concept of the rule of law. There is a spectrum, not a clear break, between 'widely-accepted' and 'controversial' values. Although some principles such as 'universal male-female suffrage' may seem uncontroversial, as late as 1928 the Privy Council had to rule on the legality of appointing women to the Canadian Senate. They rejected arguments that the 'persons' whom the Governor-General was empowered to appoint under Section 24 of the British North America Act 1867 were presumably those of the male gender only.[32]
4 An expanded list is far less likely to fit within an overarching concept and central organizing idea such as those discussed in the previous section.

5 The more we build positive values into law before it is called a law, the more difficulty we will have in overtly criticizing that law. The more positive values that must be respected before the rule of law is seen to exist, the more difficulty there will be in questioning it through the prism of other values.

Extending the reach of the rule of law

As illustrated, some writers have sought to extend the concept of the rule of law to incorporate a wide set of important but contestable values. However, the rule of law, at least in its traditional, more limited sense has also been extended recently in another way. One of the greatest developments of this century is that the institutional mechanisms for implementing the rule of law have extended to other than judicial officials. It has been applied to members of the executive with increasing fervor. For a long time it has been accepted that they should only act according to law.[33] The problem was that there were few means of determining whether they had. For this reason, administrative action has been increasingly open to scrutiny not only through monitoring bodies and appeal mechanisms, but also through the twin requirements of having to provide reasons and relevant documents – both features of judicial review. The courts have had a central role in the development of these requirements and they have made legal success against resistant administrators more possible while reducing the need to resort to formal legal action.

There has been a parallel struggle with those other wielders of great organizational power – corporate executives. The move to establish corporate governance has been about setting rules and goals for the use of corporate power – in part by governments and in part by shareholders. Both attempts have been resisted and criticized along lines that are surprisingly familiar to anyone who observed the former attempts of public service mandarins to preserve their power and shield its exercise from public scrutiny.[34]

This reflects an aspect of the widespread appeal of the rule of law. When the concept was originally outlined, the greatest source of power was the sovereign state. Sovereigns claimed absolute and paramount power. They had just fought for supremacy over other sources of power within their territories: the church, the aristocracy and foreign states. Sovereigns had sought to reduce the power of feudal lords who had previously claimed a right to autonomously control their territory. They sought to bring churches to heal in a variety of ways – from choosing the bishops to choosing the official religion. The Treaty of Westphalia itself involved a formal agreement to forbear from interfering in the internal affairs of other nations.

However, this should not blind us (as it sometimes did enlightenment thinkers) to other sources of power that can arbitrarily restrict our capacities to make and carry out life plans. The philosophers were aware of the continuing power of the aristocracy and the church. Their solution was to continue the sovereignty project and subject them to the state and the state to the people. However, they generally did not foresee the power of modern corporations and unions (although

Adam Smith's concerns about corporations and monopolies would count as honorable exceptions to this generalization). More reprehensibly, few appreciated that the women, servants and slaves in their own households generally had much more to fear from the ever-present philosopher than they had from a remote absolute monarch! One of the features of the last 300 years is the appreciation of these other sources of power and the belief that those who hold such power are responsible for its exercise and should not do so in an arbitrary fashion. Sometimes this has manifested itself in demands that the law extend into what might otherwise have been considered the 'private sphere'. However, another manifestation lies in the demands that shareholders, employees and other 'stakeholders' whose lives are affected by the decisions of large organizations that those who make those decisions are bound by, and act within, rules set by those organizations.

The rule of law deals with the way that wielders of state power use that power. However, similar arguments apply to wielders of other kinds of strong organizational power. The rule of law for a more global world is not just about international law or about the application of universal rules to sovereign states. It is about the idea that, for all forms of institutional power, there should be rules that are made subject to the Raz criteria. The sources will be different and the means of interpretation must be different. But in each case, there should be impartial arbitrators to determine whether or not the rules have been followed in letter and spirit.

The value placed on the 'thin theory'

Even though the 'thin theory' might not seem as attractive as full blown 'thick theories', many positive claims may be made about this more limited sense of the rule of law. For example:

1 Citizens must plan for their lives because the behavior of state officials is predictable.[35]
2 Some, such as Hayek, might equate this limited conception of the rule of law with 'freedom' (I would not do so).
3 The rule of law promotes stability.
4 The rule of law avoids a number of important procedural injustices of the kind Fuller indicated. This amounts to a kind of 'formal' justice.
5 As Raz argues, where rulers are prepared to be bound by their rules, it makes the law a more effective tool. Indeed, if the rulers do not tie the sanctions they apply to the rules they have established in advance, then people will be less likely to follow the rules they apply.
6 One of the most famous and impassioned defences of the rule of law was in a deeply flawed legal regime – that of eighteenth century England. At that time, democracy, rights, substantive equality and other liberal democratic values were not only not supported but their advocacy could also lead to prosecution. Nevertheless, E.P. Thomson praised the rule of law because the imposition of effective restraints on power and the defence of the citizen from power's 'all-intrusive claims' seemed to him 'an unqualified human good'.[36]

It is rare for an 'instrumental' good to be unqualified. As Raz points out, the rule of law makes laws more effective, whether we value or abhor the relevant rule. Although elements of the rule of law, especially the requirement of publicity, may be inconvenient for 'bad' laws in most societies, it is no guarantee against them. One can imagine a government passing racist or xenophobic laws to gain favor from a population with a tradition of racism that would prefer to find a supposedly justified expression of its racism than confront its racist past. In that case, open, transparent and well-publicized laws might be highly effective and politically savvy.

Nevertheless, this defect alone would not lead us to abandon the rule of law. If one is struggling to secure legislative change, one wants the legislated changes to be effective. It would merely mean that the rule of law is not the only value one should consider in deciding how to act.

Reasons for preferring 'thin' theories

I can understand why many would prefer a 'thick' theory of the rule of law to a 'thin' theory. The added values of democracy and rights are admirable and I fully endorse them. I also fully accept that the value of the rule of law is enhanced if the law is made democratically and with a desire to protect and further human rights (as rights and democracy are enhanced by the rule of law). The rule of law, democracy, rights (along with citizenship, liberty, equality, and the natural environment in which all this takes place) are a package of enlightenment values which are compromised and sometimes negated in the absence of each other.

Nevertheless, like Raz, I prefer to use a narrower concept of the rule of law – as one value among other values that is not determinative of action or preference. In general, I like to unpack the package of enlightenment values for a number of reasons:

1 If separated conceptually, they can be understood more effectively.
2 Many of them are subject to competing definitions and a variety of nuances and subtleties. If other values are included within the rule of law, then one cannot know whether the rule of law is in place unless one has settled the meaning of, say, 'democracy'. Those who adopt a different conception of democracy may deny the existence of the rule of law – or may put off its application until the other conditions are met.
3 The values can have independent worth (even if diminished as E.P. Thompson's plea makes clear).
4 It may not be possible to introduce all the relevant values simultaneously so that it appears as if no progress is being made and no praise can be given for that progress.

One of the potential reasons for preferring thick theories is the concern that fundamentally inadequate laws will receive the cachet and legitimacy of the word 'law' and be supported by 'rule of law' values. Only laws that reflect values such as 'democracy' and 'rights' should receive the honor of being called 'laws' and the legitimacy that word generates. For me, this is the right answer to an unnecessary question. Because a particular form of words can be identified as a 'law' does not mean that one has to be bound by it. One can never surrender one's conscience to any outside power. The fact that something is a law does not mean that it must be unequivocally obeyed. I am attracted to the inclinations of British positivists from Jeremy Bentham onwards. If law is seen as arising out of social facts, then one can fix it as a phenomenon for praise or blame. If law has to meet certain criteria of justice before being called law, it is harder to criticize it.

Extending the limited rule of law beyond state borders

International law emerges via different means and has a radically different extent. This has led some to say that international law is not law. If this is so, there can be no 'rule of law'. Such claims are receding into the past as various forms of international law grow in strength. Nonetheless, there are some important differences between international law and domestic law that should be borne in mind when constructing a conception of the rule of law in a globalizing society.

1. There is no body that claims a monopoly on the use of force in the way that sovereign states do within their territory. This contrast can be overstated. No sovereign state really has a monopoly on the use of force within its territory, and their claim to a monopoly of the legitimate use of force may not be shared by all or even a majority. All states allow citizens the use of force in self-defence. The United States revels in that permission, raising it to a right to bear arms[37] even though that right was historically asserted against the sovereign power against which it had revolted. Internationally, there is a right to use force in self-defence but, as a matter of international law, only the United Nations Security Council has the power to authorize the use of force for other reasons. Like all laws, such prohibitions may be breached, but the number and extent of such breaches since the World War II are very few. The biggest difference is that there are no domestic players who could breach such laws with the same degree of impunity as superpowers can breach international law. The key difference is not that of whether there are monopolies of force at domestic or international level, but the fact that the disproportion in force between sovereign and subject within states is reversed when it comes to international law.
2. Where sovereign states claim jurisdiction over all matters occurring within their borders, the subject matters which international law seeks to regulate are far more limited.[38] However, this is not so different to what a weak confederation does.
3. There are relatively few international officials. The main actors are not individual officials, such as the UN Secretary-General, but states.
4. Of the normal Humean conditions (which Hart lists as limited resources, limited altruism, and mutual vulnerability),[39] only the first two apply to states in the international community. The third involves too much variation from state to state. Some states are all but immune from interference by all but the

strongest and most unlikely of coalitions.[40] In another sense, the state is not mortal and is not as vulnerable to 'dying'.

5 Most international law is not made by 'legislatures' (e.g. the UN General Assembly) or courts, but by contract (i.e. treaties) among nation states.
6 The 'contracting parties' are sovereign states rather than citizens and their sovereign (as in Locke's model).
7 International law is of much more limited extent than the domestic law.
8 From the point of view of most liberal democratic constitutionalists, there are some severe institutional limitations in international law. There is no tripartite division of legislative, executive, and judiciary. Indeed, the UN Security Council is a potentially dangerous combination of all three with no formal legal checks and balances.
9 There is no central body charged with enforcement of international law. Enforcement is generally left up to the signatories. In fact, contracts are only enforced by the stronger party (although with some exceptions).
10 An important issue in the domestic rule of law is the 'closure rule'. Domestic jurisdictions have two contrasting closure rules to resolve legal doubts. For officials exercising power in that capacity, anything not legally authorized is prohibited, but for private individuals, anything not legally prohibited is permitted. In international law, the latter closure rule has applied to states, NGOs, and corporations. To the extent that it is relevant, the former applies to international institutions. However, it could rightly be argued that, when someone is claiming to enforce the rule of law, they are claiming for themselves the mantle of an official of international law – a police officer.

Even where the differences listed in the preceding paragraphs are sometimes overstated, the differences are legion and substantial. The real question is whether these differences mean that the rule of law is not an important ideal within international law. In general, I would argue that none of them vitiate the ideal that those who are enforcing international law should be bound by international law. To the extent that there are omissions and shortcomings, these just provide an argument for closing the gaps and addressing the shortcomings. To me, it would seem that most of the arguments in favor of the domestic rule of law run to international law. It is capable of achieving most of the virtues of a 'thin' version of the rule of law within a domestic polity – predictability, stability and effectiveness. If the major players play by the rules, others know how they must behave.

Objections to extending the limited rule of law

I will consider a number of potential arguments against extending the rule of law from domestic to international affairs. These fall into two categories (1) International versions of the arguments against the domestic rule of law, and (2) Arguments against the international rule of law *per se*.

International versions of the arguments against the domestic rule of law

1 The rule of law serves the strong and those who have made the law. The rule of law has hegemonic and legitimating effects. Further, formal equality works and masks substantive injustice. The strong might be seen as even stronger in international law. However, the requirement of consensus makes it more difficult for the strong to get their way in passing new laws that suit them. As earlier, the problem is that they will prevent new laws being passed that do not suit them.

2 International law cannot, realistically, be effectively enforced against the strongest nations. In domestic law, 'over-mighty subjects' like Mafia bosses can use more legal tricks than the average person, but ultimately Al Capone and John Gotti went to jail. But no 'international policeman' can possibly 'arrest' the United States or the People's Republic of China (unless in the future either superpower drastically declined like the Roman Empire, in which case other, more powerful rivals would be the chief 'culprits' instead). One would hope that an avowedly constitutional democracy like the USA would voluntarily exhibit 'a decent Respect to the Opinions of Mankind'.[41] But on the contrary, American leaders prefer to invoke their role as 'leader of the Free World' to ignore international law whenever it impedes their crusades against (unfriendly) dictatorships.

3 The rule of law is only one of a series of goods – and if you cannot have the other goods, it may be a bad thing. For example, the rule of law in a liberal democracy will be good, usually, because it means the laws enforced will be democratic in their origin and liberal in their content. But in a repressive theocracy or one-party state, the rule of law will not secure religious freedom or dignity. Indeed, if it means zealous judges cannot be swayed by bribes or by mercy, it would make such a regime worse.

4 Some prefer democracy before the rule of law and would prefer to wait for the former before accepting the latter. This is sometimes related to an unwillingness to give any credence to non-democratic law. A similar argument would seek the democratization of international institutions before enforcing the international rule of law. My response to this argument in international law is the same as my response to its common domestic variety:

- The rule of law has tended to precede democracy.
- Democracies need the rule of law to determine what bodies can determine laws and policy 'democratically'.
- The rule of law would have to involve the exercise of judicial power to determine and interpret international law. This would stimulate 'legislative' activity – creating treaties and securing General Assembly decisions where parties did not like the decisions reached by courts.

5 The most powerful – international business and international agencies – are not constrained. The only constraints are on individual sovereign states, especially those struggling for democracy. Business activities that were subject

not only to the rule of law but to the rule of law of democratically elected regimes, are either controlled by unelected bodies themselves controlled by one or two states (e.g. World Trade Organization) or not controlled at all.

Arguments against the international rule of law per se

It might be argued that the international rule of law is no good if it is limited, that is, if, for example, there are rules against intervention but not against ethnic cleansing. International law is very different from domestic laws because it covers so few areas of life. It does not cover many of the areas that Hart has listed as the 'minimum content of natural law' – laws allocating property and its transfer (and hence prohibiting forceful transfers outside of this provision), and laws protecting human life. Whether or not this is conceived as 'natural law' or not, they are a minimum list of what might be adequate. In the absence of such laws, it is not possible for individuals to make and carry out life plans, the ultimate justification of the rule of law. Furthermore, it could be argued that, while international law is insufficiently complete to allow ordinary individuals to make the kinds of plans that the rule of law is intended to permit,[42] it does allow those who are bent on evil to plan their evil deeds because they are secure in the knowledge that no one can touch them (or, a version of this, because a sympathetic permanent member of the Security Council will veto any action against them).

It could also be argued that international law, as the law of states, covers issues of violence (the international use of force), property (at least the vital 'real' property of sovereign territory) and its taking (invasion). However, international law is now much more than the law of states. By trying individuals for war crimes, the Nuremberg trials made individuals the subject of international law. The human rights provisions of that UN Charter and the Declarations and Covenants that followed, indicated that individual human beings could be the beneficiaries of international law. The treatment of individuals by sovereign states was once more a matter of international concern and provided for by international law.

The issue is not whether international law covers these issues but the differential enforceability of the requirements of states to respect human rights and the requirements of states to respect each other's borders. This returns us to the point that it does not allow individuals to make meaningful life plans – or even plan on living! This kind of argument may be seen as making the value of the international rule of law weaker and more easily trumped by other considerations – most notably the human rights violations mentioned. Alternatively, it may be seen as an argument that is more likely to trump the value of the rule of law in such cases. In either case, it does not suggest that the rule of law is not valuable and it does not mean that it will always be trumped. Caution needs to be taken in this case because it is only the powerful states that can do the trumping and their motives may be less than pure.

Sovereignty, historically and, still, ideologically, is an argument against the international rule of law. Sovereignty as defined by Austin, makes a point of this. The existence of an 'independent political community' largely free of outside direction is an essential requirement of sovereignty. Enlightenment values imposed the check of the rule of law, then of institutional checks and balances, and then of democracy. For a long time, the concept of sovereignty was a barrier to the introduction of similar checks and balances in international law. For those who are proud of their legal traditions, there is a danger in giving in to other laws – especially when there is a perceived democratic deficit in the making of international law. From an Anglo–American perspective, international law seems very imperfect on all the criteria by which they would seek to judge themselves and seek to be judged – democratic legitimacy, comprehensiveness, impartial judicial interpretation and judicially sanctioned enforcement and so on. However, sovereignty is breaking down. Separation of constitutional law and international law is breaking down.[43] Once that happens, there can be no doubting that traditional public law concepts (most notably the rule of law) will gain a new lease of life in international law.

The problem with strong theories of sovereignty is that they do not have room for international law. Indeed, international law is only defined through the eyes of domestic constitutional law. Sovereignty was, in fact, asserted against transnational laws and institutions (or rather laws and institutions that were only seen as transnational after the assertion of sovereignty and nationhood). It was resistance to the power of the Catholic church within the borders of the emerging states of Europe that led to initial conflict and local compromises concerning the appointment of bishops. What impelled England's break with Rome was King Henry VIII's refusal to accept Roman diktats. However immoral this Tudor Clinton may have been, it is salutary to remember that his father-in-law was in effective occupation of Rome– something that made the dispensation to allow Henry to marry his dead brother's wife in breach of church law easy and the dispensation to divorce her impossible.[44]

Governments involve more than legislators to make laws and courts to interpret them. They need a range of other institutions that the international system does not possess. This may well be true. However, the whole point of the rule of law in a domestic system is that it can be of real value even where the state is weak or limited. Indeed, many are suggesting that it is the first thing that is needed.[45] The recent Australian-led assistance to the Solomons Islands that was requested by its government, expressly aimed to restore the rule of law as a necessary first step in dealing with that country's problems.

Comparisons of the package in current circumstances present international law as seemly weak and inadequate compared with the full-blown state systems we are used to (i.e. why should the Americans, with their 'perfect' democracy with its checks and balances, culture, supreme court etc., bow to a set of laws with no legislature, no proper police force, a lesser judiciary).

Some might see the 'rule of law' as culturally grounded. It is sometimes argued that the rule of law only flourishes in a particular cultural setting. When it is pointed out that virtually all societies, western, and non-western, possess concepts akin to the rule of law, the criticism may vary. The need is for support within the domestic culture of the relevant sovereign state. However, the rule of law translates well enough into most cultures, is found within most of the relevant international treaties, and is the necessary basis for international trade. I can see no difficulty in the acceptance of the rule of law by the international community. It is those who want to flout the law who have the most difficulty with it!

The great powers would not have signed on to international treaties and institutions, if they had realized that they would have been enforced. This may well be true empirically. However, this is a subsequent assertion of bad faith that they should be estopped from making. Of course, they might argue that, in a democracy, they cannot bind their successors – this has important resonances for some of the parliamentary sovereignty cases that so concerned UK and Commonwealth countries. It could be argued that they changed the law so that, for some issues, it was necessary to do other things in order to get certain kinds of laws changed. In any case, those cases, apart from being rooted in one limited legal culture, are only relevant to the jurisdiction concerned. It may well be internally that the courts do not recognize the obligations the nation has undertaken. However, this does not mean that an international court will not recognize those obligations.

Linking the domestic and international rules of law

As argued earlier, it is important to distinguish between advocating a rule of law for all sovereign states and a rule of law for international law that overarches states. Some might insist on the former before the latter – once nation states have an internal rule of law then nation states should accept a rule of law between them. Even if this kind of argument were accepted, however, it would not mean that states could ignore their international obligations – merely that any nation which had violated the rule of law with respect to its own citizens might not be able to rely on an international rule of law to the same extent and standing and, therefore, should only be given to its citizens or their democratic representatives (where these can be determined – as they can in the case of some countries where the results of the most recent election are clear as in Burma).

However, even if the lack of a domestic rule of law in a 'rogue state' were to estop them from arguing against the intervention of international law, it does not resolve the question of whether intervening states should themselves be subject to the international rule of law. It is suggested that those who seek to intervene should subject their intervention to adjudication by the International Court of Justice (ICJ). This means that the country in which intervention takes place could take the matter to the ICJ. However, those who seek the jurisdiction of the ICJ must also submit to the jurisdiction in that matter. Accordingly, issues of human rights could also be the subject of orders by the ICJ. The mechanism for subjecting intervenors to the rule of law, desirable of itself, also deals with one of the strongest objections to it.

Conclusion

These considerations remind us that we cannot hope for as much in the international rule of law as we can from the rule of law in well-ordered liberal democracies.

The limitations of international law mean that we cannot expect to find and insist that international law conforms to a 'thick theory' of the rule of law. However, the rule of law according to the 'thin theory' remains a meaningful ideal. If it could be achieved, it would not be an 'unqualified good' – I am skeptical of any such claims for individual liberal democratic values because liberal democratic values tend to both support and qualify each other and they cannot, pace Rawls, be placed in lexical order.

However, the idea that power be subject to effective inhibitions upon power and the defence of the citizen from power's all intrusive claims, is certainly of value and is much missed by the victims of the use of illegal and brute force in international relations. Some of the institutional means by which an international rule of law might be advanced have been suggested in an earlier paper.[46] Many additional ideas are contained in the chapters that follow.

Acknowledgements

This essay was written while a Senior Fulbright Fellow at Harvard University. It is based upon papers delivered to the World Congress on Legal and Social Philosophy in June 1999 ('Sovereignty and Intervention') and at a Griffith University Symposium on 'Globalising the Rule of Law' (19 August 2000). Thanks to Virginia Berry, Margaret Palmer and Tom Round for their comments on earlier versions of this chapter.

Notes

1 Kurth, J. 'The Protestant Deformation and American Foreign Policy', paper presented to The Philadelphia Society 37th National Meeting (22 April 2001) available at: http://www.townhall.com/phillysoc/Kurth%20Speech.htm

2 1648 is generally accepted as the crucial watershed – not least because the Treaty explicitly recognized certain key features of sovereignty. Of course, economic, political, legal, and ideological forces had long been at work and the job was not completed with that one pact. See: Treaty of Westphalia (Münster, 24 October 1648), Articles 41, '... sentences pronounced during the war about matters purely secular, if the defect in the proceedings be not fully manifest ... shall not be ... void; but [their] effect shall be suspended until ... reviewed ... in a proper court ... '; 46, law and justice to be administered in all the Emperor's hereditary provinces 'without any respect as to' religion – at least for Catholics and Lutherans; and 64 '... to prevent for the future any differences arising in the politick state, all and every one of the Electors, Princes and States of the Roman Empire, are so established and confirmed in their ancient rights, prerogatives, [etc] ... that they never can or ought to be molested therein by any whomsoever upon any manner of pretence' [trans. British Foreign Office].

3 'In such condition there is no place for industry, because the fruit thereof is uncertain: and consequently ... no navigation ... no commodious building ... no arts; no letters; no society; and which is worst of all, continual fear, and danger of violent death; and the life of man, solitary, poor, nasty, brutish, and short'. Hobbes, T. *Leviathan*, Cambridge: Cambridge University Press, 1991, chapter XIII, 'Of the Natural Condition of Mankind as Concerning Their Felicity and Misery', p. 89.

'So that it appeareth plainly ... that the sovereign power ... is as great as possibly men can be imagined to make it. And though of so unlimited a power, men may fancy many evil consequences, yet the consequences of the want of it, which is perpetual war of every man against his neighbor, are much worse... And whosoever, thinking sovereign power too great, will seek to make it less, must subject himself to the power that can limit it; that is to say, to a greater'. ibid., chapter XX: 'Of Dominion Paternal and Despotical', pp. 144–5.

'Nature hath made men so equal ... that, though there be found one man sometimes manifestly stronger in body or of quicker mind than another, yet when all is reckoned together the difference between man and man is not so considerable as that one man can thereupon claim to himself any benefit to which another may not pretend as well as he. For as to the strength of body, the weakest has strength enough to kill the strongest... during the time men live without a common power to keep them all in awe, they are in that condition which is called *war*... of every man against every man'. ibid., chapter XIII: 'Of the Natural Condition of Mankind as Concerning their Felicity and Misery', pp. 86–7.

4 Europeans did not extend the same respect to non-European nations until Westphalia's 300th anniversary, but that extension was generally seen as the logical application of Westphalia rather than its contradiction.

5 I call this the 'North Atlantic' Enlightenment not merely to honor those American institutions who have been my hosts and benefactors over the last five years (including the Fulbright Commission, Harvard University, Columbia University and the Council on Foreign Relations), but to emphasize the way philosophical and institutional ideas flowed back and forth across the Atlantic, growing in strength with each passage. In particular, this term recognizes North America's breakthrough in contributing crucial thinking about the *institutional* methods of securing the enlightenment's goals.

6 'In 1725 Voltaire... was thrashed by lackeys in the presence of their noble master; he was unable to obtain either legal or honorable redress, and because he complained of this outrage, paid a second visit to the Bastille... [H]is whole life was a series of contests with arbitrary power, and nothing but his fame... saved him from penalties far more severe than temporary imprisonment'. Dicey, A.V. *An Introduction to the Study of the Law of the Constitution*, London: MacMillan & Co. Ltd., 1927, chapter IV: 'The Rule of Law: its nature and general applications', p. 186.

7 Voltaire, Diderot and Helvétius were all attracted for a time to enlightened despotism.

8 This is not to deny that institutions bequeathed by these despots have endured, for example, the *Code Napoleon.*

9 Notably: an executive completely separate from the legislature (not even Cabinet members were to be legislators); impeachment as the only way for the legislature to remove executive officials; the copying, with some undesirable variations of the UK 1688 Bill of Rights' 'right to bear arms'; and, as we shall see, much broader and less reviewable powers vested in the Head of State to act outside the nation's boundaries.

10 Montesquieu's image of it involving a three-way separation of powers was deeply flawed as a description, or even an interpretation, of the British constitution. It is one of history's great ironies that Montesquieu's description was most accurate under William III and George III, because parliamentary control over the executive was largely achieved between those monarchs' reigns but disappeared [?] with the loss of the American colonies. The Americans created a strong head of state wielding full executive power – the very thing they had rebelled against, and the British were rejecting. More importantly, one chief American objection to British rule was that they did not have the same rights as Englishmen because the Crown had more power, with fewer constraints, outside the shores of England than on home soil. Despite their objection to this feature of the British Constitution, they gave the Presidency a similarly great and largely unfettered power to act outside the United States. The legal dangers of this power are exacerbated by political factors; the President, as Head of State, not facing any official Opposition Leader in the legislature, can 'wrap himself in the flag' and depict criticism of his foreign policies as disloyalty to the nation itself. The world has reaped the consequences in recent

years as Presidents have initiated wars in apparent contravention of international law and, in the case of the current (Bush II) Administration, sought to detain and try prisoners captured in such wars, outside US soil, thereby claiming properly legislative and judicial powers without constitutional constraint.

11 In the sense that, although the rule of law alone is not sufficient, it is almost certainly a *necessary* precondition for those other features that, while external to the rule of law, are necessary for a decent society (see following notes).

12 Locke, J. 'An Essay Concerning the True Original, Extent and End of Civil Government', in Baker, E. *Social Contract: essays by Locke, Hume and Rousseau*, London: Oxford University Press, 1947, chapter IX, §131, 'Of the Ends of Political Society and Government', p. 109.

13 As I have argued elsewhere (e.g. in 'The four dimensions of rights and their means of protection' in B. Galligan and C. Sampford (eds) *Rethinking Human Rights*, Sydney: Federation Press, 1997), the process has continued, with the exposition of values on the environment and group rights being first asserted in the nineteenth century and given greater emphasis and clarity during the twentieth.

14 Although cf. Runciman, D. 'A Bear Armed with a Gun'. Review of Robert Kagan, *Paradise and Power: America and Europe in the New World Order*, *London Review of Books*, vol. 25, no. 7, 3 April, 2003, available at: http://www.lrb.co.uk/v25/n07/runc01_.html (accessed 10 March 2004).

Runciman writes: 'The adjective "Hobbesian" has become shorthand for a view that sees international politics as a scene of conflict and strife . . . But this view . . . is wrong because states are not like natural human beings. They are, as Hobbes insisted, artificial, more like giant automata than people . . . stronger, larger and more robust . . . They are not vulnerable to the same kinds of threat . . . The life of a state . . . is not solitary. Indeed, it would be hard to think of a more clubbable bunch than the society of nations, with their endless get-togethers . . . Even poor states are not poor . . . relative . . . to the poverty of the people who have to live in them . . . [S]tates are not, for the most part, nasty to each other . . . as all parties seek to keep up appearances . . . It is the whole of Hobbes's argument that states are not brutish. The law of nations is not the law of the jungle. Because they are not simply men, but machines made in the image of men, states do not share with natural men a tendency to revert to the level of beasts in their dealings with one another . . . Above all, the life of states is not short . . . Indeed, to call the Hobbesian world anarchic is to make a mockery of everything Hobbes says . . . It was Hobbes's hope that if you could build enough states, the result would be peace'.

15 One striking feature of the Westphalia Treaty is how many of its Articles were devoted to specifying, in minute detail, the titles, lands, compensation, and other privileges due to princely rulers dispossessed in the religious wars. On the other hand, several Articles (see note 3) guaranteed rights for individual citizens, such as freedom of private religious worship.

16 Hart sets out the Humean conditions for the 'minimum content of natural law', based on human biology and psychology: limited resources, limited altruism and mutual vulnerability. Hart, H.L.A. *The Concept of Law*, Oxford: Clarendon Press, 1961, pp. 189–95. The first two apply to the international community, but the last involves much variation from state to state. Some states are all but immune from interference by all but the strongest and most unlikely of coalitions.

As Runciman, op. cit. notes, states are not vulnerable to the same kinds of threat as natural individuals. He writes: 'it is very difficult to slip a knife between the shoulder blades of a state while its back is turned. You can, of course, try to attack individual rulers . . . but . . . one sovereign will immediately be replaced by another . . . This durability makes individual states more certain in their dealings with one another'. However, Daniel Skubik notes that even in a society of invulnerable creatures (turtles, perhaps?) law would still be useful, for coordination instead of protection (Skubik, D.W. *At the Intersection of Legality and Morality: Hartian law as natural law*, New York: Peter Lang, 1990).

17 Napoleon, the next who sought to establish an empire across Europe, felt it necessary to abolish the last vestiges of the Holy Roman Empire so that he could claim the Imperial title for himself. It was only after his defeat that 'Empire' came to mean simply one more, unusually powerful, state among states.

18 The term appears to have first been used by the English republican writer James Harrington, in his tracts *The Prerogative of Popular Government* (1657) and *The Commonwealth of Oceana* (1656), in slightly different terms: 'an empire of laws and not of men'. The revised version is widely used: cf., for example, Toohey, J. 'A Government of Laws, and Not of Men?' *Public Law Review*, vol. 4, no. 3, 1993, pp. 158–74.

19 See: n 33.

20 Dworkin, R.M. *Law's Empire*, London: Duckworth, 1986, p. 379.

21 Hayek, F.A. *The Road to Serfdom*, Chicago: University of Chicago Press, 1944 (1976), p. 72.

22 Hayek admits that his theory – unlike most of its rivals, for example those based on natural law or human rights – would not invalidate draconian laws worded in the proper form. However, Hayekians reply that draconian laws are unlikely to be enacted if they must satisfy Hayek's criteria (since the majority will be unwilling to oppress itself) or, if the majority does accept such a burden, this only be in such extreme circumstances, for example wartime, that the law would be justified.

23 Fuller, L.L. *The Morality of Law*, New Haven; London: Yale University Press, 1964 (1969), p. 39 ff.

24 Cass writes: 'A critical aspect of the commitment to a rule of law . . . is the promise that the government's force will be brought to bear on individuals – especially in criminal proceedings where that force is at its most fearsome – only after fair warning'. Cass, R.A. 'Judging: norms and incentives of retrospective decisionmaking', *Boston University Law Review*, vol. 75, 1995, p. 954. 'Predictability allows adjustments of individual behavior that increase societal well-being; increased predictability lowers costs associated with a decision' ibid., p. 960.

25 Walker, G. de Q. *The Rule of Law: foundation of constitutional democracy*, Melbourne: Melbourne University Press, 1988.

26 Raz, *The Authority of Law*, pp. 214–19. Raz does not specifically mention consistency and generality. Generality, however, would be affected by differences between individuals deemed sufficient to support legal distinctions, while the procedural safeguards Raz advocates would guarantee relative consistency.

27 Clause 1 of the Committee I of the International Congress of Jurists at New Delhi, 1959 cited in ibid., p. 211. Raz is critical of extending the doctrine of the rule of law to include such desiderata referring to it as a 'perversion'. He writes that the report of the committee 'goes on to mention or refer to just about every political ideal which has found support in any part of the globe during the post-war years' (ibid., pp. 211 and 210).

28 This involves a development of the 'rule of law' to the rule of *just* law – or perhaps the rule of justice. But how does justice differ from law? One common answer is that law involves at least some reliance on rules – generally, if not absolutely – whereas justice pursued *other than* 'according to law' is '*qasi* justice', invoking the trope of the Islamic judge sitting under a palm tree deciding each case according to his personal instincts. (In fact, Islamic judges are, if anything, more constrained by categorical rules than are Western judges. The *Shari'a* system of law is famously rigid).

29 John Rawls famously outlined 'thick' and 'thin' theories of 'the good' (*A Theory of Justice*, MA: Harvard University Press, 1971, pp. 118–42). I am proposing a similar distinction for the rule of law. However, the reasons for thinning out the rule of law is not because of the controversiality of some of the other additions.

30 As distinct from civil liberty. A law that prohibits smoking marijuana, for example, is a restriction of civil liberty, but does not restrict political liberty unless it also forbids or penalizes efforts to have the prohibition repealed. Compare the 'gag rule', drafted by

John Calhoun, which banned any discussion of slavery or Abolitionism on the floor of the pre-Civil War US Congress.

31 *Contra* John Hart Ely who argues that certain types of judicial activism can be democratically 'representation-reinforcing' (*Democracy and Distrust: a theory of judicial review*, MA: Harvard University Press, 1980).

32 Similarly, in the past decade many pro-choice US Senators have criticized judicial nominees opposed to *Roe v Wade* on the ground that such judges would be 'outside the mainstream'. If this were true, then a few judges who vote to overturn *Roe* would be harmless; no other judges or legislators would vote with them. It is precisely because 50–60% of Americans support various abortion restrictions that pro-choice Senators are so concerned to stop *Roe* being overruled.

33 Indeed, some lawyers are surprised to see the extent to which traditional public servants are knowledgeable of, and sticklers for, the laws under which their departments operate.

34 I sometimes think that Sir Humphrey's skills live on in much of corporate management. A new series of 'Yes CEO' might be a useful sequel!

35 Of course, planning requires much else besides – including the resources to carry out plans. Furthermore, there are other sources of power which may be exercised capriciously and unpredictably, most noticeably corporate and economic power.

36 Thomson, E.P. *Whigs and Hunters: the origin of the black act*, London: Penguin, 1990.

37 Clause 1 of the Committee I of the International Congress of Jurists at New Delhi, 1959 cited in ibid., p. 211. Raz is critical of extending the doctrine of the rule of law to include such desiderata referring to it as a 'perversion'. He writes that the report of the committee 'goes on to mention or refer to just about every political ideal which has found support in any part of the globe during the post-war years' (ibid., pp. 211 and 210).

38 See: Raz, *The Authority of Law*.

39 The 'state of nature' that states inhabit is different. 'Life', for states at war, would not be nasty, brutish and short but nasty, brutish and *prolonged* (e.g. Northern Ireland, Palestine and the Balkans). As a state does not perish when its soldiers die, it could remain at war for years. The complete collapse of a state through military defeat is extremely uncommon. (One rare recent example – the fall of Saigon and Phnom Penh – was famously applauded by anarcho-libertarian philosopher Murray Rothbard: 'Death of a State', *Reason*, July 1975, pp. 31–2). But even defeat usually means merely subjugation, not extinction. As George Orwell noted: 'It is quite true that Carthage was utterly destroyed, its buildings levelled to the ground, its inhabitants put to the sword . . . But the populations involved were tiny . . . What is the best way of killing off seventy million Germans? Rat poison?' (*Tribune*, 24 December 1943).

Our images of prolonged slaughter come from the trenches of the World War I and Russian front of the Second. However, one of history's first effective sovereign states, Sweden, was plunged by King Gustavus Adolphus into a series of wars that bled the affected populations more deeply, albeit more slowly, than either World War (Parker, G. *The Military Revolution: military innovation and the rise of the West 1500–1800*, 2nd edn, Cambridge; Melbourne: Cambridge University Press, 1996, pp. 52–61) where the maximum death rate was only 15%. Only certain units or groups in either World War – German submariners and fighter pilots, Russian soldiers who started the World War II in arms – were more devastated.

40 Thus the United States is effectively immune at this stage because no *immediately likely* alliance could stop them politically, militarily or economically. It does not follow, though, that no *possible* combination could challenge US hegemony. Collectively, Europe, China and Russia could more than match the US in military strength. The integrating European economy is of similar size US. Financially, withdrawal of Japanese deposits from the US bond market could cause enormous shocks, even more so if China, Taiwan and one or two major creditor nations joined in. Accordingly, this Humean condition does apply. It has not been evident because American diplomacy and economic policy

since the war has ensured that is has many allies and that those allies have prospered and benefited from the relationships. Most of them mentioned just now perceive more common interests than conflicting interests and the conflicting interests have generally been limited to those that fall below the threshold that would stimulate counteralliances among significant groups of other powers. Joffe argues that the nature of American power and the manner of its exercise in the twentieth century means that such counter alliances are very unlikely (Joffe, J. 'Gulliver Unbound: can america rule the world?' The Twentieth Annual John Bonython Lecture (Sydney, Tuesday 5 August 2003), available at: www.aicgs.org/c/csi.pdf).

41 *Declaration of Independence of the Thirteen United States of America*, Second Continental Congress (4 July, 1776), preamble.

42 International law deliberately excludes wide areas of policy from its ambit, by self-denying ordinance. Although, for example, it requires 'a fair and public hearing by a competent, independent and impartial tribunal', it says nothing about whether a country should adopt a British-style adversarial or a French-style inquisitorial judicial system (*International Covenant on Civil and Political Rights* (1966), Article 14(1); also *Universal Declaration of Human Rights* (1948), Article 10). International law seeks only to lay down broad principles which (however controversial their content) can be insisted upon as unchanging, universal standards. It does not prescribe policy details, which would necessarily vary over times and places. See Round, T. and Sampford, C. 'Introduction – East and West: crisis and reform', in Sampford, C., Condlln, S., Palmer, M. and Round, T. (eds), *Asia Pacific Governance: from crisis to reform*, London: Ashgate, 2002, p. 5.

43 See: Sampford, C. 'Challenges to the Concepts of "Sovereignty" and "Intervention"', in B.M. Leiser and T.D. Campbell (eds) *Human Rights in Philosophy and Practice*, Dartmouth, UK: Ashgate, 2001, chapter 16.

44 Before the Reformation, in Western Europe, '[t]o be a Christian was to be a [Catholic] Churchman and there was only one church . . . and the Pope was its head' (Bolt, R. *A Man For All Seasons*, London: Heinemann, 1974, p. vii. Afterwards, 'it was never again possible to believe whole-heartedly in the existence of a right answer to every dispute' (Milsom, S.F.C. *Historical Foundations of the Common Law*, London: Butterworths, 1981, p. 91).

45 See: Plunkett, M. 'Rebuilding the Rule of Law', in Maley, W., Sampford, C. and Thakur, R. (eds) *From Civil Strife to Civil Society: civil and military responsibilities in disrupted states*, Tokyo: United Nations University Press, 2003, pp. 207–28.

46 Sampford, C. 'Challenges to the Concepts of "Sovereignty" and "Intervention"', in Leiser and Campbell, *Human Rights in Philosophy and Practice*, chapter 16.

2 Globalizing the rule of law

Rethinking values and reforming institutions

Spencer Zifcak

> And so whoever has the Legislative or Supream Power of any Common-wealth, is bound to govern by establish'd standing Law, promulgated and known to the People, and not by Extemporary Decrees; by indifferent and upright Judges, who are to decide Controversies by those Laws; And to imploy the force of the Community at home, only in the Execution of such Laws, or abroad to prevent or redress Foreign Injuries, and secure the Community from Inroads and Invasion. And all this to be directed to no other end, but the Peace, Safety and publick good of the People.
>
> (John Locke (1689) *Second Treatise of Government*)

While in the academic literature there may be differences concerning the nature, impact and consequences of globalization, it is plain that in practice globalization, in a diversity of manifestations and spheres, is well and truly upon us. It draws great opportunity and significant difficulty in its wake.

The principal sphere of problem and promise with which I shall be concerned here relates to the 'rule of law'. The principal question that will be addressed is 'how might the rule of law, a concept so familiar in the national arena, best be understood and made operational in an increasingly international one?'

In this chapter, I shall address the question in a number of different spheres, for example, as it relates to global governance, the international protection of human rights and the regulation of the global economic order. But before examining these in greater detail, some brief introductory remarks concerning both globalization and the rule of law seems appropriate.

Globalization

Globalization, it seems to me, implies at least two distinct phenomena.[1] First, it suggests that many facets of economic, social, technological and political activity are becoming increasingly international in scope. Second, it suggests that there has been an intensification of the levels of interaction between states and societies in all of these areas.[2] Joseph Stiglitz has defined the concept succinctly as follows:

> The idea of globalization is very simple. The decrease of communication costs, transportation costs, and artificial barriers to goods and factors of production has led to a closer integration of the economies of the world. Globalization implies mobility not only of goods and services but also of capital and knowledge – and to a lesser extent of people. Globalization entails not only the integration of markets but also the emergence of global civil society.[3]

Globalization has been facilitated principally by stunning advances in technology and, in particular, information technology, and driven by the increasingly international character of many economic and social problems. The mass movements of peoples, the unbridled flow of international capital across state borders, the spread of diseases such as AIDS, the degradation of the environment, the intractability of poverty, the abuse of human rights, the drugs trade, the arms trade and the international spread of terrorist networks are each instances of pressing problems that defy purely national solution.

In response, there has been a dramatic increase in the number of international treaties and agreements designed to contain and regulate such phenomena. International law has significantly expanded its scope and reach. At the same time, there has been a tremendous proliferation of international institutions whose purpose it is to implement the new law in a manner broadly consistent with, but often transcending, statehood and sovereignty. These include many sponsored under the political umbrella of the United Nations and the economic umbrella of the World Trade Organization (WTO), the World Bank and the International Monetary Fund (IMF). They are primarily regulatory institutions yet their growth is, if anything, outpaced by that of the multinational coalitions, cartels and corporations they are designed to control and the civil society coalitions and organizations to whose representations they are increasingly required to respond.

These developments raise fundamental questions about governance, accountability and legality. Rosalyn Higgins has remarked that:

> Globalization represents the reality that we live in a time when the walls of sovereignty are no protection against movements of capital, labor, information and ideas – nor can they provide effective protection against harm and damage.[4]

If this is so, and I believe that it is, then new forms of international governance and law require development to ensure that harm and damage is limited and that the constructive potential of the newly globalizing system is maximized.

The walls of sovereignty have been crumbling in the face of many different developments but two in particular are worthy of emphasis here.[5] First, advances in technology and communications have made possible an unprecedented degree of financial and economic interdependence and the potential for economic growth.[6] As markets have become more integrated, the promise has been that trade will be liberalized, investment freed, competition enhanced, prices lowered and living standards across the globe enhanced. The promise has been only partially and very unequally fulfilled.[7] Yet in the drive to achieve it there has been a consequence of great moment – that is the sacrifice by nations of some part of their economic sovereignty in pursuit of the wider objective.

Second, at the other end of the global spectrum, in the sphere of international law and the promotion of human rights, there has been a remarkable and ethically significant shift towards the individual as the primary subject of the new international legal order.[8] Individuals, while not displacing states as the foundation of that order, have gradually come to be regarded by the international community as holding internationally material rights and interests. These rights and interests are now, as the result of developments in international treaty and customary law, beyond the scope of any single state to confer and determine. The position of individuals within the state is increasingly the subject of external scrutiny and, in extreme cases, may be the cause of external intervention. Group rights too, in the form of an international recognition of the right to self-determination and a right to development, present a similar challenge to statehood.[9]

A major consequence of these two trends has been the fragmentation of Westphalian systems of law and governance. Sovereign states now share their power with a host of international and regional, political and economic institutions and organizations. States remain at the core of the international order but the gravitational pull of the global and the individual has undermined their traditional authority. Global law and governance has become polycentric in nature, with very different and differing coalitions of regulatory actors combining in response to international economic and social problems and individual and group concerns.[10] In this polycentric world, the question of how the many international, regional and national regulatory institutions addressing a particular global issue should be drawn to account, by whom and under whose law has become ever more uncertain and critical.

That law is and will be important in forging collective transnational solutions to the kinds of problems I have just outlined, cannot be doubted. The rule of law is no less critical in a globalized world than in one dominated by sovereign nation states. Yet what this rule might mean, how it might be achieved and on what constitutional and political principles it might be founded is by no means clear.

To begin an examination of these questions, the idea of the 'rule of law' needs also to be addressed.

The rule of law

In its classical form, the rule of law is understood generally to be comprised of a number of characteristic features.[11] Hayek, for example, believed that the 'rule of law' implied that the law must be known and certain, prospective never retrospective. No individual should be coerced except in the enforcement of rules having these attributes. Individuals should be equal before the law. It must therefore be general rather than particular in its application. A system based on the rule of law must embody the separation of powers. This requires that the law's interpretation and enforcement be vested in judges independent of executive government. Their application of the law must be faithful, open and principled.[12]

Hayek is particularly clear in setting down the ethical foundations of the rule of law. Its overarching object, he argues, is to facilitate the purposive actions of the individual. It is to ensure that the individual may make informed choices affecting the directions of his or her life, without arbitrary interference by the state. In their interactions with the state and other entities, the rule of law ensures that individuals will be aware of the parameters within which their choices must be framed. The rule of law also marks out a private sphere within which the individual's choices may be pursued. It makes it unlikely that the state will interfere too invasively in this private realm by holding it as a founding principle that laws must apply generally and equally. It is this fact, that all rules apply equally to all, including those who govern, that makes it improbable that oppressive laws will be enacted.

It is important also to remark that Hayek's conception of the rule of law does not exist in a vacuum. The thought that it might pertain in an autocracy would be anathema. He cites America's great contribution to public law as the creation of a constitution that circumscribes the powers of a democratic and therefore representative legislature in the interests of protecting the people against arbitrary action. He endorses the entrenchment of higher law, law which, possessing a greater degree of generality and proceeding from a superior authority, in turn controls the contents of more specific laws that are passed by a delegated parliamentary authority. His rule of law presumes both constitutionalism and democracy.

Now, the principles and practices underlying the operation of the rule of law are reasonably well understood in national legal systems having a jurisdictionally defined, democratic and constitutional foundation. But their concreteness tends to fracture in the fragmentation, fluidity and contingency of global interconnectedness. To ascribe new and appropriate meaning to an 'international rule of law', therefore, requires that we reconsider and reapply its principal ethical and institutional underpinnings in this new context. Given the polycentric nature of the global political, economic and legal order, this is no easy task. Yet it is one that needs urgently to be undertaken.

In its landmark report, the UN Commission on Global Governance affirmed the importance of applying the rule of law in the international arena in the strongest terms:

> The rule of law has been a critical civilising influence in every free society. It distinguishes a democratic from a tyrannical society; it secures liberty and justice against repression; it elevates equality above dominion; it empowers the weak against the unjust claims of the strong. Its restraints, no less than the moral precepts it asserts, are essential to the well-being of society, both collectively and to individuals within it. Respect for the rule of law is thus a basic neighborhood value. And one that is certainly needed in the emerging global neighborhood.[13]

This statement injects into the idea of the rule of law, ideas of justice and fairness that some academic authors may with some legitimacy claim do not belong there.[14] Nevertheless, it serves to emphasize the critical importance of translating both the rationale and value of the doctrine to the global arena.

While there are, and will always be, different opinions regarding the content of the core values underlying the idea of the rule of law, in the international arena I propose five, building on Hayek's delineation, that are worthy of particular consideration. These are legality, equality, legitimacy, accountability and a commitment to fundamental human rights.[15]

The value accorded to *legality* derives from the desire to ensure that in society we should operate under a common, articulated, general and transparent framework of rules.[16] Within this framework every person and organization, while respecting the constraints these rules impose, should have an equal opportunity to pursue their own ends. In global as well as national governance, legality proscribes arbitrariness. It privileges principled over particularistic decision-making.

Legality, as understood here, also introduces the idea of *equality*. This concept goes further than asserting straightforwardly that the law should be general in its application. It requires that even a general law should refrain from making arbitrary or unjustifiable distinctions between peoples and nations, thus favoring some over others. It should eschew discriminatory treatment unless the group affected accepts the discrimination proposed as legitimate. Further, equality implies equal access as well as equal treatment. Equal legal rights and entitlements are of little tangible benefit where the opportunity for their vindication before an appropriate international forum is lacking.

The law must possess *legitimacy*.[17] While a purely formal view of the rule of law would require only that rules be known, certain and enforceable in the international arena particularly since the end of the World War II, it has increasingly and properly been insisted the law be legitimate, that is, sanctioned democratically.[18] Again, following Hayek, it should proceed hierarchically, with certain rules, universally endorsed by the community of nations and for that reason possessing constitutional standing, governing the operation of others of a more regular, legislative character. The UN Charter does not mention the word democracy. But as the former Secretary-General, Boutros Boutros-Ghali points out, the document is prefaced by the words, 'We the Peoples of the United Nations', thus rooting the sovereign authority of the member states and so, the legitimacy of the organization itself in the will of their peoples. Similarly, the Universal Declaration of Human Rights is also informed by a commitment to democracy, declaring that the 'will of the people shall be the basis of the authority of government' and then providing for foundational political and civil rights to underpin that authority and the rule of law that flows from it.[19]

The value of *accountability* is linked closely to legitimacy.[20] General international rules once adopted must be faithfully and impartially interpreted and executed. This value requires that those who exercise public power according to law be drawn to account for its use. Power holders in whom the international community have reposed their trust should act in fidelity to that trust. Accountability demands that institutional checks and balances be created such that the exercise of public power under law be independently reviewable. The doctrine of the separation of powers, therefore, is no less important globally than nationally. A fundamental commitment to the creation and maintenance of independent judicial bodies to interpret and apply diverse areas of international law is essential to international law's continuing integrity.

Finally, and again since the end of the World War II, the value accorded to *fundamental human rights* has become a foundational norm of all Western and many Eastern legal system.[21] The 'rule of law' may not stretch to the chapter and verse protection of every right and freedom contained in the UN Declaration and its principal Covenants. Nevertheless, it may reasonably be said that one of its primary functions is to promote the congruence of international legislation with core doctrines that underlie the international legal system. Consequently, the rule of law will embody respect for those human rights norms that are accepted as part of the backbone of international legal culture.[22]

Hayek himself argued that a Bill of Rights of some kind is essential to the rule of law.[23] A Charter of this kind provides protection for significant private rights occupying a discrete private realm.[24] In so doing it advances the rule of law's rationale, that is, to promote the pursuit of individual human purpose and direction and guard against its misdirection or subversion by state or society. This argument finds resonance too in more modern treatments of rights. In his recently published Harvard lectures, Michael Ignatieff, for example, argues that the fundamental idea underpinning the advancement of human rights is that their observance is an essential and non-negotiable precondition of human agency.

> Such grounding as human rights requires, I would argue, is based on what history tells us: that human beings are at risk of their lives if they lack a basic measure of free agency; that agency itself requires protection through internationally agreed standards; that these standards should entitle individuals to oppose and resist unjust laws and orders within their own states; and finally, that when all other remedies have been exhausted, these individuals have the right to appeal to other peoples, nations and international organizations for assistance in defending their rights.[25]

An international 'Rechtsstaat', in other words, cannot properly be said to exist where the capacity for choice individuals should possess in determining their lives' directions may arbitrarily be constrained, withheld or abused either by the state or in consequence of its collapse. Judith Shklar notes that:

> If one then begins with the fear of violence, the insecurity of arbitrary government, and the discriminations of injustice, one may work one's way up to finding a significant place for the Rule of Law, and for the boundaries it has historically set upon these most enduring of our political troubles.[26]

Institutional underpinnings for an international rule of law

It is one thing to agree on the values underlying the rule of law. It is quite another to translate them into a framework through which it may be made operational. Any such endeavor will no doubt provoke disagreement and contest. And the task is formidable. As James Rosenau has framed the relevant questions perceptively:

> How then to foster the authority and institutions that would bring greater degrees of democracy to governance in globalized space. How to subject its decision-makers to a modicum of accountability and responsibility. How to ensure the liberties of individuals who roam around voluntarily or otherwise in this widening domain? And equally importantly, how to begin to answer these questions without appearing hopelessly naïve, idealistic and out of touch with the realities of politics in globalized space.[27]

At the risk of falling into one or all of these errors, let me enumerate the institutional mechanisms I regard as most important in underpinning the rule of law internationally.

The first among these is a constitution. By proposing this I do not mean to suggest that a single world constitution of the kind understood as governing a nation is capable of development in any foreseeable future. Rather, the idea that one may be created should act as a beacon towards which the international community should travel and on several fronts has already commenced its journey. The idea contains within it the desire that we should work towards greater coherence across the multiplicity of treaties and rules, states and jurisdictions presently existent in order to entrench a vision of genuinely international legality. It picks up the notion that the international community should continue and advance its attempt to develop a common supra-legal structure of political action that is democratically legitimate and juridically effective. And it embodies the understanding that any such constitutional order and the laws made under it should conform to 'rule of law' principles allowing to the greatest extent possible for the exercise of human agency.

A 'constitution in progress' might do this first, by limiting by law the coercive power of institutions of global governance in a manner that permits the international subjects of that law to foresee how public power will be used; second, by making known and transparent the nature of legal constraints imposed upon those subjects; and third by defining that area of activity in which they may plan in the knowledge that their decisions will be immune from international law's impingement. More prosaically, a rule of law founded upon constitutionalism should bring some minimum order and coherence to international governance, thus making it a thing capable of being known and acted upon rationally and freely in the interests of maximizing individual agency.

A second institutional requirement is judicial review. This is the natural concomitant of a commitment to accountability. It is as much a basic principle in the international as the national arena that public power should be exercised according to the authority conferred by law. This requires that the legal boundaries of public power be defined and decided upon by an independent judicial body or bodies. It cannot be left to international institutions exercising public power under law to determine for themselves the legal parameters of its use. This is particularly the case where constitutional principles and the rules founded upon them are in question. The rights, powers, privileges and obligations exercisable by international organizations must be those and only those defined in their constituent instruments. Should international organizations act *ultra vires* or in any other way inconsistently with their charters, they must be drawn to account for doing so in an independent, impartial adjudicatory forum.

The third institutional foundation for an international rule of law is the creation of effective mechanisms for the resolution of inter-party disputes. This again requires the progressive establishment of appropriate and effective international courts, tribunals and other arbitral bodies to whom parties in conflict, whether states parties or individuals and governments, may refer their disagreements for impartial resolution and where, whether by prior agreement or otherwise, they are required to submit to judgment. Under the relevant law, all such parties must be treated equally and their access to adjudicatory bodies should be equivalently assured.

A fourth requirement is that the decisions and judgments of courts and tribunals should be enforceable. In the international arena where the sovereignty of states, although to some extent disaggregating, remains the norm, the quest for a comprehensively enforceable legal regime may still seem quixotic. And yet if respect for international law is to be engendered and equality before it maintained, there appears no alternative but to pursue gradually the goal of making judicial determinations by international judicial bodies authoritative and binding. As the Commission on Global Governance summarized the matter:

> A necessary condition for strengthening the rule of law world-wide is an efficient monitoring and compliance regime. Without this, states are tempted to embrace international norms and agreements and then not follow through on their obligations. The very essence of global governance is the capacity of the international community to ensure compliance with the rules of international society.[28]

Finally, consistent with the rule of law's incorporation of fundamental human rights, foundational human rights principles and standards should inform and infuse the law governing the work of every international organization exercising significant public power and authority. The international community recognizes certain fundamental human rights as supra-legal norms having quasi-constitutional standing. Therefore, neither political nor economic organs exercising regulatory functions in the global arena should be permitted to exercise those functions inconsistently with rights recognized as inalienable. Of course, there are legitimate differences of opinion among nations and peoples with respect to the definition of such rights and whether indeed any can be considered inalienable.[29] But nevertheless, those enumerated in the Universal Declaration and thereby endorsed in very general terms by the community of nations provide a legitimate foundation for discussion and further elaboration.

From principle to international practice

Having proposed these five institutional underpinnings for an international rule of law, I want now to explore their implications and implementation in three distinct areas of global governmental activity. These are political governance within the framework of the United Nations and its associated institutions, economic governance within the framework of the WTO and finally the UNs' institutional machinery for securing compliance with international human rights treaty obligations.

Political governance

Constitutionalism

The UN Charter is the natural starting point for the elaboration of global constitutional norms, principles and rules. It sets down the fundamental principles governing relations between states, principles that are accepted generally by the international community as the foundation stones of international peace and security. Article 2 provides for the three key principles: the sovereign equality of all UN members; the peaceful settlement of disputes; and prohibition of the threat or use of force. These were joined in 1970, in the Preamble to the UN Declaration on Friendly Relations, by four more: the ban on intervention in internal or external affairs of other States; the duty of inter-state cooperation; the principle of good faith in the performance of international obligations; and the principle of equal rights and self-determination of peoples.[30]

In accordance with the core principles, in Article 1 the Charter outlined the main functions of the UN. These are to maintain peace and security; to bring about by peaceful means the adjustment or settlement of international disputes; to develop friendly relations among nations based on respect for the principle of equal rights and the self-determination of peoples; to foster economic and social cooperation; and to promote respect for human rights and freedoms for all persons.

To effect the purposes, the Charter created an organizational structure within which the key institutions were the Security Council and the Economic and Social Council, broadly corresponding to an executive; the General Assembly, broadly corresponding to a legislature; and the International Court of Justice, being the principal organ of the international judiciary. The relations between these institutions, however, were by no means such as to create a genuine separation of powers.

Since the Charter's adoption, this framework has been supplemented by the law contained in innumerable international treaties, the continuing ripening of international norms of behavior into customary international law, and the many complementary normative pronouncements of the International Court of Justice (ICJ). This international activity has been so comprehensive and so dense that at the turn of the millennium, it would seem appropriate to identify and then codify those components of international law that are regarded as so central they may be presumed to have achieved supra-legal or constitutional standing.

The obvious point at which to begin would be with the codification of *jus cogens*. *Jus cogens* is defined in Article 53 of the Vienna Conventions on the Law of Treaties as the 'peremptory norms accepted and by the community of states as a whole from which no derogation is permitted'.[31] These are rules that emanate from and move the human conscience. Their breach is recognized as a crime by the international community as a whole. A provision of a treaty is void if it conflicts with any such norms. Defining such norms is more difficult because their inclusion in *jus cogens* depends upon the substantial agreement of states. However, it appears generally accepted that norms outlawing aggression and genocide and the principles and rules concerning the basic rights of human beings, including protection from slavery and racial discrimination, lie at its core. To these one could add others prohibiting torture, denying self-determination, outlawing massive pollution and delineating the fundamental principles of international humanitarian law.[32]

The concept of *jus cogens* has been in existence for 40 years and yet no codification has been undertaken. Instead, these peremptory norms of international law rely for their existence and authority principally upon the declarations of UN bodies such as the General Assembly and the Commission on Human Rights, the *obiter dicta* pronouncements of the ICJ and conformable pronouncements by States. Their embodiment in a written and systematic legal form would assist considerably by making them better known, more certain and recognizably general in application. It would also enhance constitutional modernization by providing a transparent textual foundation for revision and reform as new norms take shape in response to their recognition by representative States across the globe.[33]

A second point of constitutional departure should emanate from the Secretary-General, Kofi Annan's recent proposal that 25 international treaties be identified as having particular international significance and his launch at the Millennium Summit of a campaign to secure their comprehensive ratification and hence universal application.[34] The treaties he nominated reflect the key policy goals of the United Nations. Their ratification, he argued, would represent a rededication by States to the international legal framework and make a significant contribution to the promotion of the international rule of law.

The priority list of treaties included the convention on genocide, conventions to eliminate discrimination on the grounds of sex and race and to protect the rights of the child. Other instruments on the indicative list were the international covenants on civil and political rights, on economic, social and cultural rights, conventions to protect refugees, prevent terrorism and to outlaw certain conventional weapons, chemical weapons and landmines. Environmental conventions were also listed including those dealing with climate change, biodiversity and desertification. Clearly, the greater the number of signatories to these priority treaties the more forceful will be the presumption that they form part of an emerging global constitutional order.

A third component of the developing global constitutional order is contained in declarations and treaties systematizing and codifying norms governing the conduct of relationships between States. These include, for example, the Declaration on Principles of International Law concerning Friendly Relations and Cooperation among States in Accordance with the Charter of the United Nations (1970), the Vienna Convention on Diplomatic Relations (1961), the Vienna Convention on the Law of Treaties (1969) and the Statute of the International Court of Justice (1945).

A fourth and obvious component of constitutional development relates to the necessary but politically difficult task of reforming the UN institutional structure. A survey of proposals for reform in this area is well beyond the scope of the present chapter.[35] Nevertheless, the rule of law's attachment to the value of legitimacy, suggests that the direction of organizational change should be towards greater democratization.[36] One of the weaknesses of the United Nations has been its inability to adapt its institutional arrangements to the changing realities of shifts in global power over the past half century. The Security Council, for example, has retained veto power for its five permanent members despite the fact that they are no longer representative of changes in the relative wealth and power of nations. Further, the Council's membership remains dominated by nations of the North at the expense of those of the South, thereby weakening its democratic credentials. Similar criticisms may be made of the composition and operation of the General Assembly. Plainly, if new, emergent components of a world constitutional order are to be recognized, codified and eventually incorporated into a revised UN Charter, such foundational changes will require a level of democratic legitimation that the existing institutions of the United Nations cannot properly confer.

Judicial review

The existence of an effective system of judicial review is critical to any constitutional and political system founded upon the rule of law. Within the framework of the UN, however, it may be described as rudimentary at best. The problem was stated succinctly by the Commission on Global Governance:

> When the founders of the UN drew up the Charter, the rule of law world-wide loomed as one of its central components. They established the International Court of Justice at the Hague . . . as the 'cathedral of law' in the global system. But states were free to take it or leave it, in whole or in part. The rule of law was asserted and, at the same time, undermined. Each state could decide whether it was going to accept the compulsory jurisdiction of the World Court.

> And a great many did not. Thus, from the outset, the World Court was marginalized.[37]

The marginalization took two forms.[38] The first, with which I am concerned in this section, is the lack of a capacity by the Court to review the legality of the actions of the UN's principal organs and most notably those of the Security Council and the General Assembly. No explicit power is given by the UN Charter to the ICJ to review Security Council and Assembly resolutions for conformity either with the Charter or with principles of general or customary international law.

At the same time, however, Article 24(2) of the Charter provides that in discharging its duties, the Security Council shall act in accordance with the Purposes and Principles of the United Nations and consequently it must be presumed that it is not to act arbitrarily outside this framework. Further, the absence of judicial review by the ICJ has not precluded legal questions concerning the scope of the UN Charter, and the resolutions and actions of its principal organs, being considered by other UN tribunals such as those established to try alleged perpetrators of crimes against humanity. Nor, apparently, does it preclude the ICJ determining the legal conformity of resolutions adopted by political organs with Charter provisions in the context of inter-party disputation as to the meaning and application of the Charter as treaty. The Court itself has stated that 'the political character of an organ cannot release it from the observance of the treaty provisions established by the Charter when they constitute limitations on its powers or criteria for its judgment'.[39]

The question is not, then, whether the Security Council's powers are defined and limited by law. The problem resides in determining the extent of the ICJ's competence to inquire into Council resolutions. It is similar with the General Assembly.

In the *Lockerbie Case* (*Preliminary Objections*) it appears to have been accepted that the ICJ may check for conformity.[40] However, it may be impermissible for it to go further and question the Council's discretionary competence, for instance, to determine whether a genuine threat to international peace and security is present. This latter, as a political decision, might properly be considered as non-justiciable.

Is it sufficient to leave it at that? Looked at pragmatically, it is highly unlikely that, in the foreseeable future, the world's major nations will countenance fully-fledged judicial review. Nevertheless, in the context of the preceding discussion, it would clearly be desirable if some judicial intervention could be called upon where UN institutions appear to be acting in a manner calculated to undermine the Charter's core principles and purposes. So, for example, one might consider conferring a jurisdiction upon the ICJ to hear matters in which a State party claims that a UN executive organ is acting in a manner contrary to peremptory norms, or in contravention of the Charter's explicit, substantive or procedural requirements.[41]

Renewed consideration might also be given to the utilization of the Court's advisory jurisdiction. Article 65(1) of the Court's Statute provides that the Court may give an advisory opinion on any legal question at the request of any authorized UN agency. Article 96 empowers the Security Council and the General Assembly to seek such advice. A similar power could be conferred on the Secretary-General. The advisory jurisdiction may constructively be used to assist the UN's political organs to determine the proper boundaries of their powers, to resolve disputes between them and to obtain authoritative guidance on the legal framework within which their specialized agencies must act. This is not judicial review proper but if used responsibly could constitute a constructive step in moving in that direction.

Thus, for example, it would have been open to the General Assembly to seek an advisory opinion on the legality or otherwise of the invasion of Iraq in 2003. The invasion occurred purportedly in reliance upon prior resolutions of the Security Council and in conformity with the Charter. The ICJ could have been asked to advise on whether any such reliance was legally justified. Of course, there is a certain lack of assertiveness by the General Assembly and other UN organs to initiate this form of legal review, particularly where the actions of powerful nations like the USA and Britain are called into question. Nevertheless, the mechanism is there and could constructively be used in appropriate circumstances.[42]

Dispute resolution

The second source of the Court's marginalization has been the voluntary and partial nature of States' acceptance of its jurisdiction. The disputes over which it may exercise such jurisdiction relate to conflicts concerning the interpretation of any treaty, any question of international law, any breach of a recognized legal obligation and the nature and extent of reparation for such a breach.[43] But the Court may exercise this jurisdiction only where the states that are parties to a dispute have agreed to abide by its decisions. Of the United Nations' 184 member states, only 57 have opted into this jurisdiction. Of these, some have opted in only on condition that the state party taking action against them has also accepted the Court's jurisdiction. Others have agreed to accept its decisions only pursuant to their obligations under particular treaties. Still others have opted in but later withdrew when their political interests were adversely affected, most notably the United States in the *Nicaragua* case[44] and France in the *Nuclear Tests* case.[45]

Equality before the law, as a value basic to the rule of law, is clearly violated when only some parties but not others agree to abide by it. There is a strong case, therefore, for the acceptance of the compulsory jurisdiction of the World Court to become a precondition for UN membership. In the interim, however, amendments could be sought to treaties which, either because of their fundamental importance or special character, demand that States parties submit conflicts under them compulsorily to the Court for adjudication. The cause of equality would be further advanced if other non-state actors such as international NGOs with a definable interest in the outcome of the proceedings were accorded an entitlement to be joined as parties.[46]

Enforceability

Article 59 of the Statute of the ICJ provides that the Court's decisions have 'no binding force except between the parties and in respect of that particular case'. Further, pursuant to Article 38(1)(d), the Court may apply judicial decisions but, subject to Article 59, as subsidiary means for the determination of rules of law. In consequence, the judgments of the Court cannot be regarded as making law, nor is the doctrine of precedent applicable. However, it would be wrong to conclude from this that the Court's decisions possess little influence beyond the instant case. On the contrary, the principles enunciated by it in significant judgments have proven critical in the establishment of the existence of customary international law, defining its scope and content and in contributing to an understanding of what is meant by 'the general principles of law recognized by civilized nations'.[47]

Nevertheless, it remains generally true that the Court, at least in terms of enforcement, remains a somewhat toothless tiger. Again, this is unlikely to change in the foreseeable future. An interim answer, therefore, would appear to be the continuing expansion of treaty-based provisions specifying the nature of acceptable remedies and sanctions, and the prior agreement by signatory states to abide by the Court's determinations in imposing them.

The incorporation of human rights standards

By any measure, the progress made by the United Nations and its associated institutions in advancing and protecting human rights has been enormously impressive. The UN Declaration of 1948, combined with the International Covenants on Civil and Political Rights and Economic, Social and Cultural Rights, enumerate the fundamental rights of humankind and provide the quasi-constitutional foundation for their international recognition, observance and enforcement. Beyond these, a host of other more specific treaties have been negotiated most notably in relation to genocide, torture, racial discrimination, sex discrimination, refugees and the rights of the child.

Institutionally, the United Nations has established the Commission for Human Rights assisted by the UN High Commissioner for Human Rights under the auspices of the Economic and Social Council (ECOSOC), and created a plurality of human rights treaty monitoring bodies to secure States compliance with their international treaty obligations. Special International Criminal Tribunals have been established to try alleged perpetrators of crimes against humanity in Bosnia and Rwanda and most recently, the Statute of Rome creating the International Criminal Court has been adopted and awaits the appropriate number of ratifications for its commencement. UN Special Rapporteurs have been despatched to various parts of the globe to report upon and endeavor to ameliorate egregious abuses of rights. And a concerted attempt has been made by relevant UN agencies to encourage the creation of regional human rights conventions and the creation of national rights charters and associated human rights commissions. The effectiveness of some of these treaty bodies in ensuring compliance with international human rights obligations will be addressed presently.

Here, however, I am concerned with a different facet of human rights promotion. That is, the incorporation of human rights standards in the work of the UN itself. As the pivotal international institution having responsibility for the spread of a human rights culture globally, it is only reasonable to expect that the UN and its associated organs will give due consideration to human rights concerns in every aspect of its own deliberations and actions.

In this regard, I have space here only to sketch two issues for consideration. The first relates to the tension that will inevitably arise in the Security Council between its Chapter VII obligation to maintain peace and security and the more general commitment of the wider organization to preserve human dignity and human rights. While the maintenance of peace and security is an absolute precondition for human rights observance, the two objectives may sometimes conflict. Intervention to secure peace, for example, may require forceful military intervention, an incident of which may be significant and unavoidable civilian casualties. Alternatively, as was demonstrated tragically in the Somalian case, the deployment of UN peacekeepers possessing a principally humanitarian brief without the additional authority and personnel to secure order by engaging in necessary military action to achieve it can result in a military quagmire. The balance is a delicate one. The matter is complicated further by the political character of the Security Council which tends to make its decisions to intervene on humanitarian grounds on criteria that are highly selective. This in turn conflicts with the universal character of international humanitarian and human rights obligations.[48] So, the goal should be to ensure that the Security Council acts in accordance with its fundamental obligation to protect human rights worldwide but clearly its achievement in conflict situations will not always be straightforward.[49]

Second, the United Nations has been slow to incorporate human rights considerations into its deliberations concerning the regulation of the international economy and international economic actors. Indeed, it has been argued persuasively that the organization's attention has been captured increasingly by neo-liberal ideology and free-market economic policy to the detriment of advancing the human rights agenda.[50] Institutionally this has been reflected in the separation of global financial institutions such as the World Bank, the IMF and the WTO from ECOSOC and its associated human rights treaty bodies and commissions, and other environmental and developmental agencies. This institutional fragmentation has contributed, among other things, to a diminution of the importance of economic and social rights in the deliberations of the international economic regulatory agencies.[51] This is an issue to which I return in the next section of the chapter that explores the 'rule of law' in relation to the world trade regime.

Economic governance

Constitutionalism

The agreement establishing the WTO is perhaps the most important and comprehensive development in global governance since the adoption of the UN Charter.

The Uruguay Round's Final Act of 1994 strengthened the General Agreement on Tariffs and Trade's (GATT) institutional machinery through the creation of the WTO. The WTO is a single institutional framework encompassing GATT together with all the agreements and legal instruments negotiated in the Uruguay Round and other agreements relating to trade in goods; the General Agreement on Trade in Services (GATS); the Agreements on Trade-Related Property (TRIPs); and on Trade-Related Investment Measures (TRIMs); and The Understanding on Dispute Settlement; among others. The WTO has, in the short time since its creation, become the focal point for the promotion of global trade and development.

The founders of the new international trading regime recognized that the opportunities of economic globalization could be exploited only if agreed, reliable, transparent and generally recognized international rules were adopted to regulate trading relationships between nations and only where those rules applied equally to all. Consequently, the rule of law was central to the new international economic enterprise from the outset. In 1995, the Director-General of the Organization argued that without a firm framework of rules and disciplines, openness of trade would descend into anarchy. Open trade must therefore be trade within the rule of law. The constitutional structure of the organization is a clear reflection of a commitment to this ideal and provides a marked, albeit understandable, contrast to the problems that beset the development of an international constitutional order in the global political arena.[52]

The successful constitutional development of the organization lies principally in its members' adherence to certain fundamental norms and values. The overriding value is a commitment to free trade within free markets across international borders.[53] The principal norms that underpin this commitment are first, most favored nation treatment, meaning that a nation will not in its trading relationships treat any one nation more or less favorably than any other. The second is that relating to national treatment. This involves an agreement by all member nations that they will not discriminate against foreign products, services or nationals in a manner that may disadvantage them in relation to their domestic equivalents. The third is market access for services. This involves the agreement by members that they will not place unnecessary burdens on the passage of foreign services, and the entities that supply them, into relevant domestic markets.

To make these norms operational, the WTO regulates and supervises the operation of the key trade treaties previously mentioned. Its task is to provide the forum in which members may conduct further negotiations and develop additional agreements designed to facilitate their multilateral trading relationships. All of the existing treaties are founded upon the fundamental norms and principles and rules that derive from them. Membership of the WTO, therefore, is contingent not only on accession to the Agreement Establishing the WTO but also upon submission to the treaties, together with the Trade Policy Review Mechanism and the Understanding on Rules and Procedures Governing the Settlement of Disputes (about which more will be said in the following paragraphs).

To support the treaties and trade negotiations, the WTO has adopted a common, comprehensive and constitutionally governed organizational structure headed by a Director-General who has similar standing to the heads of the World Bank and the IMF. Its principal forum is a Ministerial Council consisting of representatives of all the members. Between meetings, the business of the Organization is undertaken by a General Council. The General Council convenes two important specialist bodies – the Trade Policy Review Body and the Dispute Settlement Body. It has also established several high level Councils to oversee trade treaties concerning specific subject matters. The constitution also regulates voting procedures, among other things, by providing that the constitutional norms providing the Organization's rationale can be changed only with the authority of every member.

In short, the constitutional framework for world trade regulation is firmly established thus underpinning the primary foundation for the adoption of a global rule of law in the economic arena. As one commentator has noted:

> The initial success of . . . the WTO . . . lay in its single minded pursuit of a simple goal: the development of a universal framework of rules and procedures dedicated to liberalization and non-discrimination, enforced through mutual respect amongst its members for the rule of law. Its success is attested both in its growing membership and in its steady progress in widening and deepening liberalization and strengthening the rules and procedures to back it up.[54]

As we explore the other relevant institutions and principles, however, the achievements with respect to conformity with the rule of law become distinctly more variable.

Judicial review

Given the thoughtful and comprehensive nature of the WTO's constitutional settlement, it is striking that its Articles of Agreement contain no provision for the judicial review of the constitutionality of its resolutions, decisions and actions. Although a comprehensive machinery of dispute resolution between member states has been constructed, the broader question as to whether the Organization has acted within its Charter curiously has not been given to judicial solution. Contrary to the rule of law value of accountability, the interpretation of the Articles of Agreement is left to the Ministerial Council itself to determine.[55] Given the very substantial impact the decisions of the Organization may have on nations and peoples throughout the world, this is an omission that should be remedied. The WTO is an organization affiliated with the United Nations. Perhaps, therefore, it should amend its Articles of Agreement to provide that the interpretation of the Articles and the validity of actions taken under them should be determined by the ICJ.

Dispute resolution

The WTO has adopted an innovative and effective system for the resolution of treaty disputes between its members. The Understanding on Rules and Procedures

Governing the Settlement of Disputes (DSU) promotes the rule of law value of legality in many different ways.

In summary, the dispute resolution procedures are as follows.[56] Upon receipt by a member of complaint that another member has adopted trade measures affecting the substantive provisions of a trade agreement, the Organization notifies the member complained against and seeks a response. Should this response fail to achieve a mutually satisfactory solution, the dispute is referred to an independent dispute resolution panel. The panel will usually consist of three members each of whom are recognized experts in international trade law or policy. They are not judges but experts serving in their individual capacity and must not come from the member states involved in the disputation. The panels are subject to strict time lines for the completion of both conciliation and litigation. In making their determinations, the panels are guided principally by the terms of the treaty or treaties with which they are concerned but may also take into consideration GATT jurisprudence and that developed by the WTO's appellate body. The parties to the dispute are the member states in disagreement together with any other member state whose trading interests may be affected by the outcome. Having heard submissions from each of the parties, the panel transmits a report to the WTO's Dispute Resolution Body. The report is adopted by that Body unless it decides by consensus that the report should not be adopted or if one of the parties decides to appeal the panel's conclusions. Where an appeal is lodged, it is heard by a seven-member Appellate Body appointed by the Dispute Resolution Body. The Appellate Body is limited to determining questions of law. In so doing, it is bound by the interpretations of multilateral trade agreements adopted by the Ministerial Conference and General Council, interpretations endorsed by three-quarters of the total membership. Reports of the Appellate Body are adopted automatically by the Dispute Resolution Body unless it decides by consensus not to do so. The Dispute Resolution Body is charged with the responsibility of determining how to implement the relevant reports.

The procedure is a resourceful combination of conciliation, negotiation and litigation, its emphasis being upon achieving a mediated outcome wherever possible. With certain exceptions, the process resembles a judicial one and the basic rules of procedural fairness are observed. Nevertheless, there remain a number of evident deficiencies. The main one concerns the lack of transparency in proceedings. The panel and appellate hearings are conducted in camera, depriving the legal process of the openness so important to the achievement of accountability. As Stiglitz has argued persuasively:

> At the WTO, the negotiations that lead up to agreements are all done behind closed doors, making it difficult – until it is too late – to see the influence of corporate and other special interests. The deliberations of the WTO panels that rule on whether there has been a violation of WTO agreements occur in secret. It is perhaps not surprising that the trade lawyers and ex-trade officials who often comprise such panels pay, for instance, little attention to the environment; but by bringing the deliberations more out into the open,

> public scrutiny would either make the panels more sensitive to public concerns or force a reform in the adjudication process.[57]

Standing to appear is confined to member states. It does not extend, as perhaps would be desirable, either to individuals or organizations whose interests may also be affected adversely by the outcome of the proceedings. Nor does it extend to other international organizations, including those of international civil society, whose representations could be expected to bring a broader range of associated and relevant perspectives to bear on the treaty disagreements in question.[58] Further, it remains to be seen whether member states will have equal access to the dispute resolution mechanisms. In the first years of its operation, it has clearly been wealthier nations who have been its principal users. Should this trend continue, consideration may have to be given to supporting developing nations to pursue complaints and similar assistance will certainly be required if the standing rules are relaxed to permit civil society organizations to make the representations they demand.

Enforcement

As in most other spheres of international law, mechanisms for the enforcement of these quasi-judicial trade-related decisions are relatively weak although in this instance they do not lack influence. The adoption of a panel report does not bind the parties to implement its recommendations. Instead, the decision is referred to the Dispute Resolution Body whose task then is to attempt to secure by persuasion the withdrawal of the measures that have been held to be incompatible with the agreements. Should the defaulting party fail to withdraw, an obligation is placed upon the parties to negotiate an appropriate amount of compensation. The payment of compensation, however, is also voluntary. Where the payment of compensation is refused, the complaining party may approach the Dispute Resolution Body with a request for the authorization of countermeasures. The countermeasures approved can involve the suspension of concessions or other benefits conferred by the relevant treaty either in the same sector or by cross-retaliation in another. Of course, whether or not such countermeasures are applied remains more in the nature of a political than a legal decision. Certainly, this extended process of adjudication is a significant advance upon any other yet developed to settle disputes in the global community and yet from the perspective of the rule of law values of accountability, equality and fairness, it has not yet produced an entirely satisfactory outcome.

To this it should be added that the corpus of law developed by the Appellate Body has become increasingly influential in determining the decision-making of dispute resolution panels, promoting consistency between them. In addition, by developing an extensive framework of relevant principles and rules, the Dispute Resolution Body has encouraged greater convergence in the trading behavior of WTO members themselves, thus generating greater confidence and stability as the backdrop to the making of economic choices.

Human rights

While the WTO may have been successful in establishing a general, known and certain framework of law within which to conduct its global activities, the massive, disruptive demonstrations conducted at its recent meetings provide more than ample evidence that the content of its decision-making is the subject of considerable contention.[59] The objections and anger directed at the Organization come from groups representing an eclectic array of interests including individuals and organizations concerned about the widening North–South divide, the associated gap between rich and poor nations and peoples, a deterioration in international labor conditions and standards, consumer protection and ecological degradation. While criticisms of the WTO from each of these perspectives can be justified, and each relates, to some degree, to issues linked to human rights, my discussion here will of necessity relate only to economic and social rights since these are of the most direct relevance to the Organization's Charter.

My argument in this respect is the same as it was in the previous section. Consistent with the values underlying the rule of law, the WTO's Charter and operations should require it at every stage of its deliberations to consider the effect of its policies, rules and practices upon the economic and social rights possessed universally by the peoples of the world and protected explicitly by the UN Charter and its associated Covenant on Economic, Social and Cultural Rights.

There are considerable obstacles, however, to the achievement of this objective. The first, already referred to, is the institutional division created in the existing structure of global governance between international political and economic organizations. While the UN as the apex of the political structure has specific Charter responsibility for the promotion and protection of economic, social and cultural rights, no such specific mandate is given to the WTO whose concerns have been almost exclusively economic in nature. This has allowed it to de-emphasize if not altogether exclude matters concerning the eradication of third-world poverty, labor standards and cultural preservation from its agenda. These, it may be argued, remain within the province of the political wing.

Second, the juridical framework of the WTO may itself have contributed to the neglect of the consideration of economic, social and cultural rights. These rights have proven notoriously difficult to translate into tangible categories of entitlements capable of enforcement by law. The puzzlement of the international legal community at large and trade law specialists in particular about how to realize these rights, provides at least a partial explanation for continuing inaction on this front.

Third, and perhaps most obviously, the philosophy underlying the WTO is founded upon the profound (ideologically grounded) belief that global welfare, and hence economic, social and cultural rights, is best promoted by enhancing free markets in trade, finance and investment. Regulation, in the form of a requirement to modify economic regimes to cater for the needs of developing countries and their citizens can, on this view, only inhibit the achievement of the very goals to which the reformers aspire. This is a form of economic and ideological blindness that makes the cause of promoting human rights in this sphere an enormously difficult and problematic one.[60]

Nevertheless, there remain institutional mechanisms within the WTO framework through which the cause may be promoted however gradually. It should become obligatory, for example, for human rights impact statements to be prepared prior to the adoption of major treaties, policies and decisions. The sources of law that can be taken into consideration by dispute resolution panels and the Appellate Body should be expanded to include the general principles of international law, including that contained in both the major human rights covenants. And there should be movement towards the greater democratization of the Organization by institutionalizing its relationships with civil society. This could be effected by providing for the accreditation of internationally recognized and respected NGOs with an interest in the Organization's activities. Once accredited, they should be entitled to make representations when significant treaties are negotiated or amended and when new policies are being considered. They should also be afforded standing before dispute resolution panels and in cases having significant precedential consequences before the Appellate Body.

If the rule of law is genuinely to be globalized, it cannot be permissible for certain institutions of international governance to ignore or downgrade critical principles and values that underpin it. Instead, these values and principles must be incorporated into every aspect of their work. For all of its success in founding global economic governance upon legal principle and practice, the WTO can be no exception to this overarching principle. Consequently, the promotion of human rights in general, and of economic, social and cultural rights in particular should occupy a central place in its global reform agenda.

The UN human rights treaty monitoring system

Constitutionalism

The final institutional arena I wish to consider is the system developed under the auspices of the United Nations to monitor and secure human rights globally. Since the topic is large, I can touch upon it only in summary in the context of the more general discussion of the rule of law with which this chapter is concerned. While there have been many significant developments in this sphere, not the least of which has been a developing doctrine of international humanitarian intervention to prevent crimes against humanity perpetrated by sovereign states and the conclusion of the Rome Statute establishing the International Criminal Court, I have chosen here to focus on the United Nations' Human Rights Treaty Monitoring System.[61]

The constitutional components of this system may straightforwardly be described. They consist first of the major human rights treaties and conventions ratified by member states of the United Nations and in particular the UN Declaration of Human Rights and its associated Covenants on Civil and Political Rights and Economic, Social and Cultural Rights. These and the many other treaties concerned with preventing human rights violations in more specific fields such as race, sex and disability, provide a known, certain and generally applicable documentary foundation for this quasi-constitutional regime. In the first 50 years of the UN's existence, the proliferation of relevant treaties and their extensive ratification by nations across the globe has constituted one of its most remarkable achievements. However, from the perspective of the rule of law, many substantial challenges remain to be met.

The principal challenge is that of ensuring that states, having ratified the relevant treaties, are made to meet their obligations under them. Unlike the position that pertains in relation to the WTO, it is not a condition of UN membership that States parties ratify and comply with treaties, even those relating to matters as fundamental as the protection of human rights. As it is, the significant majority of nations have ratified the principal human rights conventions but most still choose to evade their legal and political strictures. Far fewer have signed the very important Optional Protocol to the Civil Rights Covenant, which provides a means whereby individual victims of human rights abuse may complain to an international body, the Human Rights Committee. Regrettably, among those that have refused to sign are the United States, Britain and China. Further, no such protocol exists or is likely to be accepted under the Covenant protecting Economic, Social and Cultural Rights. The primary reason for this lack of cooperation has been stated succinctly by Richard Falk:

> The most serious of all constraints bearing on the application of international human rights norms . . . is perhaps the one least brought to light. It is, in essence, the staunchly realist orientation of the political elites who have continued to control the shaping of foreign policy on behalf of most states, and especially on behalf of those states that play the most active geopolitical roles. The realist frame of reference entertains extremely serious, principled doubts about the relevance of law and morality to the proper operation of the state system.[62]

It is this realist orientation that provides the context for the further consideration of the monitoring system that follows.

The principal institutional mechanism established to promote state compliance with treaty obligations is the system of Human Rights Monitoring Committees. Each treaty creates such a supervisory Committee. For the Civil Rights Covenant and its Optional Protocol, the monitoring body is the Human Rights Committee. For the Economic Rights Covenant, the monitoring body is the Committee on Economic, Social and Cultural Rights. For the Convention on the Elimination of all Forms of Discrimination against Women, the Committee with the same name and so on. These Committees have three principal functions. They receive and examine periodic reports submitted by States; they receive and consider upon inter-state complaints; and, under the Optional Protocol procedures, they hear and make recommendations in relation to complaints lodged by individuals or groups alleging treaty violations by a particular State. The functions, powers and procedures of these Committees are considered further in the following section on Dispute Resolution.

Judicial review

The stark reality of the international treaty monitoring system is that States have been entirely unwilling to submit their actions to international judicial scrutiny. The reason is plain – allegations of human rights abuse are politically extremely sensitive and if found proven may engender very significant diplomatic and economic costs. Consequently, the idea that an international court might be established to make definitive rulings with respect to complaints about human rights violations has barely registered on the international political and legal agenda. In this matter, considerations of state sovereignty continue to dominate.

In the result, the international community has favored an essentially administrative rather than judicial system of monitoring States' compliance with their international human rights obligations. And because the system is principally administrative rather than judicial in character, the issue of the judicial review of Committee procedures and views simply has not arisen.

One of the most compelling question facing those concerned with making progress towards a global rule of law is how best to move towards a more rigorous, judicially founded resolution of individual complaints of human rights abuse internationally.

Dispute resolution

The monitoring Committees established to act as guardians of the human rights treaties to which they relate have three principal functions. They request and consider State reports, they receive and consider State communications and, where there is an appropriate Optional Protocol in place, they receive and make recommendations with respect to individual complaints. Speaking generally, the purpose of the monitoring process is to create a dialogue between the Committees and States parties with a view to improving the latter's levels of compliance and reducing the need to resort to State or individual complaints. The purpose of the communications process is to attempt to resolve State and individual complaints concerning alleged infringements of treaty provisions.[63]

The monitoring process established differs from a judicial one in several important respects.[64] The Committee members are elected by the States parties and serve as 'experts' in their individual capacities. Most have a particular expertise in international human rights law but the degree to which they act independently of the views of their sponsoring governments varies. Except in the case of the Optional Protocols, an aggrieved party does not initiate proceedings. Instead, a discussion takes place founded upon the periodic progress reports the Committees require States parties to tender. With very limited exceptions, oral evidence is taken only from the State party whose report is being considered. Those who advocate an opposing perspective, such as international and domestic human rights NGO's, may submit written comments on a party's report but are not generally invited to speak. The outcome of the process does not involve the making of rulings or determinations. Rather, it consists of a written response by the Committee to the relevant State report together with generally stated observations and recommendations for further action. No clear mechanism has been developed to follow-up Committee observations and recommendations.

The procedures for the receipt and determination of individual complaints, for example, under the Optional Protocol to the Civil Rights Covenant, also possess features that depart significantly from the judicial or quasi-judicial.[65] Committee members serve part-time and not infrequently hold senior positions with the national government by which they have been nominated, thus creating potential conflicts of interest. The Committees deal with individual complaints only on the basis of written submissions. These are provided solely by the parties. Committee meetings on complaints are held in camera and the pleadings are regarded as confidential. The Protocol contains no explicit provisions about the effect of the Committee's legal views or about any remedy that may be afforded.

It will be apparent from this brief comparison that Committee monitoring procedures fall well short of those which would normally be considered appropriate for securing States' compliance with their international treaty obligations and hence with the rule of international law. Similarly, the protocol procedures are quite inadequate to achieve the transparent, fair and effective resolution of individual human rights complaints.

To this catalogue of difficulties, a number of political and administrative deficiencies may also be added.[66] The effectiveness of the monitoring procedures has been hampered significantly by many States' recalcitrance and tardiness in producing their periodic reports. The Committees themselves have been starved of adequate time and resources to undertake their supervisory functions in detail and with the seriousness they demand. Committees have been reluctant to engage in trenchant criticisms of States, even where such criticisms may be appropriate, for fear of alienating not only the particular States concerned but others whose cooperation is valued or whose entry into the system is desired.

The Protocol procedure has had similar problems in attracting reasoned and helpful responses from States complained against. There is a considerable backlog of cases to be considered which, because of the delay, lessens significantly the impact of any written views it may express in any individual case. Most significantly, the disparity between the well-known extent of human rights violations that occur across the globe and the veritable trickle of petitions received under the Protocol provides ample evidence that the procedure lacks relevance and credibility.

Taking all this into consideration, Anne Bayefsky, in her report on the Committee system commissioned by the UN High Commissioner for Human Rights, summarized her conclusions as follows:

> The gap between universal right and remedy has become inescapable and inexcusable, threatening the integrity of the international human rights legal regime . . . . The system is characterized by overwhelming numbers of overdue

> reports, untenable backlogs, minimal individual complaints from vast numbers of potential victims and widespread refusals of states to provide remedies where violations of rights are found.[67]

It is tempting to conclude that the UN human rights treaty monitoring system is irredeemably flawed.[68] Stymied by the contemptuous attitudes of States, debilitated by compromised Committee membership, undermined by a lack of institutional support and resources, and shunned by potential complainants across the globe, the capacity of the system to effect the international rule of law's commitment to accountability and to the protection of fundamental human rights would appear to be compromised almost fatally.

Yet one should not also fail to appreciate the magnitude of the difficulties facing the international community in securing the compliance of States with a regime of international law designed of its very essence to constrain the exercise of their power and to generate global condemnation for its misuse. Nor should it be forgotten that, taking a longer term perspective, much, though not nearly enough, has been achieved. As the former Secretary to the Committee on Economic, Social and Cultural Rights, Philip Alston has remarked:

> The human rights treaty system has come a very long way in a relatively short time. As recently as 1969, there was not a single human rights treaty body in existence. States were extremely reluctant to subject their human rights record to any sort of external scrutiny. The terms agreed in the text of the several treaties that had been adopted envisaged a minimalist approach to monitoring. No treaty-based individual complaints system existed and the prospects of any coming into force were not considered good. The only human rights reporting exercise that had been tried had yielded almost nothing. Thirty years later, the system has developed so rapidly that it has problems of which human rights proponents in earlier eras could only have dreamed. Those problems are certainly considerable, but they must be viewed against the background of the historical evolution of the system as a whole.[69]

Given the staunchly realist orientation of existing political elites, the idea that immediate, radical reform of the system would be feasible is questionable. It would be more likely than not to generate further political reticence, new treaty reservations, frank refusals to cooperate and, ultimately, state withdrawals from the system in its entirety. However regrettable it may seem from a rule of law perspective, a more cautious approach to reform would therefore appear warranted. Much could be done to strengthen the existing system procedurally and administratively without generating a profound alienation from it. The ultimate aim should remain the construction of a judicially enforceable international Bill of Rights. But this is a distant objective.

In the short- to medium-term then, the following suggestions for reforming the monitoring process should be considered. The Committees' work should be far better coordinated. It might be best simply to amalgamate them and have one overarching Committee meet throughout the year, rather than as now infrequently and for short, relatively unproductive periods. A greater degree of coordination is also required with other UN human rights agencies.[70] The Commissioner for Human Rights commissions studies and despatches fact-finding missions to report on immediate and continuing patterns of human rights abuse. These studies and reports should be fed into the Committees' deliberations as a matter of course. The Committees' views and recommendations similarly should inform the work of the Commission on Human Rights and ECOSOC. The system of electing Committee members should be reformed to ensure that they are without exception expert and impartial. The Committees' agendas should become more focused and selective. The routine examination of cursorily produced country reports should be replaced by specific requests to nominated countries to provide answers to carefully framed, pre-determined questions. The sources of information upon which the Committees rely should concomitantly be broadened. The United Nations should authorize Committees to send their own fact-finding missions where such a course of action is deemed necessary to respond to suggestions of present and widespread human rights abuse. National Human Rights Commissions and affiliated NGOs should be accorded standing to appear and give evidence before Committees concerning the human rights performance of nations whose progress is under examination. The entire system, finally, must be given adequate human and financial resources to undertake the critical task in which they are engaged.

The individual complaints procedures could also be altered constructively. To avoid unnecessary duplication and confusion, a single, separate Committee to hear and determine individual complaints should be established. Care should be taken to ensure that members elected possess the relevant legal qualifications and well-founded reputations for impartiality. The Committee should possess the capacity to pick and choose between communications to ensure that it deals as a matter of priority with those relating to serious allegations of human rights abuse and those that are most likely to create significant legal precedents. Its hearings should be open and capable of hearing oral as well as written evidence. It should be able to appoint *amicus curiae* and afford standing to affiliated civil society organizations and other parties who may provide evidence of direct relevance to the resolution of the complaint. Once again, it will need to be provided with the resources necessary to complete its work effectively.

Enforcement

It follows from the argument pursued in the preceding section that currently, to invest the UN, and the ICJ on its behalf, with the power judicially to enforce States parties' obligations under international human rights treaties remains an unrealistic and hence very distant objective. Nevertheless, there have been a number of developments towards the achievement of this aim in the international arena that are positive and should briefly be mentioned for the sake of completeness.

First and most obviously, the force and standing of international criminal law has been substantially advanced by the creation of the International Criminal Tribunals in relation to Bosnia and Rwanda and the subsequent conclusion of the Rome Statute establishing the International Criminal Court. It remains, however, a blight in this regard, that a lack of international political will has prevented the establishment of a third specialist Tribunal in relation to offences against international humanitarian and human rights law allegedly committed by Indonesian forces in East Timor.

Second, there has been significant progress in establishing regional human rights conventions that have explicit provision for judicial review and enforcement. The model in this regard is the European Convention on Human Rights under which complainants, having exhausted all internal remedies, may appeal to the European Court situated in Strasbourg. The Court may hear and determine the complaints and its decisions are implemented by States parties under supervision. There is also an Inter-American system with a Convention, Commission and Court that covers many Latin American and Caribbean members of the Organization of American States. This Court also has the power to issue binding decisions. The United States, unfortunately, while ratifying the Convention has refused to submit to the Court's jurisdiction. There is also an African Charter on Human and Peoples Rights with a commission to monitor and to receive complaints about its breach which is headquartered in Banjul in Gambia and falls under the general supervision of the Organization of African Unity. Without a Court, and lacking any worthwhile political support, it has been much less successful than its European and Inter-American counterparts.

Third, to put the matter in perspective it needs to be remembered that to a very great extent the task of protecting and enforcing human rights is still undertaken nationally rather than regionally or globally. Particularly in the past 10 years, there has been a huge proliferation of countries across the globe that have incorporated Bills of Rights into their constitutions or statutes.[71] A significant number of these charters are judicially enforceable. Still more nations have established national human rights commissions of one kind or another to receive, conciliate and arbitrate on complaints. At least in part, this impressive array of activity is a response by States parties to the treaty obligations they have assumed under international human rights law. This suggests that both national and international systems for the protection of human rights could be strengthened by reciprocal cooperation. The international human rights monitoring system would benefit significantly, for example, from structured input into its deliberations by national human rights commissions that could provide an informed, educative and sometimes critical perspective on country reports. National systems could benefit from carefully framed and targeted recommendations from UN Committees encouraging the further development of domestic mechanisms for human rights protection and promotion.[72]

Clearly, then, while judicial enforcement of human rights obligations remains almost non-existent at supra-national level, the trend nationally should be considered as broadly positive when viewed in historical perspective.

Conclusion

In its landmark report, the Commission on Global Governance placed great weight on the need to strengthen the rule of law worldwide. Its chapter containing its own analysis of the problems in doing so and making recommendations for appropriate reform marked the starting point for a continuing and constructive discussion of the subject. In the report the Commission concluded that:

> The world must strive to ensure that the global neighborhood of the future is characterized by law, not by lawlessness; by rules that all must respect; by the reality that all, including the weakest are equal under the law and that none, including the most powerful is above the law. This, in turn, requires a will to lead by those who can, and willingness by the rest to join and help in the common effort.[73]

This chapter, and the book which it prefaces, is an endeavor to contribute to a continuing, political and legal dialogue concerning the values that should underpin the global rule of law and the institutional reforms that need, however gradually, to be implemented to sustain it. It forms part of the common effort that the Commission has called for and that is so demonstrably required.

Acknowledgements

I wish to acknowledge the invaluable work of Helen Wheatley who acted as my research assistant during the writing of this chapter and the book of which it forms part.

Notes

1 Two illuminating, practical, treatments of globalization by prominent actors in the field are Soros, G. *The Crisis of Global Capitalism,* London: Little Brown, 1998; Hutton, W. and Giddens, A. (eds) *On the Edge: living with global capitalism,* London: Johnathan Cape, 2000.

2 This definition and the discussion that follows has been influenced significantly by the work of David Held. See for example: Held, D. *Democracy and the Global Order: from the modern state to cosmopolitan governance*, Cambridge: Polity Press, 1995; Archibugi, D., Held, D. and Kohler, M. (eds) *Re-imagining Political Community*, Cambridge: Polity Press, 1998; Held, D., McGrew, A., Golblatt, D. and Perraton, J. *Global Transformations: politics, economics and culture,* Cambridge: Polity Press, 1999; Held, D. and McGrew, A. *The Global Transformations Reader*, Cambridge: Polity Press, 2000, chapter 1. See also: Mittelman, J. *The Globalization Syndrome: transformation and resistance,* Princeton: Princeton University Press, 2000.

3 Stiglitz, J. 'Globalization and Development' in D. Held and M. Koenig-Archibugi, *Taming Globalization: frontiers of governance*, Cambridge: Polity, 2003, p. 37.

4 Higgins, R. 'International Law in a Changing International System', *The Cambridge Law Journal*, vol. 58, issue 2, March 1999, p. 77.

5 See: Camilleri, J. and Falk, J. *The End of Sovereignty? the politics of a shrinking and fragmenting world*, Hants: Edward Elgar, 1992; Kelsey, J. 'Globalization, State and Law: towards a multi-perspectival polity', *Law In Context*, vol. 14, 1996, p. 31; Slaughter, A. 'The

Real New World Order', *Foreign Affairs*, vol. 76, issue 5, September–October 1997, pp. 183–97; Sur, S. 'The State Between Fragmentation and Globalization', *European Journal of International Law*, vol. 8, no. 3, 1997, p. 421.

6 See generally: Castells, M. *The Information Age*, vol. 1: *The Rise of the Network Society*, Oxford: Blackwells, 1996; Dicken, P. *Global Shift: transforming the world economy*, 3rd edn, London: Paul Chapman, 1998; Beck, U. *What is Globalization?* Cambridge: Polity Press, 2000.

7 See generally: Gray, J. *False Dawn*, London: Granta Publications, 1998; Stiglitz, J. *Globalization and its Discontents*, London: Allen Lane, The Penguin Press, 2002; Singer, P. *One World: the ethics of globalization*, Melbourne: Text Publishing, 2002; Monbiot, G. *The Age of Consent: a manifesto for a new world order*, London: Flamingo, 2003.

8 See generally: Cassese, A. *International Law in a Divided World*, Oxford: Oxford University Press, 1986; Bobbio, N. *The Age of Rights*, Cambridge: Polity Press, 1996; Robertson, A. and Merrills, J. *Human Rights in the World*, 4th edn, Manchester: Manchester University Press, 1989; Cassese, A. *Human Rights in a Changing World*, Cambridge: Polity Press, 1990; Alston, P. and Steiner, M. *International Human Rights in Context*, 2nd edn, Oxford: Oxford University Press, 2000; Falk, R. *Human Rights Horizons: the pursuit of justice in a globalizing world*, London: Routledge, 2000; Ignatieff, M. *Human Rights as Politics and Idolatry*, Princeton: Princeton University Press, 2001.

9 See: Crawford, J. (ed.) *The Rights of Peoples*, Oxford: Clarendon Press, 1992; Baxi, U. *Membrino's Helmet? human rights for a changing world*, New Delhi: Har-Anand Publications, 1994; Felice, M. *Taking Suffering Seriously: the importance of collective human rights*, Albany: State University of New York Press, 1996; McCorquodale, R. 'Human Rights and Self-Determination', in M. Sellers (ed.) *Sovereignty, Human Rights and the Self-Determination of Peoples*, Oxford: Berg, 1996.

10 See: Jayasuriya, K. 'Globalization, Law and the Transformation of Sovereignty: the emergence of global regulatory governance', *Indiana Journal of Global Legal Studies*, vol. 6, issue 2, Spring 1999, p. 425.

11 There is a wealth of literature on the rule of law. In developing the framework the following books and articles were of particular assistance: Marsh, N. 'The Rule of Law as a Supra-National Concept', in A.G. Guest (ed.) *Oxford Essays in Jurisprudence: a collaborative work*, Oxford: Oxford University Press, 1961; Fuller, L. *The Morality of Law*, New Haven: Yale University Press, 1964; Raz, J. 'The Rule of Law and its Virtue', *Law Quarterly Review* vol. 93, 1977, p. 197; Dworkin, R. *Taking Rights Seriously*, London: Duckworth, 1977, chapters 2 and 3; Dworkin, R. *A Matter of Principle*, Cambridge: Harvard University Press, 1985, chapter 1; Finnis, J. *Natural Law and Natural Rights*, Oxford: Oxford University Press, 1980, chapter 10; Hayek, F.A. *Law, Legislation and Liberty: a new statement of the liberal principles of justice and political economy*, London; Melbourne: Routledge and Kegan Paul, 1982, chapters 4 and 5; Harden, I. and Lewis, N. *The Noble Lie: the British constitution and the rule of law*, London: Hutchinson, 1986, chapters 2 and 10; Allen, T.R.S. *Law, Liberty and Justice*, Oxford: Clarendon Press, 1993, chapter 2; Jowell, J. 'The Rule of Law Today', in J. Jowell and D. Oliver (eds) *The Changing Constitution*, 3rd edn, Oxford: Oxford University Press, 1994; Crawford, J. *Democracy in International Law*, Inaugural Lecture, Cambridge: Cambridge University Press, 1994; Raz, J. *Ethics in the Public Domain: essays in the morality of law and politics*, Oxford: Oxford University Press, 1995, chapter 17; Mason, K. 'The Rule of Law', in P. Finn (ed.) *Essays on Law and Government*, vol. 1, Sydney: Law Book Co., 1995; Habermas, J. *Between Facts and Norms*, Cambridge: Polity Press, 1996, chapter 4; Craig, P. 'Formal and Substantive Conceptions of the Rule of Law: an analytical framework', *Public Law*, 1997, p. 467; Brownlie, I. *The Rule of Law in International Affairs*, The Hague: Martinus Nijhoff, 1998; Kay, R. 'American Constitutionalism', in L. Alexander (ed.) *Constitutionalism: political foundations*, Cambridge: Cambridge University Press, 1998; Shklar, J. *Political Thought and Political Thinkers*, Chicago: University of Chicago Press, 1998, chapters 1 and 2; Dyzenhaus, D. 'Form and Substance in the Rule of Law'; in C. Forsyth (ed.) *Judicial Review and the Constitution*, Oxford: Hart Publishing, 2000; Watts, A. 'The Importance

of International Law', in M. Byers (ed.) *The Role of Law in International Politics*, Oxford: Oxford University Press, 2002.

12 Hayek, F.A. *The Constitution of Liberty*, London: Routledge, 1960, chapter 14.

13 Commission on Global Governance, *Our Global Neighbourhood*, Oxford: Oxford University Press, 1995, p.303.

14 See: Dicey, A.V., *An Introduction to the Study of the Law of the Constitution*, 10th edn, London: MacMillan, 1959, chapter 4; Raz, J. 'The Rule of Law and its Virtue', p. 195; Summers, R. 'A Formal Theory of the Rule of Law', *Ratio Juris*, vol. 6, no. 2, July 1993, p. 127.

15 See to similar effect: Watt, A. 'The Importance of International Law', in Byers (ed.) *The Role of Law in International Politics*, p. 7. Watt argues that: 'The rule of law in international affairs involves the existence of a comprehensive system of law, certainty as to what the rules are, predictability as to the legal consequences of conduct, equality before the law, the absence of arbitrary power, and effective and impartial application of the law'.

16 See in particular: Fuller, *The Morality of Law.*

17 John Rawls puts it eloquently: 'Political power is legitimate only when it is exercised in accordance with a constitution (written or unwritten) the essentials of which all citizens, as reasonable and rational, can endorse in the light of their common human reason. This is the liberal principle of legitimacy. It is a further desideratum that all legislative questions that concern or border on those essentials, or are highly divisive, should also be settled, so far as possible, by guidelines and values that can be similarly endorsed'. Rawls, J. *Justice as Fairness: a restatement*, Cambridge, MA: Harvard University Press, 2001, p. 41.

18 See: Franck, T. 'The Emerging Right to Democratic Governance', *American Journal of International Law*, vol. 86, no. 1, 1992, p. 46.

19 Boutros-Ghali, B. *An Agenda for Democratization*, New York: The United Nations, 1996.

20 For an analysis of global governance in the context of the general principle of accountability see Keohane, R. 'Global Governance and Democratic Accountability', in Held and Koenig-Archibugi (eds) *Taming Globalization.*

21 This is not of course to deny that there are competing perspectives on the proper content of human rights. For a recent treatment of the principal competing schools, see Mutua, M. 'Politics and Human Rights: an essential symbiosis', in M. Byers (ed.) *The Role of Law in International Politics*, and, more generally, Bauer, J. and Bell, D. *The East Asian Challenge for Human Rights*, Cambridge: Cambridge University Press, 1999.

22 On the role of rights in the rule of law domestically and internationally see: Lauterpacht, H. *International Law and Human Rights*, London: Stevens & Sons, 1950; Dworkin, R. *A Matter of Principle*, chapter 1; Dworkin, R. *Law's Empire*, London: Fontana Press, 1986, chapter 7; Laws, J. 'Is the High Court the Guardian of Fundamental Constitutional Rights?', *Public Law*, 1993, p. 59; Laws, J. 'Law and Democracy', *Public Law*, 1995, p. 72; Kriegel, B. *The State Under the Rule of Law*, Princeton: Princeton University Press, 1995, chapter 2; Laws, J. 'The Constitution: morals and rights', *Public Law*, 1996, p. 622; Robertson, G. *Crimes Against Humanity: the struggle for global justice*, London: Allen Lane, The Penguin Press, 1999, chapter 3; Rosenau, J. 'The Drama of Human Rights in a Turbulent, Globalized World', in A. Brysk (ed.) *Globalization and Human Rights*, Berkeley: University of California Press, 2002; Donnelly, J. 'Human Rights, Globalizing Flows and State Power', in Brysk (ed.) *Globalization and Human Rights.*

23 Hayek, *The Constitution of Liberty*, chapter 14.

24 It is doubtful, however, that Hayek would have countenanced the inclusion in such a Charter of economic, social and cultural rights. Such an inclusion would have offended his forceful advocacy of free market liberalism. See further Shklar, *Political Thought and Political Thinkers.*

25 Ignatieff, *Human Rights as Politics and Idolatry*, p. 55.

26 Shklar, *Political Thought and Political Thinkers*, p. 36.

27 Rosenau, J. 'Governance and Democracy in a Globalizing World', in Archibugi, Held and Kohler (eds) *Re-Imagining Political* Community, pp. 39–40.
28 The Commission on Global Governance, *Our Global Neighbourhood,* p. 326.
29 See for example: Ignatieff, M. *Whose Universal Values? The Crisis in Human Rights*, The Hague: Foundation Horizon, 1999; Van Ness, P. (ed.) *Debating Human Rights: critical essays from the United States and Asia*, London: Routledge, 1999.
30 Declaration on Principles of International Law Concerning Friendly Relations and Co-operation Among States in Accordance with the Charter of the United Nations (1970).
31 The Vienna Convention on the Law of Treaties (1969) which entered force on 27 January 1980.
32 See: Cassesse, *International Law in a Divided World*, chapter 5.
33 Re *Jus Cogens* see generally: Cassese, *International Law in a Divided World,* chapter 6; Brownlie, I. *Principles of Public International Law*, 4th edn, Oxford: Oxford University Press, 1990, chapter 25; Dixon, M. and McCorquodale, R. *Cases and Materials on International Law*, London: Blackstone Press, 1991, chapter 3; Harris, D.J. *Cases and Materials on International Law*, 4th edn, Sweet and Maxwell, 1991, chapter 10; Shearer, I. *Starke's International Law,* 11th edn, London: Butterworths, 1994, chapter 3; Robertson, *Crimes Against Humanity*, chapter 3. Shelton, D. 'International Law and Relative Normativity', in Evans, M. (ed.) *International Law*, Oxford: Oxford University Press, 2003, chapter 5.
34 Secretary-General's Press Release, SG/2063 L/T/4345, 17 May 2000, 'Secretary-General to Encourage Universal Participation in Multilateral Treaty Framework During Upcoming Millennium Summit'.
35 The literature is voluminous but see, in particular: Childers, E. and Urquart, B. *Towards a More Effective United Nations*, Uppsala: Dag Hammaskjold Foundation, 1992; Childers, E. and Urquart, B. *Renewing the United Nations System*, Uppsala: Dag Hammarskjold Foundation, 1994; Bertrand, M, 'The UN as an Organization: a critique of its functioning', *European Journal of International Law*, vol. 6, no. 3, 1995, p. 352; Falk, R. 'Appraising the UN at 50: the looming challenge', *Journal of International Affairs*, vol. 48, 1995, p. 625; Falk, R. *On Humane Governance: toward a new global politics*, Cambridge: Polity Press, 1995; Franck, T. *Fairness in International Law and Institutions*, Oxford: Oxford University Press, 1995; Boutros-Ghali, *An Agenda for Democratization*; Paolini, A., Jarvis, A. and Reus-Smit, C. *Between Sovereignty and Global Governance: the United Nations, the state and civil society*, London: MacMillan, 1998; Aksu, J. and Camilleri, J. (eds) *Democratizing Global Governance*, Basingstoke: Palgrave MacMillan, 2002; Krasno, J. (ed.) *The United Nations: confronting the challenges of a global society*, Boulder: Lynne Reinner, 2004.
36 A polemical, if somewhat impractical, agenda for global democratization, including for the democratization of the UN is contained in Monbiot, *The Age of Consent.*
37 Commission on Global Governance, supra, p. 303.
38 See: Franck, T. *Judging the World Court*, New York: Priority Press, 1986; Thirlway, H. 'The International Court of Justice' in Evans, M. (ed.) *International Law*, Oxford: Oxford University Press, 2003.
39 *Admission of a State to Membership in the United Nations (Advisory Opinion)* ICJ Reports (1948) p. 64.
40 *Aerial Incident at Lockerbie Case (Provisional Measures) (Libya v. US and UK)*, Reports (1992) p. 3. See further the discussion in Brownlie, *The Rule of Law in International Affairs*, chapter XV.
41 See further: Gowlland-Debbas, V. 'The Relationship between the International Court of Justice and the Security Council in the Light of the Lockerbie Case', *American Journal of International Law*, vol. 88, 1994, p. 663; and Gowlland-Debbas, V. (2002) 'Functions of the UN Security Council', in Byers (ed.) *The Role of Law in International Politics* supra.
42 See further: Weeramantry, C. *Armageddon or Brave New World?: reflections on the hostilities in Iraq*, Ratmalana: Vishva Lekha, 2003.

43 Statute of the ICJ, Article 36.
44 Nicaragua v. US, 1984 *I.C.J. Reports* 392.
45 Australia v. France; New Zealand v. France, ICJ Reports (1974) p. 253.
46 See further: Bowett, D., Crawford, J., Sinclair, I. and Watts, A. 'The International Court of Justice: efficiency of procedures and working methods', *International and Comparative Law Quarterly Supp.*, vol. 45, 1996, s24; and Seidl-Hohenveldern, I. 'Access of International Organizations to the International Court of Justice', in A.S. Muller, D. Raic and J.M. Thuránszky (eds) *The International Court of Justice: its future role after fifty years*, The Hague: Kluwer, 1997; Nowrot, K. 'Legal Consequences of Globalization: the status of non-governmental organizations under International Law', *Indiana Journal of Global Legal Studies*, vol. 6, issue 2, 1999, p. 579.
47 For some critical examples see: Cassesse, A. *International Law*, Oxford: Oxford University Press, 2001, pp. 159–60.
48 See: Chinkin, C. 'International Law and Human Rights', in T. Evans, (ed.) *Human Rights Fifty Years On: a reappraisal*, Manchester: Manchester University Press, 1998; Koskenniemi, M. 'The Police in the Temple: order, justice and the United Nations: a dialectical view', *European Journal of International Law*, vol. 6, no. 3, 1995, p. 325.
49 For a recent detailed inquiry into the merits and demerits of humanitarian intervention and the criteria for justified military intervention see: International Commission on Intervention and State Sovereignty, *The Responsibility to Protect*, Government of Canada, 2000.
50 Falk, R, 'Appraising the UN at 50: the looming challenge', p. 625.
51 Latham, R. 'Globalization and the Transformation of Economic Rights', in B. Gills (ed.) *Globalization and the Politics of Resistance*, London: MacMillan, 2000.
52 I am indebted in this section to the discussion of the WTO's constitution and organization contained in Arup, C. *The New World Trade Organization Agreements: globalizing law through services and intellectual property*, Cambridge: Cambridge University Press, 2000; and see further: Qureshi, A. *The World Trade Organization: implementing international trade norms*, Manchester: Manchester University Press, 1996.
53 See generally: Palmeter, D. and Navrodis, P. 'The WTO Legal System: sources of law', *American Journal of International Law*, vol. 92, 1998, p. 398.
54 Hart, M. 'The WTO and the Political Economy of Globalization', *Journal of World Trade*, vol. 31, no. 5, 1997, p. 83.
55 Articles of Agreement, Article IX(2).
56 For more detailed treatment, see: Davey, W. 'The WTO Dispute Settlement System', *Journal of International Economic Law*, vol. 3, issue 1, March 2000, p. 15.
57 Stiglitz, *Globalization and its Discontents*, pp. 227–8.
58 See further: Scholte, J. *et al*, 'The WTO and Civil Society', *Journal of World Trade*, vol. 33, no. 1, 1999, p. 107; Tripley, D. 'Safe Trade and the WTO', *Amicus Curiae*, issue 28, June 2000, p. 8; Nelson, P. 'Information, Location and Legitimacy: the changing bases of civil society involvement in international economic policy', in M. Edwards and J. Gaventa (eds) *Global Citizen Action*, London: Earthscan Publications, 2001.
59 See generally: Thomas, C. 'International Financial Institutions and Social and Economic Rights: an exploration', in Evans, *Human Rights Fifty Years On*.
60 A perceptive and more detailed critique of the WTO's performance and its seeming incapacity to take environmental and human rights concerns seriously into account is contained in Singer, *One World*.
61 For extensive discussions of the UN Treaty Monitoring System see in particular: Alston, P. *The UN and Human Rights*, Oxford: Clarendon Press, 1992; United Nations, *The United Nations and Human Rights (1945–1995)*, Blue Book Series, vol. VII, New York: UN Publications; and Alston, P. and Crawford, J. (eds) *The Future of the UN Human Rights Treaty Monitoring*, Cambridge: Cambridge University Press, 2000.
62 Falk, *Human Rights Horizons*, p. 41.
63 See: Alston, P. 'Critical Appraisal of the UN Human Rights Regime', in Alston (ed.) *The UN and Human Rights*.
64 See further: Cassese, *International Law in a Divided World*, chapter 8.

65 See: Steiner, H. 'Individual Claims in a World of Massive Violations: what role for the human rights committee', in Alston and Crawford (eds) *The Future of UN Human Rights Treaty Monitoring*.
66 See: Crawford, J. (2000) 'The UN Human Rights Treaty System: a system in crisis?' in Alston and Crawford, *The Future of UN Human Rights Treaty Monitoring*.
67 Bayefsky, A. (2001) *The UN Human Rights Treaty System: universality at the crossroads*, available at: http://www.bayefsky.com (accessed 24 February 2004).
68 For powerful expressions of this position see, for example: Bayefsky, A. 'Making the Human Rights Treaties Work', in L. Henkin and J. Hargrove (eds) *Human Rights: an agenda for the next century*, Washington, D.C.: American Society of International Law, 1994; and Robertson, *Crimes Against Humanity*.
69 Alston, P. 'Beyond Them and Us: putting treaty body reform into perspective', in Alston and Crawford, *The Future of UN Human Rights Treaty Monitoring*.
70 See: Samson, K. 'Human Rights Co-ordination within the UN System' in Alston, *The UN and Human Rights*.
71 See generally: Alston, P. (ed.) *Promoting Human Rights Through Bills of Rights: comparative perspectives*, Oxford: Oxford University Press, 1999.
72 For an illuminating discussion of proposals for reciprocal interaction, see Gallagher, A. (2000), 'Making Human Rights Treaty Obligations a Reality: working with new actors and partners', in Alston and Crawford, *The Future of Human Rights Treaty Monitoring*.
73 The Commission on Global Governance *Our Global Neighbourhood*, p. 332.

3 Globalizing the rule of law? Global challenges to the traditional ideal of the rule of law*

*The Hon. Justice Michael Kirby AC, CMG***

Tradition and reality

The traditional ideal of the rule of law in a society such as Australia, is relatively straightforward. Law represents the ultimate authority and expression of power of the nation state. Formally, it derives its legitimacy by being traced, or traceable, to the national constitution. In a federal country, that constitution will provide for a federal or national polity and sub-national polities. These enjoy powers in respect of each other as provided by the constitution. Conventionally, there are three branches of government in each polity that makes up the nation. These are the legislature, the executive and the judiciary. Whereas the judiciary is independent of the other two branches in the parliamentary system, the executive is dependent on the legislature. Ministers in the executive government must, within a short time of their appointment, be elected to the legislature.

Each branch of government makes law that must be respected by everyone. That law may, ultimately, be enforced coercively by the agencies of the state. The major lawmaker is the legislature, but it may delegate powers of law-making to the executive. The main function of the judiciary is to interpret the constitution and the laws and to vindicate the claims that are made under the law. But even the judiciary has, in the minor key, a power of law-making. In a common law country, the judges have the responsibility of declaring the principles of the common law. Subject to the constitution and valid statute law, those principles must be obeyed.

It is left to the judiciary to settle disputes about the boundaries of law. These include disputes concerning the validity of national and sub-national laws (in the case of a federation). They also include disputes concerning the meaning of the constitution, of statute law and of the residual common law that operates in the society. Once the judiciary has spoken on the subject, the other branches of government, and those who comprise them, conform to the judicial pronouncement. So must ordinary individuals – both natural persons and corporations.

Everyone is taken to be subject to the law. No one is so high as to be above it. Obedience to law permeates society. It renders everyone in society ultimately accountable. Subject to the constitution, laws made by the legislature, the executive or the judicial branch may be changed at the will of the people. If they do not like a law they can secure the passage of amendments, thereby reflecting the democratic will. Even where the constitution stands as a barrier to such change of the law, the people's will can ultimately be vindicated in accordance with the procedures for constitutional amendment. Such procedures may be relatively straightforward, as they are under the Basic Law of the Federal German Republic.[1] Or they may be weighted in favor of the status quo and resistant to change, as is the case with the constitution of the United States of America and Australia.[2]

The symbol of the rule of law is the declaration, chiselled in marble on the façade of the Supreme Court building in Washington and expressed in a more low key way in a country such as Australia. It reads 'Equal Justice Under Law'. Because the law is ultimately accountable to the people it is expected to reflect the people's sense of justice. Where it does not, it is assumed that the democratic process will change the law so that justice may be secured in the future. Increasingly, it is accepted for these reasons, that within the nation state the people are sovereign, whatever may be the formal legal arrangements. The monarch may be called a sovereign. The legislature may be called sovereign. But, ultimately, in a modern nation state it is the people who are taken as sovereign because, ultimately, in the matter of law, their will can be done.

There is much truth in the forgoing description of the rule of law, at least so far as Australia is concerned. But the realities are often somewhat different from the appearances. The 'sovereign' parliament has lost power in recent decades to the executive government. The executive government, in turn, has lost much power and influence to the cabinet and the head of government to political parties, as well as to the permanent officials who 'advise' government and strongly influence law and policy-making. The judiciary is not always accessible to ordinary citizens. Vindication of the rule of law may exist on paper but, as a matter of practice, may sometimes be out of reach. Proposals for reform to secure justice under law may be ignored by all branches of government. The law that rules may be out of date, out of touch, unjust. Increasingly within the nation state other realities are recognized. These include the great power of bodies difficult to subject to law: the multinational corporations and the media, not for nothing called the fourth estate.

In addition to such internal challenges to the rule of law to which I have referred, now the nation state must increasingly face challenges from beyond its borders. These may come from the international bodies of growing significance in connection with global and regional trade and economics (such as the World Trade Organization (WTO), the World Bank, the International Monetary Fund (IMF), the Organization for Economic Cooperation and Development (OECD)). Or they may come from the international agencies of human rights (such as the Commission on Human Rights, the UN Human Rights Committee, the Special Rapporteurs and Representatives of the United Nations and particular agencies of that Organization). The power and influence of such bodies and of the political arms of the United Nations are felt increasingly within the borders of the nation state.[3]

Even the most powerful nations cannot ignore the actions of international bodies. Sometimes such bodies reflect and direct changes which narrow the scope for law-making by the organs of government of the nation state. To the extent that this happens, the old paradigm is challenged. The lawmakers of the nation state are no longer fully able to control the legal destiny affecting the persons living within the borders of the nation state. This development presents a number of problems for the assumptions about government that have been held until now. Those assumptions have been based on an organization of the world around its nations. The impact of globalism and regionalism affects the capacity of the law-making organs of the state to respond to the democratic will of its people.

The recognition that this has happened, in a comparatively short space of time, has a number of consequences. We need to revise the institutional model for the rule of law. What is the law that rules if those who make that law are not directly accountable to the people governed by it? If they are not removable where the people are discontented with their law? How can the international organs of rule-making avoid the perils of unaccountability? How can they be made humble by periodic review and challenge? In short, how does the notion of the rule of law operate in the realities of the world we now live in?

Others with different experience or a yearning to preserve the certainties of the past may be pessimistic about the paradigm shift that is occurring. The reasons for such pessimism, and even for anxiety, are understandable enough. However, my thesis is two-fold. First, the shift is unstoppable. It is urged forward by developments in technology (whether nuclear fission, cyberspace or the genome) and by a recognition of many problems which simply cannot be solved within the boundaries of a nation state (such as genocide, global weather change and responding effectively to HIV/AIDS).

My second thesis is that we need not be unduly pessimistic about what is. In fact, the developments are natural to the realities of the world we live in. They respond to the features of that world.

I cannot speak of the political agencies of the United Nations or of the trade and security bodies, global and regional, that have such a large and growing impact on the governance of every nation. But I can describe other places where the paradigm shift is happening. I refer to the international agencies and municipal courts in which, today, the influence of international law is growing and strengthening. My own observations lead me to a sense of optimism. I will recount what I have myself seen. I will do so, not because my role is, in the large picture, important. Instead, I do so because my experience may help to illustrate the highly practical, useful and right respecting character of international law as it is now being felt in a country such as Australia. I will start first with some experiences in international agencies. Then I will mention a few experiences in which, in the Australian courtroom, international legal questions arise and inform the Australian legal system directly, in a way that is useful and even beneficial.

The agencies

For me, it all began when I was appointed chairman of the Australian Law Reform Commission 25 years ago. Soon afterwards, the Commission was required by the Federal Attorney-General to prepare a report for the Australian Parliament on privacy protection. This task coincided with the establishment by the OECD of an

Expert Group to develop guidelines on privacy protection in the context of transborder data flows. That was an unusual task for the OECD. Looking back, we can see it as an early portent of the increasing moves in recent years of hard-nosed economic and trade bodies into areas of governance without which economic advancement will be a hollow achievement, if it is attainable at all.[4]

I was elected chairman of the OECD group. We prepared our guidelines.[5] They were adopted by the Council of the OECD. They were as much designed to prevent the economic inefficiency of disparate municipal regulation of the new information technology as to defend fundamental human rights. Eventually most OECD countries, including Australia, accepted the guidelines. In Australia they provided the basis for privacy principles incorporated in privacy protection legislation.[6] Through the Law Reform Commission, I was able to see the highly practical way in which a legal project at an international level could assist and influence municipal law-making. After that, I could never accept that international law – even soft law – was a matter for scholars and theorists alone. In countries as far apart as Japan, the Netherlands and Australia, the deliberations of our group in Paris had a real, practical and beneficial effect on local law and international cooperation.

In the manner of these things, one engagement leads to another. Soon after the OECD work was completed I took part in the general conference of UNESCO, also in Paris. That organization was in the bitter throes of what became the withdrawal of the United States and the United Kingdom, the former only recently repaired. One of the given reasons for the United States' withdrawal was the insistence of Director-General M'bow that UNESCO should continue the exploration of the meaning in the common first articles to the International Covenant on Civil and Political Rights, the International Covenant on Economic, Social and Cultural Rights which promise the self-determination of peoples. Who were a 'people' for this purpose?

It was strange that the United States should have opposed the exploration of this idea, given the famous opening words of its Declaration of Independence. But the United States quit UNESCO and, to its great credit, that organization went on with examining the issue of self-determination. I was appointed to the group, and ultimately elected as rapporteur and chairman. Ours was, and is, a highly controversial topic. It is uncongenial to many nation states. It is even unwelcome to some people in Australia. But who can doubt, looking at the real causes of conflict in the world today, that this is one of the great issues of international law – from East Timor to Acheh; from Burma to Tibet; from Palestine to Kosovo; from Corsica to Ulster; from the Falklands to Nunavut; and most recently from Fiji, Bougainville, West Irian and Solomon Islands to Aboriginal Australia. This is an issue that circles the earth. It goes to the heart of most contemporary dangers to international peace and security. It concerns the rights of peoples but also the human rights of the individuals who make up those peoples.

The UNESCO expert group completed its task. It identified four elements necessary to constitute a 'people' for international law purposes.[7] It is a misfortune that many who are unaware of the body of international law on this subject mistake self-determination for total national independence. That is a possible, but not a necessary, attribute of self-determination. This is a message from international law that needs to be learned in many countries.

By the time the work of the UNESCO groups was completed the HIV/AIDS pandemic was upon the world. I was called to serve on the World Health Organization Global Commission on AIDS. The Global Commission established principles for the management of the HIV epidemic, now being pursued by that unique inter-agency body, UNAIDS. Implementing the guidelines has been by no means easy, given the cultural and religious impediments that exist in various countries. It has fallen on some of the participating agencies, such as the UN Development Programme (UNDP) to attempt to persuade governments and bureaucracies in affected countries to adopt the bold strategies that will help reduce the spread of the virus. Significantly, those countries which have done so (including Australia) have seen the graph of sero-conversions to HIV plateau and even fall. Those countries which have not (particularly in sub-Saharan Africa and parts of Asia) have witnessed rapid escalation in the spread of the virus.

UNAIDS guidelines[8] worked out in 1997 at meetings held in concert with the UN Centre for Human Rights which I chaired, provide reflections of consensus amongst the most informed public health and epidemiological experts in the world. The guidelines afford a stimulus to the recalcitrant or the ignorant leaders and officials of nation states. This is not international law in the traditional sense. But the influence of such guidelines, carried into municipal bureaucracies by WHO and UNAIDS experts, fired with a zeal to prevent the ravages of AIDS, can sometimes have a direct local impact far greater than high-sounding treaties or well-meaning laws. This is international cooperation and principle turned to the vital effort to save human lives. It can influence local law and policy in profound and useful ways, beyond local popularity. Without international law and international agencies it would just be a dream.

In two other specialized agencies of the United Nations, I have also witnessed the practical helping hand that can sometimes be offered to domestic law-making. In 1991–2 I participated with two other judges in the International Labour Organization (ILO) Fact-Finding and Conciliation Commission on Freedom of Association. Our particular task, just before the achievement of constitutional change, was to examine the labor laws of South Africa and to advise on the standards they had to attain in order to conform to ILO Conventions. Having walked out of the ILO rather than be expelled during the apartheid years, South Africa's labor laws had fallen into serious disrepair. South Africa was keen to repair its relationship with international legal norms. The ILO mission examined closely the letter and practice of the South African law. Its report, delivered to the de Klerk government, was subsequently acted upon by the Mandela government. A new Labour Relations Act was adopted, complying with ILO standards.[9]

In 1994, UNDP arranged my participation in a number of meetings leading up to the constitutional conference in Malawi. It was that conference which agreed on the text of constitutional changes designed to usher in a multiparty democracy in the place of the one-party rule of President Hastings Banda. After a referendum and elections, a peaceful change of government was accomplished in Malawi. I pay tribute to the fine officers of UNDP and other agencies who facilitated this remarkable change in Malawi and in other lands. This was truly a translation of the universal principles of human rights into action in a particular country. I do not believe that it could have happened without the skills of UN agencies which I saw in operation at first hand.

In more recent years I have served in the International Bioethics Committee of UNESCO. That body has been grappling with some of the most difficult legal and ethical questions confronting humanity. I refer to the quandaries presented by genomic science and the development of the Human Genome Project. The UNESCO Committee in 1998 adopted the Universal Declaration of Human Rights and the Human Genome. This contains a number of basic norms aimed to provide a framework for a global response to legal and ethical questions relevant to the entire human species.[10] It is possible that, in due course, this Universal Declaration will lead on to a treaty, as others in the past have done. The point to be made is that an international agency, calling on diverse expertise and viewpoints from different religions and cultures, is seeking to design an effective universal response. The difficulties of securing such a response in a world of so many different starting points and where large investments and differing national intellectual property regimes apply, is not to be underestimated.

In April 2000 I was called to Vienna by the UN Office for Drug Control and Crime Prevention. Under the aegis of that agency, a Global Programme Against Corruption was been established. Since then, several international agencies, including the OECD, the World Bank, the IMF and the WTO, have concerned themselves with the problem of corruption and its insidious effect on municipal governmental institutions.

At the same time, a judicial group on strengthening judicial integrity was established in Vienna to work directly with the UN office there. This group comprised four chief justices from Asia and four from Africa. I acted as its rapporteur. Its task was to draw up a universal minimum code of judicial conduct. Wisely, the project was left to the judges themselves, supported by research and other staff, as well as by informed non-governmental organizations such as Transparency International in London and the Centre for the Independence of Judges and Lawyers within the International Commission of Jurists in Geneva. The group developed a draft code which was then disseminated widely among judges and judicial organizations in both common law and civil law systems. It was essential that it be scrutinized in this way to ensure that it could assume the status of a duly authenticated international code of judicial conduct. A revised draft was then placed before a Round-Table meeting of Chief Justices from the civil law system, held in The Hague in November 2002. This meeting finalized what are now known as *The Bangalore Principles of Judicial Conduct (2002)*. The principles contained therein are derived from the core values of independence, impartiality, integrity, propriety, equality, competence and diligence.[11] This document may fairly be considered as the first global statement of the appropriate standards of ethical conduct for judges wherever they may sit. Whether these principles will lead to treaty obligations or be given effect as conditional requirements imposed by the OECD, the World Bank, the IMF or the WTO remains to be seen.

Effective international law cannot be dismissed. Pursuant to an OECD Convention, long-arm legislation has been enacted both in the United States and Australia, to render it a crime for nationals of those countries to engage overseas in corruption of foreign officials. The point to be made is that, once again, an issue of common concern has attracted a universal response under and outside the aegis of the United Nations. The development may override powerful local interests which resist effective rules against corruption. The sharing of research and knowledge and the pooling of ideas will contribute to global standards and hopefully effective action, not just papers and talk. The beneficiaries, it may be hoped, will ultimately be the people.

I tell these stories to illustrate, by reference to some activities with which I am familiar, the rapid advance of international initiatives, many of them relevant to law, indeed the rule of law. What, only 40 years ago, was basically the concern and responsibility of the nation states has increasingly become an issue for international cooperation, the development of universal guidelines, the involvement of people and their organizations and, sometimes, international law. These developments gather pace. We are witnessing the opening phase of them. But we are privileged, in effect, to be present at the creation.

Policing universal human rights

One of the most remarkable developments of international law in recent decades, which has clearly affected local rule-making, has been the growing impact of international human rights treaties on municipal law and practice. I have observed this at three levels. I want to mention each. I acknowledge that each challenges the unbridled power of the branches of government in nation states to do as they please, including where what they please offends the universal norms of human rights. But it has been my experience that the changes that are occurring are beneficial, uphold fundamental norms, emphasize basic rights and stimulate the legal systems of nation states to do likewise.

The special rapporteurs and special representatives

Between 1993 and 1996 I served as Special Representative of the Secretary-General of the United Nations for Human Rights in Cambodia. That function arose in the aftermath of the successful completion of the United Nations Transitional Authority in Cambodia (UNTAC) phase, as a requirement agreed between Cambodia and members of the international community and given effect in the Paris Peace Accords.[12] Twice a year, in Geneva in April and in New York in November, it was my duty to report on the state of human rights in Cambodia to the Commission on Human Rights and to the General Assembly. I was one of about thirty UN Special Representatives and Special Rapporteurs. I saw at first hand the operations of the UN Centre for Human Rights. I worked closely with the High Commissioner for Human Rights. The criteria for my visits and reports were not intuitive beliefs of my own about civilized standards. They were the principles laid down in the international treaties which together establish the basic framework of international human rights law.

Despite various difficulties, I have no doubt that my work and that of the UN Office of Human Rights in Cambodia, stimulated, cajoled and encouraged domestic law and practice in that country to conform with the international treaty obligations which Cambodia increasingly accepted. In a land that had been racked by revolution, war, genocide and invasion, there was a deep thirst for guidance and support. This is not the occasion to tell you of the noble servants of the United Nations with whom I worked during those years. Of 'Shorty' Coleman, an Australian soldier supervising landmine clearance. Of Christoph Peschoux, human rights officer, who investigated dangerous cases of abuse of power. Of Basil Fernando, who instituted programmes for training prison officers and police. Of Ms Kek Galebru who helped establish non-governmental organizations to assert and uphold the rights of women.

Let no one say that the United Nations is only made up of time servers. I have seen with my own eyes the dedicated and idealistic servants of international human rights law, often working in most trying and even dangerous situations. That work goes on. Many of the Special Rapporteurs of the United Nations have suffered retaliation for their actions, including the Special Rapporteur on the Independence of the Judiciary (Dato' Param Cumaraswamy) whose case was taken to the International Court of Justice.[13] The bureaucracy of the United Nations is often trying. The frustrations and defeats are sometimes dispiriting. But let no one say that it is all talk. At least in the case of Cambodia, there was action. Even for more oppressive nation states, it is a salutary requirement of international institutions and practice today that the autocrats and their representatives must come before the bar of the United Nations and answer to charges of infractions of international human rights law. There is progress in that fact alone.

The ICCPR First Optional Protocol

My second illustration brings little credit on me. Soon after it was announced that Australia would sign the First Optional Protocol to the International Covenant on Civil and Political Rights (ICCPR) (thereby rendering itself accountable to the UN Human Rights Committee on the communication of an individual), I was asked whether the gay and lesbian reform group in Tasmania should mount a complaint to the United Nations concerning the Tasmanian criminal laws against adult homosexual conduct between males.[14] I am ashamed to say that I expressed a view that such a communication was bound to fail. The intended complainant, Nicholas Toonen, had not been charged with an offence under the Tasmanian laws. He had not exhausted domestic remedies because no domestic process had been taken against him. I told him that his complaint was hopeless.[15] In fact, the Human Rights Committee upheld Mr Toonen's complaint against Australia.[16] In the ultimate result, the Australian Federal Parliament enacted a statute overriding the Tasmanian laws.[17] Those laws were repealed and replaced by the non-discriminatory provisions now in force. Now, nowhere in Australia is there any law imposing criminal sanctions for adult private sexual conduct, although there are still inconsistencies in the definition of who is an adult for this purpose.

The lessons of the Toonen Case are many.[18] For my immediate purposes, they show once again the practical operation of international human rights law, at least in a country such as Australia which has signed the First Optional Protocol to the ICCPR and is a good international citizen. As Australia does not have a general constitutional Bill of Rights and as there is no regional human rights court or commission for Asia or the Pacific,[19] the importance of the ICCPR could not be overstated. Indeed, the significance of the Toonen decision runs far from Tasmania and Australia which, ultimately, would have corrected their legal aberration on homosexual offences. It brings hope to people in countries where individuals are still oppressed by reason of their sexuality.[20] Because I am homosexual myself, I understand that oppression; indeed it helps me to understand all oppressions based on irrational and irrelevant grounds. I applaud the fact that two Australians, Nicholas Toonen and Rodney Croome, politely ignored my opinion and pressed on with their communication, invoking international law.[21]

I do not pretend that the Toonen decision, and its reasoning, passed without criticism in Australia or elsewhere. For example, some have seen it as an unwarranted and premature intrusion into Australia's domestic concerns and federal governmental arrangements, indeed to the rule of law in Australia. Some, of the other view, have considered that it did not go far enough. Thus, it has been suggested that it is fundamentally erroneous to rest a human rights response to oppression on the ground of sexuality on notions of privacy rather than on notions of full equality. This has been seen, by some observers, as little more than the 'freedom' of a closeted human identity and one which tolerates the very public violence and discrimination suffered by many homosexual citizens when they move out of the privacy of the kind that ICCPR protects.[22] Australia's rule of law was challenged and tested. But the outcome was reform of that law which, now, most would regard as enlightened and just.

Bangalore principles on domestic application of international law

A most important development has occurred in Australia in the use that is being made of international human rights norms. It is a development new in a country which has hitherto adhered strictly to the 'dualist' notion: that the norms of international law do not become part of the domestic law unless made so by the municipal lawmaker.[23] The development to which I refer is sometimes described by reference to the Bangalore Principles.[24] These were adopted at a conference mainly attended by Commonwealth judges in Bangalore, India in 1988. These Bangalore Principles acknowledge the dualist rule. International law is not in most countries, as such, part of domestic law. But, in respect of international human rights norms, the Bangalore Principles accept that judges of the common law tradition may properly utilize such international rules in construing an ambiguous statute or in filling the gaps in the precedents of the common law.

In a former judicial post, I frequently invoked the Bangalore Principles, sometimes with, and sometimes without, the support of judicial colleagues.[25] An important breakthrough occurred in Australian thinking on this subject in the Mabo decision which, for the first time, upheld the rights of indigenous peoples in Australia to title in land with which they could prove long association.[26] One strand in the reasoning which led the majority of the High Court of Australia to reversing past judicial holdings and upholding that claim, was the serious breach that would otherwise arise in respect of Australia's international human rights obligations. Justice Brennan, who wrote the leading opinion in the Mabo Case,[27] said:

> The common law does not necessarily conform with international law, but international law is a legitimate and important influence on the development of the common law, especially when international law declares the existence of universal human rights. A common law doctrine founded in unjust discrimination in the enjoyment of civil and political rights demands reconsideration. It is contrary both to international standards and to the fundamental values of our common law to entrench a discriminatory rule.

The High Court in Mabo acknowledged the impact which the powerful influence of the Covenant would increasingly come to play upon Australia's common law. This appreciation obliges a shift in the understanding of the dualist principle. In the past, it has ordinarily been voiced in terms that municipal law must await incorporation of international law by the municipal legislature. In a common law country, it should, I think, be candidly accepted that the judiciary also has a role. In the exercise of that role, the judiciary of the common law tradition may, in appropriate cases, play a part in moulding the common law to universal principles expressed in international human rights law. In doing so, they should not simply incorporate a complete treaty 'by the back door'.[28] However, the legitimate role of judicial elaboration using international law as an influence upon municipal common law is now increasingly understood and decreasingly controversial. This process will, I have no doubt, continue to gather pace. It is not a breakdown in the rule of law. It is simply a new way of expressing the rule.

In my reasons in a number of in the High Court of Australia, I have suggested that the Bangalore Principles might be appropriate for incorporation into reasoning about the meaning of the Australian Constitution itself.[29] I have suggested that the Court 'should adopt the meaning which conforms to the principles of universal and fundamental rights rather than an interpretation that it would involve a departure from such rights'.[30] In elaborating this view I have suggested:[31]

> Where there is ambiguity, there is a strong presumption that the constitution, adopted and accepted by the people of Australia for their government, is not intended to violate fundamental human rights and human dignity.... The Australian Constitution ... speaks to the people of Australia. But it also

> speaks to the international community as the basic law of the Australian nation which is a member of that community.

In due course I believe that this opinion will be vindicated. Indeed, the universal need for ambiguity must be doubted. But it must be acknowledged that views of the kind which I have mentioned have attracted criticisms, especially from those who adhere to the 'originalist' school of constitutional interpretation,[32] which I regard as a form of legal ancestor worship.[33]

A number of other Australian developments should also be stated. One has been the introduction of a Bill designed to overcome a decision of the High Court and to render, as part of Australian federal law, the rule that 'entering into an international treaty is not reason for raising any expectation that government decision-making will act in accordance with the treaty if the relevant provisions of the treaty have not been enacted into domestic law'.[34] The Bill has not been made law.

The second development was the institution by the Australian government of a review of Australia's participation in six UN committees which oversee human rights treaties.[35] This review followed, in point of time, criticism of Australia in the Committee on the Elimination of All Forms of Racial Discrimination in respect inter alia of mandatory sentencing laws that were partly copied from the United States. The work of the UN human rights committees was defended by the then President of the Australian Human Rights and Equal Opportunity Commission.[36] The outcome of the review is not known as it has not been made public. However, its consequence has been that Australia has withdrawn a measure of cooperation from the UN committees and has agitated instead for their reform.[37]

So far as domestic application of international law by the judges is concerned, Professor Hilary Charlesworth has said, accurately I believe, that the suggested 'threat of international law to the Australian legal system is much exaggerated'.[38] She has described the highest court as being 'very cautious in its embrace of international law; it has kept its gloves and hat on at all times'.[39] If, occasionally, I have lifted my hat to pay passing respect to international law it is because my experience over 20 years has brought me into close familiarity with the operations of international law and international institutions – especially in the field of human rights. That operation is by no means alien to lawyers of the Anglo-American tradition. The influence of such lawyers upon the texts and jurisprudence, from the beginning of Mrs Roosevelt's Universal Declaration of Human Rights up to the present time, has been profound. In a sense, as Judge Buergenthal said in 1997:[40]

> It is ironic that western countries which have a cultural and geopolitical interest in global respect for human rights, have lately come to apply brakes to the domestic application of international norms. By way of contrast, some States which have suffered from past dictatorial regimes have played an important role in encouraging the adoption of domestic constitutional mechanisms that strengthen the power of the independent judiciary to enforce international human rights guarantees in conflict with national law and to implement the rulings of international tribunals.

Conclusion

No sitting of the High Court of Australia now passes without some relevant international legal principle being invoked as an aspect of a domestic legal problem. For example, on 4 August 2000, the Court refused special leave to appeal from a decision of the Full Court of the Federal Court in Nulyarimma v. Thompson.[41] That was a case in which a number of Australian Aboriginals had complained that they had suffered 'genocide' in terms of the Genocide Convention and international customary law. They contended that the applicable principles of international law were reflected in, and recognized by, Australia's municipal law. The 'genocide' of which they complained was a form of 'cultural genocide' arising from alteration of their native title rights to land and a decision of the federal government not to proceed with listing certain traditional lands on the World Heritage List. The Court (comprising Justices Gummow, Hayne and myself), in refusing special leave, expressed no opinion on the general question of the incorporation of international law in municipal law otherwise than by treaty or on the special question of the incorporation of the universal crime of genocide. The Court acknowledged that these were important legal questions but held that they did not arise in the instant case. It is in this way that, typically, issues of this nature come to be considered before Australian courts.

Many cases come before the High Court concerning the Refugees Convention which, in Australia, has been incorporated into municipal law in respect of the definition of 'refugees'.[42] Beyond this, important questions are regularly presented to the courts concerning extradition law,[43] the Convention on the Civil Aspects of International Child Abduction,[44] the international intellectual property protection regimes,[45] various conventions of the International Labor Organization to which Australia is a party,[46] the Hague Rules and the Brussels Convention for the Unification of Certain Rules of Law Relating to Bills of Lading,[47] and the Closer Economic Relations Treaty between Australia and New Zealand.[48] Most of these cases are collected each year in the Year Book of International Law. Each year this chapter grows larger.

Even if today municipal judges in countries such as Australia were personally disinclined to lift their eyes to the burgeoning growth of international law, their ordinary judicial duties will increasingly confront them with the realities that come with global transport, interactive technology and international problems. International law is no longer a realm of princes, diplomats and nations. The global economy and the global village have brought international law into the courtrooms at every level. It is inevitable that, in this way, international law comes increasingly to affect the rule of law in Australia.

The old ideology of the traditional concept of the rule of law in the nation state was flawed by weaknesses within each nation. Increasingly that ideology has been challenged from outside in the form of transnational corporations and media. Now the challenges are being felt from global and regional organizations, especially in the field of economics and trade but also in the contexts of international security and human rights.

The nature of the interconnected world, with global and regional problems, makes it impossible to turn back the clock. Accordingly, there will thus be no return to the idealized notion of the rule of law in the nation state with the 'sovereign' people of each state able to control, without restriction, the law by which they are governed. Even the strongest of the 'strong' states of the world is now unable to ignore the dynamic of globalism.[49] This is because the dynamic grows out of universal phenomena – global technology and the urgent need for solutions to global problems in which the world or many states are concerned.

This being the case, the growing interaction of municipal legal systems and international law is inevitable. Its impact on the rule of law is inescapable. In my experience, at least in the field of human rights, it is usually beneficial. Whether this is universally so, and in particular in matters of trade and economics where the big players have a disproportionate clout, remains to be seen.

The challenge before us is to readjust our thinking within nation states to the reality of the world in which those polities, and their law-making institutions, must now operate. And to inculcate, in global and regional institutions, the mechanisms for effective accountability, a respect for matters in which there is, or should be, sharing about the common heritage of humanity and deference to universal principles of human rights which should lie at the heart of the New World Order.

Notes

* Parts of this chapter are based on an address at the Opening Session of the Joint Meeting of the Australian and New Zealand Society of International Law and the American Society of International Law in Sydney on 26 June 2000.

** Justice of the High Court of Australia.

1 Young, K. 'The Implementation of International Law in the Domestic Laws of Germany and Australia: federal and parliamentary comparisons', *Adelaide Law Review*, vol. 21, no. 2, 1999, p. 179. The Basic Law, Art 79(2) requires a two-thirds majority in both the Bundestag and Bundesrat for amendment of the constitution. This procedure has been successful on 40 occasions. Amendment of the Australian Constitution has only been achieved in accordance with s 128 eight times in 44 proposals since 1901; Blackshield, T. and Williams, G. *Australian Constitutional Law and Theory*, 2nd edn, Sydney: The Federation Press, 1998, p. 1183.

2 Palmer, K.E. (ed.) *Constitutional Amendments – 1789 to the Present*, Gale Group, 1999, p. 591.

3 Sampford, C. *Democratic and Global Challenges to the Concepts of 'Sovereignty' and 'Intervention'*. Paper presented at the 19th World Congress on Philosophy of Law and Social Philosophy, New York, June 1999.

4 Kelsey, J. 'Global Economic Policy-making: a new constitutionalism?' *Otago Law Review*, vol. 9, no. 3, 1999, p. 539.

5 OECD, *Guidelines on the Protection of Privacy and Transborder Flows of Personal Data*, Paris, 1980. Cf. 'Privacy in Cyberspace' in M.D. Kirby, *Through the World's Eye*, Annandale, N.S.W.: Federation Press 2000, chapter 5.

6 Privacy Act, 1988 (Cth), s 14. By the operation of s 5 each Principle is treated as if it were a section of the Act.

7 UNESCO, International Meeting of Experts for the Elucidation of the Concepts of Rights of Peoples (1985–91) (Final Report SHS–85/Conf.613/10). See also: UNESCO, Report of the International Conference of Experts, Barcelona 21–27 November 1998,

'The Implementation of the Right to Self-Determination as a Contribution to Conflict Prevention' (1999).

8 UNAIDS/Centre for Human Rights Guidelines on Implementation of HIV/AIDS Strategies (Geneva, 1997).

9 International Labour Organization, Report on the Mission to South Africa (1992).

10 Universal Declaration on Human Rights and the Human Genome (1998). Cf. 'The Human Genome' in Kirby, *Through the World's Eye*, chapter 4.

11 See further: on the Code of Judicial Conduct and judicial accountability generally Das, C. and Chandra, K. (eds) *Judges and Judicial Accountability*, Commonwealth Law Association, 2003.

12 The 1991 Paris Peace Agreements are referred to and the work of the author as Special Representative explained in 'Cambodia: the struggle for human rights', in Kirby, *Through the World's Eye*, chapter 3.

13 International Court of Justice, Difference Relating to Immunity from Legal Process of a Special Rapporteur of the Commissioner on Human Rights, (United Nations v. Malaysia), Advisory Opinion (1999), ICJ Reports 62.

14 Criminal Code (Tas), ss 122 and 123.

15 In this respect I made the same mistake as was made by Justice Powell in the Supreme Court of the United States of America in Bowers v. Harwick 478 US 186 (1986): He reportedly changed his opinion about the challenge in that case to the validity of a Georgia statute penalising sodomy on the basis that he was convinced that, because the statute was not being enforced the case was 'frivolous'. He later regretted his opinion, as I do mine. See: Leslie, C. R. 'Creating Criminals: the injuries inflicted by "unenforced" sodomy laws', *Harvard Civil Rights, Civil Liberties Law Review*, vol. 35, Winter 2000, pp. 107–8.

16 Toonen v. Australia (1994) 1 International Human Rights Reports 97 (No. 3) Steiner, H.J. and Alston, P. *International Human Rights in Context: law, politics, morals: text and materials*, Oxford: New York: Clarendon Press; Oxford University Press, 1996, p. 545. See also: 'Same-Sex Relationships', in Kirby, *Through the World's Eye*, chapter 6.

17 Human Rights (Sexual Conduct) Act 1994 (Cth). See also: Croome v. Tasmania (1997) 191 Commonwealth Law Reports (hereafter *CLR*) 119.

18 Evatt, E. *National Implementation – The Cutting Edge of International Human Rights Law*, ANU Centre for International and Public Law, Law and Policy Paper No 12, 24.

19 The creation of an Asian Human Rights Commission under the aegis of ASEAN has been mooted but 'not in the near future'. See: Sunday Nation (Bangkok) 23 July 2000, p. 2.

20 See for example: Report of the Special Representative on Iran, UN Doc E/CN.4/1991/35 paras 59–60 recording how homosexual people are executed in the Islamic Republic of Iran based on the Islamic Shariat. See: extract in Steiner and Alston, *International Human Rights in Context*, p. 415.

21 See: initiatives of Amnesty International, P. Baehr, 12 Neths QHR 5, in Steiner and Alston, *International Human Rights in Context*, 1994, p. 485.

22 Morgan, W. 'Sexuality and Human Rights: the first communication by an Australian to the Human Rights Committee under the optional protocol to the International Covenant on Civil and Political Rights', *Australian Yearbook of International Law*, vol. 14, 1993, p. 277; Morgan, W. 'Identifying Evil for What it is: Tasmania, sexual perversity and the United Nations', *Melbourne University Law Review*, vol. 19, no. 3, June 1994, p. 740; Mathew, P. 'International Law and the Protection of Human Rights in Australia: recent trends', *Sydney Law Review*, vol. 17, no. 2, June 1995, p. 185.

23 Higgins, R. *Problems and Process: international law and how we use it*, Oxford: Clarendon Press, 1994, chapter 12; Buergenthal, T. 'Modern Constitutions and Human Rights Treaties', *Columbia Journal of Transnational Law*, vol. 36, 1997, p. 213.

24 Cf. Bangalore Principles, *Australian Law Journal* vol. 62, 1988, p. 531; *Commonwealth Law Bulletin*, vol. 14, no. 3, July 1988, p. 1196; *Judicial Colloquium*, April 1989; Harare, Zimbabwe, on Domestic Application of International Human Rights Norms, *Australian Law Journal*, vol. 63, 1989, p. 497.

25 Gradidge v. Grace Bros Pty Ltd (1988) 93 FLR 414; Young v. Registrar, Court of Appeal [No 3] (1993) 32 NSWLR 262. Cf. Kirby, M.D. 'The Australian Use of International Human Rights Norms: from Bangalore to Balliol, a view from the Antipodes', *University of New South Wales Law Journal*, vol. 16, no. 2, 1993, p. 363.

26 Mabo v. Queensland [No 2] (1992) 175 *CLR* 1.

27 (1992) 175 *CLR* 1 at 42.

28 Minister for Immigration and Ethnic Affairs v. Teoh (1995) 183 *CLR* 273 at 288 per Mason, C.J. and Deane, J. Cf. Bouwhuis, J. 'International Law by the Back Door?' *Australian Law Journal*, vol. 72, no. 10, October 1998, p. 794.

29 Cf. Petersmann, E.-U. 'How to Constitutionalize International Law and Foreign Policy for the Benefit of Civil Society', *Michigan Journal of International Law*, vol. 20, no. 1, Fall 1998, pp. 1–30; Yoo, J.C. 'Globalism and the Constitution: treaties, non self-execution and the original understanding', *Columbia Law Review*, 99, 1955.

30 Kartinyeri v. The Commonwealth (1998) 195 *CLR* 337 at 417. Cf. Newcrest Mining (WA) Ltd v. The Commonwealth (1997) 190 *CLR* 513 at 655–657.

31 Kartinyeri (1998) 195 *CLR* 337 at 418 [166]–[167] citing South West Africa Cases (2nd phase) [1966] ICJR 3 at 293; cf. Petersmann, 'How to Constitutionalise International Law and Foreign Policy for the Benefit of Civil Society'.

32 Craven, G. 'The High Court of Australia: a study in the abuse of power', Alfred Deakin Lecture Trust, Melbourne, 1997, cited in Charlesworth, H. 'Dangerous Liaisons: globalisation and Australian public law', *Adelaide Law Review*, vol. 20, no. 1, 1998, p. 65.

33 Kirby, M.D. 'Constitutional Interpretation and Original Intent: a form of ancestor worship?' *Melbourne University Law Review*, vol. 24, issue 1, April 2000, p. 1. Cf. Grain Pool (WA) v. The Commonwealth (2000) 202 *CLR* 479 at 522–530.

34 Administrative Decisions (Effect of International Instruments) Bill (1999) (Cth).

35 'UN urges Howard to review state jail laws', *Sunday Telegraph*, 26 March 2000 p. 19.

36 Tay, A. 'Walk Tall in a Wicked World', *Sydney Morning Herald*, 26 March 2000 p. 17.

37 Zifcak, S. *The New Internationalism: Australia and the United Nations Human Rights Treaty System* The Australia Institute, Discussion Paper 54, April 2003.

38 Charlesworth, 'Dangerous Liaisons: globalisation and Australian public law', *Adelaide Law Review*, Vol. 20, no. 1, 1998, p. 66.

39 Ibid.

40 Buergenthal, 'Modern Constitutions and Human Rights Treaties', pp. 212–13.

41 (1998) 165 *Australian Law Reports* (ALR) 621.

42 See for example: Applicant A v. Minister for Immigration and Ethnic Affairs (1997) 190 Commonwealth Law Reports (*CLR)* 225; Minister for Immigration and Ethnic Affairs v. G (1998) 191 *CLR* 559; Minister for Immigration and Ethnic Affairs v. Wu Shan Liang (1996) 185 *CLR* 259. Cf. Ward, C. 'A v. Minister for Immigration and Ethnic Affairs: Principles of Interpretation Applicable to Legislation Adopting Treaties', *Federal Law Review*, vol. 26, no. 1, 1998, p. 207; Matthew, 'International Law and the Protection of Human Rights in Australia', p. 177.

43 Director of Public Prosecutions (Cth) v. Kainhofer (1995) 185 *CLR* 528; Attorney-General for the Commonwealth v. Tse Chu-Fai (1998) 193 *CLR* 128.

44 De'L v. Director General (Department of Community Services) (1996) 187 *CLR* 640.

45 Telstra Corporation Ltd v. Australasian Performing Right Association Ltd (1998) 191 *CLR* 140; Phonographic Performance Co of Australia Ltd v. Federation of

Australian Commercial Television Stations (1998) 195 *CLR* 158; Grain Pool (WA) v. The Commonwealth (2000) 202 *CLR* 479.

46 Victoria v. The Commonwealth (1996) 187 *CLR* 416; Qantas Airways Ltd v. Christie (1998) 193 *CLR* 280.

47 Great China Metal v. Malaysia Shipping (1998) 196 *CLR* 161.

48 Project:1998 Project Blue Sky Inc v. Australian Broadcasting Authority (1998) 194 *CLR* 355.

49 The recent citation of international human rights law in the elaboration by the Supreme Court of the United States of American constitutional norms represents an important development in harmony with my thesis. See Lawrence v. Texas, 539 US 558 at 562, 567 (2003) per Kennedy J for the Court. See also Koh, H.H. 'International Law as Part of Our Law' (2004) *American Journal of International Law*, p. 43.

Part II

Human rights and the rule of law

4 Whose rule? Women and the international rule of law

Hilary Charlesworth

Introduction

Feminist theorists have generally been suspicious about the rule of law. The rule of law, the claim that law provides an impartial and objective system of justice and that everyone is treated equally before the law, has been analyzed in many different contexts.[1] It has regularly appeared as a slogan without substance. The Australian Law Reform Commission's report on Equality before the Law, for example, illustrated not only the practical obstacles that many women faced in using the legal system but also the ingrained, unseen biases against women inherent in legal rules and doctrine.[2] A.V. Dicey considered arbitrary or biased judgment the antithesis of the rule of law[3] and yet most legal systems retain this quality with respect to women. What force do these criticisms of the rule of law have in an international context?

The notion of an international rule of law proposed by Spencer Zifcak in Chapter 2 of this book has five institutional features: a constitutional order; judicial review of the exercise of power; effective dispute resolution; enforcement of judicial decisions; and respect for foundational human rights. Zifcak finds elements of each of these features present in the international order, leading him to conclude that an international rule of law is within our grasp if a number of institutional reforms are achieved. Looking at the rule of law using a feminist lens, however, leads to a less optimistic assessment of its utility and attainability.

Women worldwide suffer from a great range of injustices. Statistics gathered for the 1995 World Conference on Women, Beijing present a global system of disadvantage. Economically, politically, socially, culturally, physically and legally, women fare less well than men.[4] In both the developed and developing world, men's quality of life rates consistently better than women's and there are few signs of improvement over time. The United Nations Development Programme (UNDP) has noted that: 'Ironically, what unites countries across many cultural, religious, ideological, political and economic divides is their common cause *against* the equality of women – in their right to travel, marry, divorce, acquire nationality, manage property, seek employment and inherit property'.[5]

In this context of global injustice, the value of Zifcak's institutional features promoting the rule of law will depend on their definition. For example, a constitutional order may be of value if it includes a substantive commitment to the equality of women. Judicial institutions at national and international levels have thus far only sporadically acknowledged the structural disadvantages that confront women. Moreover, all existing international courts and tribunals are largely male in composition.[6] Unless we scrutinize the gendered perspectives represented on these international decision-making bodies, the Diceyan hope of unbiased judgment is impossible to realize.

In this chapter, I focus on the fifth feature of the international rule of law identified by Zifcak: respect for foundational human rights. Zifcak argues that 'neither political nor economic organs exercising regulatory functions in the global arena should be permitted to exercise those functions inconsistently with rights recognized as inalienable'.[7] What does this aspect of the international rule of law offer to women's lives? Are the human rights of women included in the category of inalienable rights?

The norm of non-discrimination on the basis of sex

The most widely recognized human right of women in international law is the norm of non-discrimination on the basis of sex. It is included in the Universal Declaration of Human Rights,[8] the International Covenant on Civil and Political Rights (ICCPR)[9] and all regional human rights treaties.[10] The right is elaborated in the Convention on the Elimination of All Forms of Discrimination against Women of 1979 (Women's Convention).[11] Non-discrimination on the basis of sex has been defined as prohibiting both direct and indirect forms of discrimination.[12]

Non-discrimination on the basis of sex is a limited response to the disadvantaged position of women. The norm promises non-discrimination in the public spheres of life: when men and women are in the same position, they should be treated in the same way. The Women's measures will be temporary techniques to allow women eventually to perform exactly like men.[13] The fundamental problem for women is not, however, simply discriminatory treatment compared with men. Women are in an inferior position because they lack real economic, social or political power in both the public and private worlds. Noreen Burrows has said that:

> For most women, what it is to be human is to work long hours in agriculture or the home, to receive little or no remuneration, and to be faced with political and legal processes which ignore their contribution to society and accord no recognition of their particular needs.[14]

The notion of discrimination contained in the major human rights treaties does not then necessarily respond to the problems women face worldwide. The non-discrimination approach of the Women's Convention was translated directly from the 1966 Convention on the Elimination of Racial Discrimination (Race Convention).[15] Although this was a strategy to ensure the international acceptability of the Women's Convention, the appropriateness of the model can be questioned. Indeed, one of the obstacles faced by women in the area of international law is the general consensus at the state level that oppression on the basis of race is considerably more serious than oppression on the basis of sex.[16]

The discrimination prohibited by the Women's Convention is, with the exception of the obligation to suppress all forms of traffic in women and exploitation of prostitution of women,[17] confined to accepted human rights and fundamental freedoms. If these rights and freedoms are themselves defined in a gendered way, as discussed in the following paragraphs, access to them will be unlikely to promote any real form of equality.

The male-centred view of non-discrimination offered in international law is reinforced by the focus in the Women's Convention on public life, the economy, the legal system, education, and the treaty's only limited recognition that oppression within the private sphere, that of the domestic and family worlds,[18] contributes to women's inequality. It does not, for example, explicitly prohibit violence against women perhaps because of the conceptual difficulty of compressing a harm characterized as private into the public ambit of the Convention, or perhaps because it does not fit directly into the frame of non-discrimination. The monitoring body created by the Women's Convention, the Committee on the Elimination of Discrimination Against Women, has, however, described gender-based violence as a form of discrimination against women, underlining the significance of the private sphere as a site for the oppression of women.[19]

In 1995, the Beijing Declaration and Platform for Action elaborated in detail the international understanding of women's equality.[20] Equality is presented as women being treated in the same way as men, or at least having the same opportunity to be so treated, with little consideration of whether the existing male standards are appropriate. The Platform calls for women's equal participation in a wide range of areas – from the economy and politics to environmental management. The assumption appears to be that women's inequality is removed once women participate equally in decision-making fora. This account of equality does not acknowledge the underlying structures and power relations that contribute to the oppression of women. While increasing the presence of women is certainly important, it does not of itself transform these structures. It allows women access to a world already constituted by men, not to a world transformed by the interests of women. Dianne Otto has noted that the endorsement of affirmative action programmes by the Women's Convention is problematic since,

> [i]n the absence of a recognition that the decision-making structures must themselves change, it is not clear what difference women's equal participation would make. Ultimately, it may merely equally implicate women in the perpetuation of the masculinist liberal forms of minimalist representative democracy and capitalist economics.[21]

In any event, it is not clear that the international norm of non-discrimination on the basis of sex has foundational or inalienable status at the international level. Peremptory, or *jus cogens*, norms in international law must be 'accepted and recognized by the international community of States as a whole as a norm from which no derogation is permitted'.[22] Non-discrimination on the basis of race is usually accepted as a *jus cogens* principle, but the prohibition on sex discrimination rarely qualifies for this status.[23] The foundational character of the prohibition of sex discrimination is undermined by the relatively weak obligations imposed by the Women's Convention. The operative language of the Convention is much weaker, compared, for example, with the Race Convention. Most of the obligations imposed on States parties to the Women's Convention involve taking 'all appropriate measures', a term that leaves considerable discretion to individual states. The Race Convention contains more immediately binding obligations. The qualified language of the Women's Convention is further weakened by the large number of far-reaching reservations and declarations that have been made to its terms by States parties.[24]

'General' human rights norms

How well do 'general' human rights norms, expressed to be relevant to women and men, respond to the lives of women? The Beijing Declaration and Platform for Action acknowledged that women's rights were human rights and described the human rights of women and the girl child as an inalienable, integral and indivisible part of all human rights and fundamental freedoms.[25]

A major limitation of human rights law is its dependence on various distinctions between public and private worlds. These distinctions can muffle, and often completely silence, the voices of women. In the sphere of human rights, a number of actors have an interest in preserving dichotomies between public (regulated) action and private (unregulated) action. For example, powerful entities in the private arena, such as religious and commercial institutions, benefit from lack of international human rights scrutiny.

Many provisions of the international human rights treaties do not address the political, economic, social and cultural context in which most women live. For example, the definition of the right to just and favorable conditions of work in Article 7 of the International Covenant on Economic, Social and Cultural Rights (ICESCR) is confined to work in the public sphere. Much economic activity by women all over the world is rendered invisible precisely because it is performed by women without pay and considered within the private, domestic sphere.[26] Article 7's guarantee to women of 'conditions of work not inferior to those enjoyed by men, with equal pay for equal work' does not respond to the low valuation of the extent and economic value of women's domestic work. Further, even within the paid, public sector, the sexual division of labor that clusters women in typically low-paying jobs that are deemed 'suitable' for women, means that there is often no male comparator, underlining the deficiencies of the non-discrimination paradigm. Thus, homeworking is perceived as a leisure activity pursued by housewives, while the marketing and distribution of the finished products, which is mainly performed by men, is categorized as economically productive.[27] Another example is the right to food, set out in Article 11 of the ICESCR. The elaboration of this right has not taken account of the many transactions involving providing, preparing and serving food that are integral to the lives of women.[28]

Women's economic, social and cultural rights have been deeply affected by the structural adjustment programmes imposed by the international monetary institutions in the name of globalization. Indeed, it has been argued that the severity of the socio-economic conditions caused by structural adjustment programmes in Africa undermines the relevance and utility of rights discourse for African women.[29] For example, such programmes in Ghana were designed to stimulate economic growth, enhance production, strengthen the balance of payments and increase domestic saving and investment. Currency devaluation increased the cost of imported goods, and higher taxes meant increased petroleum and utility tariffs. Basic food prices increased, employment levels were reduced and government spending was cutback. Emphasis on export of agricultural commodities reduced the land available to women for subsistence farming while increasing the total burden of their work.[30] Akua Kuenyehia has written:

> For women in Ghana and other African countries facing structural adjustment, the problems seem endless. They continue to have the responsibility for child care, producing food, gathering fuelwood and water, and taking care of sick members of the family. These functions are economically invisible and yield little or no cash. Additionally, they have to engage in economic ventures to earn income in a climate that has been rendered increasingly hostile by a process of adjustment that has completely marginalized their productive activities.[31]

This situation works against all aspects of women's rights: reduction in access to health, sanitation and education has primary impact on women. Compliance with structural adjustment programmes has also given governments an excuse not to implement obligations under the Women's Convention.

The international legal definition of the right to development provides another example of the privileging of a male perspective and a failure to accommodate the realities of women's lives.[32] The problematic nature of current development practice for women in the South goes, of course, much deeper than the international legal formulation of the right to development, but the rhetoric of international law reflects and reinforces a system sustaining the domination of women. The 1986 UN General Assembly Declaration on the Right to Development describes the content of the right as the entitlement 'to participate in, contribute to and enjoy economic, social, cultural and political development, in which all human rights and fundamental freedoms can be fully realized'.[33] The right is apparently designed to apply to all individuals within a state and is assumed to benefit men and women equally. Article 8 of the Declaration states that 'effective measures should be undertaken to ensure that women have an active role in the development process'.

Despite this specific reference to women, the Declaration fails to take the realities of women's lives into account. First, the Declaration does not specify discrimination against women as a major obstacle to development, nor to the fair distribution of its benefits. For example, one aspect of the right to development is the obligation on states to take 'resolute steps' to eliminate 'massive and flagrant violations of the human rights of peoples and human beings'.[34] The examples given of such violations include apartheid and race discrimination but do not include sex discrimination. Although subsequent UN deliberations have referred to the gender implications of the right to development, these concerns are generally presented as discrete, soluble by the application of special protective measures, rather than as central to development.[35]

A second problem with the Declaration is the model of development on which it rests. Although the formulation of the right to development includes a synthesis of all recognized human rights, its core is redress of economic inequality. Development is taken to mean industrialization and a market economy. The domination of women by men within the family and in society does not enter the traditional development calculus. The limitations of the idea of development enshrined in international law are highlighted by research that has documented the critical role women play in the economies of the South, particularly in agriculture, and at the same time the widespread inequality of women within their families and communities.[36] 'Development' has delivered little to women because economic visibility depends on working in the public sphere. Unpaid work in the home or the subsistence economy is categorized as 'unproductive, unoccupied, and economically inactive'.[37]

The failure to value 'private' women's work is one basis for the observation that overall, the process of development exacerbates the problems of women in the South. Jean Drèze and Armartya Sen have pointed to the significance of perceptions of relative economic contributions in the familial division of food, resources and health care in the developing world.[38] Paid employment is regarded as more significant than unpaid work. The differential valuation of the work of women to that of men often means that, within the family, women will not have an equal claim to food and other necessities. The narrow notion of development endorsed by international law thus operates to exclude women from some aid programmes because they are not considered workers, or because they are regarded as less productive than men. When aid is provided to women, it is often because of their identity as mothers. Another consequence of the economic paradigm of development is that women may be regarded as providing a lesser return on training and education.

The international formulation of the right to development, then, reinforces gendered public/private distinctions. It does not regard systemic discrimination on the basis of sex as a barrier to development, despite the global evidence of the disparity between the economic position of women and men. Moreover, in using the 'neutral' language of development and economics, international law reinforces the pervasive, and detrimental, assumption that women's work is of a different value to men's.

Trade liberalization promoted by international institutions such as the World Trade Organization (WTO) has undermined the effectiveness of human rights discourse for women. Vandana Shiva has argued that economic globalization 'is deeper and wider than Structural Adjustment Policies or GATT [The General

Agreement on Tariffs and Trade] – it is the ruling ideology that centres on the replacement of governmental and state planning by corporate strategic planning and the establishment of global corporate rule'.[39] She has pointed out that although the process of globalization is made to appear 'natural, spontaneous and inevitable', in reality it is deeply political and shaped primarily by the interests of transnational corporations.

The forces of economic globalization are not accountable under the traditional state-centred structures of international law. From the perspective of women, globalization turns on its head the public/private distinction of traditional human rights law, because it redefines understandings of the role of the public sector, facilitates privatization and requires governments to act primarily in accordance with the imperatives of the market rather than those of social justice and human rights. Investment and export processing can increase women's access to paid employment, although the forms of employment created may be oppressive and exploitative.[40]

The influence of cultural relativism

Cultural relativism has deeply influenced approaches to the human rights of women and challenges their status as 'foundational'. The claim of cultural relativism is that if international human rights norms conflict with particular cultural standards, the particularity of culture must take precedence over universalizing trends. Critics of universal human rights standards point to the Western ethical basis of human rights law and reject this as a basis for commitments in other traditions.[41] At the same time, Western states have developed their own form of cultural relativism in the human rights area in arguing for very broad 'margins of appreciation' in implementing their human rights obligations, based on the particularity of their national circumstances.

While concerns of cultural relativism arise with respect to human rights generally, 'culture' is much more frequently invoked in the context of women's rights than in any other area. An example is *Md Ahmed Khan* v. *Shah Bano Begum*.[42] An Indian Muslim woman who was divorced after 40 years of marriage claimed the maintenance payments under the Indian Code of Criminal Procedure rather than those lower payments available under Muslim personal status law. After the Supreme Court of India upheld her claim, opposition and protests from within the conservative Muslim community ultimately persuaded the government to reverse the decision through the inaccurately named Muslim Women (Protection of Rights on Divorce) Act 1986. Another example is the *Vos* case brought against the Netherlands under the Optional Protocol to the ICCPR.[43] The case involved discrimination between women and men with respect to access to a disability pension on the death of a spouse. Dutch law enabled disabled men to retain a disability pension when their wives died, but disabled women were only eligible for a less generous widow's pension in the same circumstances. Ms Vos had been divorced for 22 years at the time of her former husband's death and had been supporting herself at the time she had become disabled. The Human Rights Committee found that the Dutch law was not discriminatory. It accepted the Dutch government's explanation of the distinction between women and men as reasonable and objective on the grounds of consistency with Dutch culture – the assumption that men were the primary breadwinners for their families. The Human Rights Committee seemed to assume that there must be some sort of discriminatory intent for the legislation to violate the prohibition of sex discrimination in the ICCPR, rather than examining the actual effect of the legislation.

The Vienna Declaration of 1993 expressed 'respect' for cultural and religious diversity, but reaffirmed the universality of human rights.[44] It considered cultural and religious practices in the context of violence against women, but did not offer any resolution of the tension between rights to culture and religion on the one hand and women's rights on the other. The Declaration called only for the eradication of conflict between women's rights and 'the harmful effects of certain traditional or religious practices, cultural prejudices and religious extremism' without stipulating that the resolution of the tension should promote women's rights.[45] Extensive debate over the relative priorities of women's rights and religious and cultural beliefs was also a feature of the 1995 Beijing Conference on Women. During the negotiations over the text of the Beijing Platform for Action, it was proposed that a footnote be inserted to ensure that all the actions in relation to health not be considered universally applicable, but be made subject to national laws and priorities consistent with 'the various religious and ethical values and cultural backgrounds of its people'. The footnote was eventually deleted, in a trade-off for the deletion of all references to 'sexual orientation' in the Platform.[46] The final text of the Platform repeats the ambiguous language of the Vienna Declaration with respect to culture.[47]

A major conceptual difficulty with cultural relativism is that the notion of culture is itself endlessly mutable. All social values and hierarchies in their own time frames can be described as forms of culture. In this sense, 'to argue from culture is to prove too much'.[48] If all cultures are seen as special, resting on values that cannot be investigated in a general way, it is difficult to make any assessment from an international perspective of the significance of particular concepts and practices for women.

Cultural relativism is concerned with narrowing the scope of international law in that it places culture in a 'private' sphere outside international regulation. Feminists have pointed out that we need to investigate the gender of the 'cultures' that relativism privileges. Relativism is typically concerned with dominant cultures in particular regions and these are, among other things, usually constructed from male histories, traditions and experiences. Arati Rao has argued that the notion of culture favored by international actors is 'a falsely rigid, ahistorical, selectively chosen set of self-justificatory texts and practices whose patent partiality raises the question of exactly whose interests are being served and who comes out on top'.[49] Rao has proposed a series of questions to assess claims of culture, particularly those used to counter women's claims of rights: whose culture is being invoked? what is the status of the interpreter? in whose name is the argument being advanced? and who are the primary beneficiaries of the claim?

An international rule of law for women?

Does the concept of an international rule of law offer more hope for women than the domestic version? While the international law of human rights provides a very limited response to the injustices and inequality many women face, it has allowed at least some individual victories in national courts. Even the circumscribed notion of non-discrimination on the basis of sex offered by international law may be useful in particular national contexts. One example is the case of Unity Dow in Botswana, where Dow argued successfully that the Botswanan Constitution should be read in light of the international law principle of sex equality.[50]

How can the idea of an international rule of law respond to the disadvantages women face around the world? First, it requires that attention be given to the nature of the official international institutions of justice. The composition of all the major law-making bodies in the international arena is overwhelmingly male: for example, the International Court of Justice (ICJ) has one woman judge out of its 15 members, and the International Law Commission has two women members out of 45. The creation of a complaints mechanism for the Women's Convention has been hailed as a contribution to a woman-conscious international rule of law.[51] The Optional Protocol to the Women's Convention allows women in states that accept the Optional Protocol to invoke international standards and scrutiny when national laws are inadequate. It will also generate a body of jurisprudence interpreting the Women's Convention, although the fact that no cases have yet been brought under the Optional Protocol almost three years after its entry into force suggests that it may be a very limited measure.

A strategic dilemma exists with respect to women's position within international legal structures. On the one hand, the attempt to improve the position of women through more generally applicable measures has allowed women's concerns to be submerged by what are regarded as more 'global' issues. On the other, the price of the creation of separate institutional mechanisms and special measures dealing with women within the UN system has typically been the creation of a 'women's ghetto', given less power, fewer resources and a lower priority than 'mainstream' human rights bodies. The creation of a specialized 'women's' branch of human rights law, of which the Women's Convention is the flagship, exemplifies this tension. It has allowed valuable attention to be given to the lives of women. On the other hand, 'mainstream' human rights institutions have generally not understood the complexities of applying human rights norms to women's lives.[52]

One response to the problems women face in the international human rights system has been the policy of 'gender mainstreaming'. At the Vienna Conference on Human Rights in 1993, it was accepted that the human rights of women should form 'an integral part of the United Nations human rights activities'. The Office of the High Commissioner for Human Rights has made efforts to integrate gender into all human rights activities and is cooperating on this project with the UN Division for the Advancement of Women. The Office has developed a policy on gender and on strategies for its effective implementation. Economic and Social Council (ECOSOC) and the Commission on Human Rights have requested and encouraged the country-specific and thematic Special Rapporteurs, experts and working groups to include sex-disaggregated data in their reports, to address women-specific violations of human rights and to cooperate and exchange information with the Special Rapporteur on violence against women.

Guidelines designed to 'mainstream' gender perspectives in the international human rights system were formulated in 1995 by the annual meeting of the Chairpersons of the human rights treaty bodies. The reaction of the treaty monitoring bodies to calls for gender mainstreaming has been varied, however.[53] The reactions appear to depend on the presence of at least one or two committee members who have a real commitment to the issue. At one end of the spectrum, there have been significant advances. For example, the Committee on Economic, Social and Cultural Rights has generally taken the task of gender mainstreaming seriously, referring to the position of women regularly in its concluding observations on States parties reports and in general comments. Its reporting guidelines are, however, uneven with respect to gender issues. For example, gender is not referred to with respect to some important articles such as the right to free primary education. By contrast, the Committee on the Elimination of Racial Discrimination (CERD) has been slow to address gender considerations in its concluding observations or general comments, although the intersection of race and sex discrimination is an important and controversial area.[54]

The Human Rights Committee, which monitors the ICCPR, is regarded as one of the most progressive of the treaty monitoring bodies with respect to women. It has adopted a number of useful General Comments on articles of the ICCPR that show a sensitivity to gender issues, and in 1995 the Committee amended its reporting guidelines to request States parties to provide information on the position of women. The Committee is not however, consistent in its concern with gender.[55] Thus, overall, gender mainstreaming has had a mixed fate. It has been relatively easy to obtain revision of reporting guidelines and much more difficult to obtain practical follow-through, for example, through the systematic questioning of states.[56]

A second major challenge in developing an international rule of law to respond to the situation of women is to enlarge the category of 'foundational' human rights. The boundaries of the traditional human rights canon must be redefined to accommodate women's lives. Can the human rights canon usefully respond to women's concerns across the globe? Campaigns for women's rights to be recognized as human rights can play a useful, strategic role in advancing women's equality, particularly when used in conjunction with other political and social strategies, but that the limited nature of the discourse of rights must be acknowledged. Rights discourse offers at least a recognized vocabulary to frame political and social wrongs, but we must be conscious of its 'constricted referential universe'.[57] The need to develop a feminist rights discourse so that it acknowledges gendered disparities of power, rather than assuming all people are equal in relation to all rights, is crucial. The challenge is then to invest a rights vocabulary with meanings that undermine the current skewed distribution of economic, social and political power. In societies of the South, this task may be particularly complex. In South Asia, for example, Radhika Coomaraswamy has pointed out that 'rights discourse is a weak discourse', especially in the context of women and family relations. She has argued that the very notion of rights has little resonance in many cultures, for example the countries of South Asia, and that the discourse of women's rights assumes a free, independent, individual woman, an image that may be less powerful in protecting women's rights than other ideologies, such as 'women as mothers'.[58]

Adetoun Ilumoka has made a similar observation with respect to Africa, pointing out that the enforcement of rights is rarely an arena of struggle, and that the language of freedom, justice and fair play is considerably more powerful. In the African context, Ilumoka has argued, 'addressing the problem of poverty is a priority human rights issue . . . [and] international economic policies . . . are a main source of violation of [women's] human rights'.[59] She has suggested that the language of rights may have a particular force in this context because the generators of the international economic policies, UN agencies and the developed North, also see themselves as guardians of human rights.

The language of rights is thus a complex instrument at an international level and ways of adapting it to respond to local and regional circumstances need to be devised. The Vienna and Beijing discourse about women's human rights gives prominence to civil and political rights of women at the expense of economic and social rights. Health and reproductive rights were particularly controversial at Beijing. The feminization of poverty, although clearly acknowledged in the Beijing Platform, was not placed in a rights context. It has been noted that the Platform 'assumes . . . that capitalism has the ability to deliver economic equality to the poor women of the world and . . . that the obligation of states to guarantee certain economic and social rights is made redundant by the more "efficient" processes of free market forces'.[60] For many women, a focus on economic and social human rights would offer an alternative vocabulary to that of the demands of international global capital and allow some resistance to it, even if only at the margins.

As other chapters in this collection indicate, the international rule of law has developed beyond a narrow Diceyan framework. Indeed, Radhika Coomarawsamy has noted that the notion of the international rule of law proposed by international institutions is more connected to the western Enlightenment project than to Dicey, bringing the ideas of representative government, an independent judiciary and respect for human rights to rehabilitate 'failed' or emerging states.[61] While these elements are valuable, it is also important to recognize their politics, limits and silences. Who is a government representative of? What is a judiciary independent of? Whose human rights are being respected? We need to investigate the identities of those staffing these institutions and consider their priorities and blindspots. The commitments of the international rule of law can all too easily be translated in a way that can mask and even exacerbate the injustices confronting women.

Notes

1 See for example: O'Donovan, K. 'Engendering Justice: women's perspectives and the rule of law', *University of Toronto Law Journal*, vol. 39, 1989, p. 127.
2 Australian Law Reform Commission, *Equality Before the Law*, Sydney: Australian Government Publishing Service, 1994.
3 Dicey, A.V. *Introduction to the Study of Law of the Constitution*, 10th edn, London: Macmillan, 1959, pp. 184–203.
4 Charlesworth, H. and Chinkin, C. *The Boundaries of International Law: a feminist analysis*, Manchester: Manchester University Press, 2000, pp. 4–14.
5 United Nations Development Programme (UNDP), *Human Development Report*, New York: Oxford University Press, 1995, p. 43 (emphasis in original).
6 Linehan, J. (2002) 'Women in Public International Litigation', available at: http://www.pict–pcti.org/activities/meetings/London_07_01/Women1.pdf (accessed 25 February 2004).
7 Zifcak, S. 'Globalizing the Rule of Law: rethinking values and reforming institutions', p. 39.
8 Article 7.
9 Article 26.
10 See for example: European Convention on Human Rights and Fundamental Freedoms 1950, Article 14; African Charter of Human and Peoples' Rights 1982, Article 2.
11 1249 United Nations Treaty Series (UNTS) 13.
12 UN Human Rights Committee, General Comment 8, 21 November 1989.
13 Article 4.
14 Burrows, N. 'International Law and Human Rights: the case of women's rights', in T. Campbell (ed.) *Human Rights: from rhetoric to reality*, New York, NY; Oxford, UK: Blackwell, 1986, p. 82.
15 660 UNTS 195.
16 Charlesworth and Chinkin, *The Boundaries of International Law*, p. 230.
17 Article 6.
18 Article 16.
19 General Recommendation 19, UN Doc A/47/38, 30 January 1992.
20 UN Doc A/CONF 177/20, 15 September 1995.
21 Otto, D. 'A Post-Beijing Reflection on the Limitations and Potential of Human Rights Discourse for Women', in K. Askin and D. Koenig (eds) *Women and International Human Rights Law*, vol. 1, Ardsley, NY: Transnational Publishers, 1999, p. 127.
22 Vienna Convention on the Law of Treaties 1969, Article 53.
23 See for example: The American Law Institute, *Restatement (Third) of the Foreign Relations Law of the United States*, 1987, para. 702.
24 Charlesworth and Chinkin, *The Boundaries of International Law*, pp. 103–13.
25 Para. 213.
26 Waring, M. *Counting for Nothing: what men value and what women are worth*, North Sydney; Wellington, NZ: Allen & Unwin, 1988.
27 Mohanty, C. 'Women Workers and Capitalist Scripts: ideologies of domination, common interests, and the politics of solidarity', in M. Alexander and C. Mohanty (eds) *Feminist Genealogies, Colonial Legacies, Democratic Futures*, New York : Routledge, 1997, p. 12.
28 Chinkin, C. and Wright, S. 'The Hunger Trap: women, food and development', *Michigan Journal of International Law*, vol. 14, no. 2, Winter 1993, p. 262.
29 Kuenhehia, A. 'The Impact of Structural Adjustment Programs on Women's Human Rights: the example of Ghana', in R. Cook (ed.) *Human Rights of Women: national and international perspectives*, Philadelphia: University of Pennsylvania Press, 1994, p. 422.
30 Ibid., p. 425.
31 Ibid., p. 431.

32 Charlesworth and Chinkin, *The Boundaries of International Law*, pp. 241–42.
33 GA Res 41/128, para. 1.1.
34 Para. 5.
35 See for example: UN Doc E/CN.4/1990/9.
36 See for example: Drèze, J. and Sen, A. *Hunger and Public Action*, Oxford: Oxford University Press, 1990, chapter 4.
37 Ibid., p. 57.
38 Ibid., p. 52.
39 Shiva, V. *Women, Ecology and Economic Globalisation: searching for an alternative vision*, Indian Association of Women's Studies, 1995, pp. 4–5.
40 Mohanty, 'Women Workers and Capitalist Scripts'.
41 See for example: Pollis, A. and Schwab, P. *Human Rights: a Western construct with limited applicability*, Pennsylvania: Pennsylvania State University Press, 1980.
42 [1985] 3 SCR 844.
43 Communication 218/1986.
44 UN Doc A/CONF 157/23.
45 Para. 38.
46 Otto, 'A Post-Beijing Reflection on the Limitations and Potential of Human Rights Discourse for Women', p. 19.
47 Para. 9.
48 Binion, G. 'Human Rights: A feminist perspective, *Human Rights Quarterly*, vol. 17, issue 3, 1995, p. 522.
49 Rao, A. 'The Politics of Gender and Culture in International Human Rights Discourse', in J. Peters and A. Wolper (eds) *Women's Rights Human Rights: international feminist perspectives*, New York; London: Routledge, 1995, p. 174.
50 *Attorney-General of Botswana v. Unity Dow* [1992] LRC (Const) 623.
51 Evatt, E. 'Reply to Radhika Coomaraswamy', in C. Saunders and K. Le Roy (eds) *The Rule of Law*, Annandale, NSW: Federation Press, 2003, p. 176.
52 Charlesworth and Chinkin, *The Boundaries of International Law*, pp. 218–20.
53 See: Gallagher, A. 'Ending the Marginalisation: strategies for incorporating women into the United Nations human rights system', *Human Rights Quarterly*, vol. 19, issue 2, 1997, p. 283; and Connors, J. 'General Human rights Instruments and their Relevance to Women', in A. Byrnes, J. Connors and L. Bik (eds) *Advancing the Human Rights of Women*, Commonwealth Secretariat, 1997, p. 33.
54 See: General Recommendation on Gender Dimensions of Racial Discrimination UN Doc CERD.
55 Connors, 'General Human rights Instruments and their Relevance to Women'.
56 Ibid.
57 Williams, P. *The Alchemy of Race and Rights*, Cambridge, MA: Harvard University Press, 1991, p. 159.
58 Coomaraswamy, R. 'To Bellow Like a Cow: women, ethnicity and the discourse of rights', in Cook (ed.) *Human Rights of Women*, 1994, p. 55.
59 Ilumoka, A. 'African Women's Economic, Social, and Cultural Rights: toward a relevant theory and practice', in R. Cook (ed.) *Human Rights of Women: national and international perspectives*, Philadelphia: University of Pennsylvania Press, 1994, p. 319.
60 Otto, 'A Post-Beijing Reflection on the Limitations and Potential of Human Rights Discourse for Women', p. 127.
61 Coomaraswamy, R. 'Broken Glass: women, violence and the rule of law' Saunders and Le Roy (eds) *The Rule of Law*, 2003, p. 144.

5 The universalizing of human rights and economic globalization

What roles for the rule of law?

*David Kinley**

Introduction

The phenomenon of globalization grips us. Everyday, and almost at every turn, we encounter directly the practical effects of its impact. Certainly, such encounters are evidence enough of the empirical fact of its existence, even if the concept of globalization remains nebulous. The process of its inductive construction continues as we try to make sense of our increased global interconnectedness on at least two levels. On one, the process is concerned with charting the causes of, and consequences for, our social lives as we live them. On another level, it is concerned with the conceptual placement of globalization – that is, how the phenomenon relates to, impacts upon and is constituted by the myriad of other conceptual constructs that we use to understand, explain or promote the human, social condition. It is with the second level that this chapter is principally concerned, and specifically with two of these other conceptual constructs – the rule of law and human rights.

This chapter can be seen as part of the wider concern to identify, explain and analyze the fit between law and globalization.[1] Such a quest is, on its own, significant because of the central placement of the rule of law within notions of fair, just and usually democratic government – indeed it is by law that we are ruled, not by whim or caprice. However, the particular concern here is with the interrelationship between the rule of law and the protection and promotion of human rights – within the context of globalization.

The globalization knot that ties the two notions has, at least since the advent of the modern (post-1945) iteration of universal human rights norms, been clear and crucial,[2] even if sometimes overwhelming.[3] In that sense, it is by the development of human rights laws (both international and domestic) upon which so much of the promotion of human rights has relied over the past 50 years, even if the protection of human rights is still wanting.

Given that, one might ask, how is the notion of the rule of law faring today and how might it fare in the future as we become more aware and attuned to globalization as it affects and is affected by the universalizing objects of human rights? To what extent, in other words, must we now reinterpret the nature of the rule of law/human rights relationship and redraw the lines that mark out their synergy?

To try to answer these questions, it is necessary first to analyze the relationship between human rights globalization and the globalization of the rule of law. And second, it is necessary to analyze the implications of this relationship within the context of a globalizing economy. These, broadly, are the aims of this chapter.

Finally, on a point of definition and distinction, it must be emphasized that though generally I shall be dealing with an undifferentiated body of human rights (in the sense that they are interdependent and indivisible), I shall at times highlight economic, social and cultural rights where their particular place in the quest to reconcile the disparate discourses of globalization, commercial enterprise, human rights and the rule of law is especially significant.[4]

My analysis proceeds by way of four steps:

1 a discussion of certain perspectives of, and trends in, globalization;
2 an analysis of the relevant features of the notion of rule of law;
3 an analysis of the complexities of human rights globalization; and
4 consideration of the future utility of the rule of law in human rights protection.

Perspectives of globalization

The concern in this section is not to provide an account of all, or even the principal, globalization perspectives and theories, but rather to pick out those that are amenable to addressing the rule of law's impact upon the protection and promotion of human rights.

At the broadest level, the globalization theories that are most accommodating of the rule of law are those which highlight both the external and internal dimensions of globalization, for this resonates strongly with legal theory's own orthodox fixation with the binary of national and international law. Globalization is both an 'out there' and an 'in here' phenomenon, blending the distant with the local.[5] Furthermore, it is a two-way process. As Anthony Giddens puts it, the globalization process 'link[s] distant localities in such a way that local happenings are shaped by events occurring many miles away and vice versa'.[6] Such a taxonomy applies equally to the interrelationship between national and international law.

An alternative perspective on the same theme is that of Boaventura de Sousa Santos's separation of two strands of the globalization process in an effort to source that which is perceived to have been globalized.[7] The first strand he terms 'globalized localism', which occurs when essentially local phenomena are exported or propagated globally.[8] Examples of this abound, but certainly include soccer, certain retail brands (e.g. McDonalds, Sony, Manchester United Football Club merchandise and Coca-Cola), the English language, American intellectual property laws, Scotch whiskies, European Union (EU) data protection laws, Chinese cuisine, and Anglo-American popular music. The second he calls 'localized globalism', which occurs where global phenomena are adopted locally – for example: tourist catering, free trade policies/laws, environmental degradation, internet penetration, human rights standards and satellite television.[9]

Though beguilingly simple and alliterative, we can have little use for such a division as an analytical tool if taken at face value, for the two strands do not operate on a linear plane, running, as it were, in opposite directions.[10] Rather, the best way to make sense of them is to view them as operating in perpetual circular motion – that which is (already) global and now is being localized, was itself, in some form, originally a local phenomenon made subject to globalization! The cycle is depicted therefore, as one of global practice leading to local impact, adaptation and export which leads to global impact, adaptation and practice. What is most useful about the Santos characterization is that it helps us to identify where, at any one time, a product, concept, genre or effect is in the cycle of globalization. It is to this end that I employ the Santos typology in respect of the notion of the rule of law later in this chapter.

In addition to the important provision of analytical tools to aid us in charting the relationship of globalization and the rule of law, globalization theory also, to some degree, directly addresses the substantive issue itself. Gunther Teubner's 'global law' thesis counters Kant's perception of an orderly procession towards a transcendental legal order for all mankind (by way largely of an international convention to that effect) on the simple basis that evidently it has not been borne out in practice. In its stead he sees '[t]oday's globalization . . . [as] a highly contradictory and . . . fragmented process',[11] where the extent to which there is a globalization of the rule of law is as a consequence of 'lawyers' law' (or 'living law')[12] in practical decision-making, especially in regard to trans-global commercial contracts (*lex mercatoria*). And important though this is, for Teubner it is the exception that proves the rule, in that in the absence of any centralized, sovereign global law-making authority, the law's centre of gravity is still the nation state.[13]

Jean-Philippe Robé, writing alongside Teubner in the same volume, expands the details of the latter's analysis to include two important additional loci of globalized law, both of which he sees as challenges to States' self-proclaimed monopoly of law creation.[14] One arises out of the 'construction of global deterritorialized legal orders – in other words, multinational enterprises'.[15] The other, which is clearly linked to the first, is that of the national laws which have extraterritorial effect – specifically, in Robé's view, 'the exportation by other states of their norms through international economic exchange, and in particular through multinational enterprises'.[16]

Together, these perspectives of the legal dimensions of globalization reflect the pluralist roots of global law. Thus, as William Twining points out, it is not surprising that, despite the almost exclusively municipal framework within which legal pluralism has been historically forged, it has much to offer any global law project.[17] This is so principally because of two key characteristics of legal pluralism: first, its obvious openness to other legal cultures and perspectives, and second, its openness to non-state sources of law. Together, these features of legal pluralism provide for a suitably textured canvas upon which the shape of international or global law can be traced.[18]

Globalization trends

Among the many globalizing areas in which one can discern a specific and significant trend, there are two that stand out – namely, corporate/commercial enterprise and human rights/humanitarian standard-setting. The corporate/commercial enterprise is characterized by the patent aggrandizement of the power of multinational enterprises, the influence of capital markets,[19] and the concomitant expansion of international regimes for trade regulation – such as the World Trade Organization (WTO), the North America Free Trade Agreement (NAFTA) and the EU – and for economic development – such as the International Monetary Fund (IMF), the World Bank and the regional development banks of Africa, Asia and South America.

Human rights standard setting is characterized by the spreading, though not unqualified, acceptance across states[20] of the universality and indivisibility of human rights. It is also characterized by the emergence of new regional human rights regimes beyond the European[21] and American[22] progenitors – that is, in Africa,[23] the Arab States[24] and in rudimentary form in Asia.[25] What is of interest in the present context is the question: to what extent do these two trends compete with each other, complement each other or simply co-habit?

To be sure, there exists a perplexing dissonance between these two trends that haunts (or at least should haunt) all those concerned about globalization, the rule of law and human rights. Consider, for instance, the perspective of those who protested in Seattle, Davos, Melbourne or Genoa against what they see as the facilitating role in commercial/corporate globalization of such institutions as the WTO, the IMF, the World Bank and the economic clubs of G8 and the Western Economic Forum in particular. One might also consider the potentially degrading effect such globalization has on local economies and culture everywhere (but especially in developing countries), to the benefit of a very few, already powerful, corporate elites in the West.[26] However, many of those same protestors were and are at the same time strong supporters of the globalization (or spreading universalism) of human rights standards.[27] Whilst in terms of desired outcome such a stance need not necessarily be contradictory, there is on its face, some inconsistency.

Of course, the most immediate response to this situation is to point out that it is not globalization *per se* that is the problem, but rather the nature of the phenomenon being globalized. It is argued, for example, that the commercial/corporate axis of globalization is to be resisted precisely because it distributes its benefits unequally – that is, to the few (mainly in the West) at the expense of the many everywhere.[28] On the other hand, human rights globalization is to be supported precisely because of its universalist nature – rights being available (or applied) to all, everywhere, at all times. To put it even more crudely, the claim is that whereas the former promotes inequality, the latter promotes equality.

In reality, these two phenomena are unlikely to be so starkly divergent, in that the current perception, though not without foundation, is due as much to the problem of it not being recognized that the two are both players on the same field of globalization. In the following section I consider whether by analyzing these two globalizing trends through the prism of the rule of law any light can be shed on how they do, will, or should overlap.

Relevant dimensions of the notion of the rule of law

In order to analyze these trends through the rule of law, there is no need here to embark on an exegetical voyage into the notion of the rule of law; not least because of the prodigious output of those that have gone before. Certainly, Lon Fuller captured the essence of the notion in a classically pithy statement coming out of his own substantial work on the subject, that 'law is the enterprise of subjecting human conduct to the governance of rules'.[29] Most, if not all, modern formulations of the rule of law have common base elements, even if their categorization, and the reasons for such, differ between leading commentators.[30] These are that the notion comprises rules of general application; that government is bound by rules; and, that rules are prospective and publicly accessible such that the legal implications of one's future actions may be predicted.

Be that as it may, what is of specific interest in the present context is the narrower question of the role of the rule of law in these two fields of globalization. Drawing on the previously mentioned local/global typology, it can be argued that law associated with the commercial/corporate axis of globalization is local–drawn principally from the liberalist philosophy of Western social, economic, political and legal thought, or, more specifically, from the competition policies, commercial laws and corporate codes of the United States and Europe. The utility of law in this context is simultaneously to enhance free trade and freedom of contract and to exert commercial (i.e. transactional) order through the extraterritorial imposition of Western municipal law,[31] multinational enterprise practice and Western-style regulatory regimes, backed by free-market ideology. Of the key principles that classically comprise the formal notion of the rule of law, the one here emphasized is that of the publicized and relatively predictable operation of laws and legal system.[32] In its orthodox formulation, this requires a system where the government 'is bound by rules fixed and announced beforehand', such that its actions are in theory knowable, allowing individuals and other legal persons to plan their own actions accordingly.[33] This principle's substantive object of mitigating arbitrariness is achieved when, as Martin Krygier felicitously puts it:

> [T]he law in general does not take you by surprise or keep you guessing, when it is accessible to you as is the thought that you might use it, when legal institutions are relatively independent of other significant social actors but not of legal doctrine, and when the powerful forces in society, including the government, are required to act, and come in significant measure to think, within the law; when the limits of what we imagine our options to be are set in significant part by the law and where these limits are widely taken

seriously – when the law has integrity and it matters what the law allows and what it forbids.[34]

In accordance then with the typology of the formal conception of the rule of law, the concern here is with the prospect of surety that flows from the existence of the legal process itself. The law's instrumental integrity is more relevant than the substantive content of the law. Such a focus draws on the essential systemic rationality of law being a means, as Cotterrell puts it, 'by which human beings impose reason, to the limits of their ability, on the otherwise chaotic conditions of their social existence'.[35] Thus, in respect of this chapter's concern with the commercial, corporate and regulatory drivers – both national and transnational – of the globalizing economy, this dimension of the rule of law is vital to the pursuit of their objects.[36]

The law associated with globalized human rights standards, on the other hand, is not so specifically sourced.[37] The claims to universality of human rights (and therefore human rights law) mark them out as inherently 'global' in origin as well as application.[38] Above all, international human rights regimes draw upon the rule of law's innate recognition of equality before the law, which forms an integral part of the fundamental concept of equality that underpins the concept of human rights itself.[39] But insofar as the notion of the rule of law implies more than the formal, architectural concerns of its strictly formal incarnation and includes also stipulations as to substance, the imperative of equality takes on added significance.

Of course, debate continues over the degree of this necessary leakage of substantive considerations into the formal conception of the rule of law.[40] However, it is significant that commentators such as Philip Selznick[41] and even Joseph Raz, the doyen of the formal conception, embrace certain substantive claims within their view of the ambit of the rule of law. Raz, for example, in his more recent work, maintains the necessary presupposition of 'civil rights' in the notion of the rule of law.[42] In the same vein, but further still, Ronald Dworkin includes the protection of moral rights within his 'rights conception' of the rule of law.[43] It is then, where the rule of law promises (at the very least) substantive equality, above merely formal equality that the most certain bond between globalizing human rights standards and the notion of the rule of law is fashioned.

There can be no doubt that these two features of the rule of law – the formal and the substantive – are distinct, but they are not, and cannot be, unrelated. The very fact that of the existence of a rule–producing system that is itself bound by rules is a substantive outcome, and one that is both desirable and necessary.[44] I raise this point here (I return to it in the section, The role of the rule of law, that follows) so as to stress its importance and to ensure it is borne in mind. For, I now proceed to assess the effect of distinctive dimensions of rule of law relied on in the different globalizing forums of corporate and commercial enterprise and human rights.

If, in these two fora, the rule of law, or at least different aspects of it, is being globalized, what can we say about the nature of such globalization and its implications? Here again we can adopt the modified Santos categorizations such that the two categories operate within a cyclical relationship. It might be said that the category which most closely fits the role played by the rule of law in recent history of human rights globalization is 'localized globalism' – on account of the equality claims made of it in underpinning the idea of the proclaimed universality of human rights. In contrast, the appropriate category for the place of the rule of law in the globalizing commercial/corporate axis is 'globalized localism' – on account of its locally-sourced properties of certainty and predictability that underpin the global scope of secure commercial transactions and corporate enterprise.

What this characterization enables us to see is that the ends to which the rule of law is put by the two globalizing trends are apparently starkly divergent. On the one hand, it is avowedly a process of colonization by which local commercial laws and corporate practice are capturing the global market. On the other, in contrast, it is the project of globally situated human rights standards to seek to capture the local. One is imperial and hegemonic; the other is normatively based and universal.

However, as is so often the case with simple dichotomies of complex issues, the lines that divide these two globalizing phenomena and the conclusions that can be drawn from them are not as clear in practice. It is in this grey domain that there is potential not only to find common ground between the two but also to establish some form of mutually beneficial alliance.

The complexity of globalization and human rights

There are many dimensions to this clouding of the distinction. Here I highlight four especially important ones, which separately and together have the effect of focusing our attention on human rights as a whole as well as the particular situation of economic, social and cultural rights. Together, the first two dimensions tend to obscure the normative claims made of human rights and thereby their characterization as global phenomena locally adopted (i.e. 'localized globalism'). The latter dimensions challenge the assumption that commercial/corporate globalization is necessarily and always antithetical to the promotion of universal human rights observance. The four dimensions are discussed in the following sections.

Human rights categorization

Not all categories of human rights are 'globalized', or at least globally accepted, to the same extent. Most importantly, there is a fundamental difference between the status and treatment of civil and political rights on the one hand, and economic, social and cultural rights on the other. The Universal Declaration of Human Rights' coverage of both sets of rights marks the apogee of the international community's commitment to their indivisibility.

Since 1948, and despite proclamations to the contrary,[45] the two sets of rights have been essentially separated (initially and fundamentally, in the form of the two separate UN Covenants in 1966)[46] with the result that civil and political rights have taken centre stage in the programme of human rights globalization. Civil and political rights are still frequently referred to – and in a hierarchical sense, are believed to be – 'first generation' rights. Economic, social and cultural rights are considered to be 'second generation' rights.

In terms of the relative legal standing of the two Covenants, this distinction is borne out in practice. By far, the greatest body of human rights jurisprudence in the international arena concerns civil and political rights. The three busiest and most influential international human rights tribunals have custody over the civil and political rights instruments – namely, the European Court of Human Rights (the European Convention on Human Rights),[47] the UN Human Rights Committee (the International Covenant on Civil and Political Rights)[48] and the Inter-American Court on Human Rights (the American Convention on Human Rights 1969).[49] And although the Human Rights Committee is not a court – its conclusions are views, not judgments and are non-binding – the generally high regard in which the Committee's views are held coupled with the sheer volume of its output assures their legal importance.

In stark contrast, the Committee on Economic, Social and Cultural Rights has no competence to hear individual complaints regarding violations of the Covenant's provisions and as such has no equivalent body of jurisprudence.[50] Further, proponents of economic, social and cultural rights have to battle against the powerful rhetorical claims that such rights are not even rights at all, or at any rate are non-justiciable, being expressed more in the form of policy aspirations and non-binding provisions which are not amenable to curial enforcement.[51] However, such a stance can hardly be sustained in the face of what role the law (and the courts) actually plays in the realization of human rights. For it is fundamentally the same legal vehicle by which implementation is supervised for *all* human rights (whether civil and political, or economic, social and cultural) – namely, the remedies available through administrative law or due process.[52] In regards to both sets of rights, it is insistence on the fairness of the procedures by which decisions are made concerning the substantive elements of a rights claim that is the key justiciable concern, not the allocation of resources required for the right's protection.

At the domestic level too, the great majority of legal provisions protecting human rights (whether constitutional, legislative or judge-made) address civil and political rights rather than economic, social and cultural rights. This preponderance is most marked regarding Western human rights charters and laws in both civil code and common law jurisdictions. Thus, since the courts of the West have produced the bulk of the case law on domestic human rights protection, the dominance of civil and political rights is further entrenched.[53]

Challenges to human rights universality

The conceptual structure of human rights is not monolithic; nor are human rights themselves hermetically sealed imperatives. Neither at the general nor specific levels are human rights stated unambiguously and applied unquestioningly – they never have been, nor will they ever be.

Therefore, claims as to the universality of human rights are not simply understood, let alone simply accepted or rejected. This indeterminacy has fuelled the continuing and occasionally raging debate over the extent to which the assertion as to the universality of human rights is rebutted or qualified by relativist (usually cultural relativist) arguments. If it is the case that specific cultural groups derive their governing social norms (including human rights) from their own internal frame of reference, does this mean that universalist and cultural relativist arguments are mutually exclusive?[54] Or to put it another way: is not the argument for human rights universalism dealt a fatal blow by any significant admission of the cultural contingency of human rights in terms of meaning or application?

The intuitive reaction to this for many is to support universalism by way, in part at least, of an attack on cultural relativism. This, in turn, provokes a redoubling of efforts on the part of relativists to bolster their position . . . and so the cycle goes on. However, the depiction, as well as the fact of such a causal relationship, is premised on a basic misconception – namely that the full nature, extent and form of human rights are somehow identifiable. On the contrary, it is only once they have been identified that we are in a possession of that which is universally recognized. To question this premise is not to deny universalism, nor to champion cultural relativism; indeed, quite the reverse. It is to provide the ground upon which one might construct a fuller understanding of the relevance of human rights to all human beings, not as a conceptual strait-jacket into which we all must fit, but rather a garment that is still in the process of being fitted. It is to recognize that differing cultural perspectives necessarily contribute to both their design and fabric, not to mention that such inclusiveness *must* to some significant degree exist if the universal application of human rights is to be backed by their universal origins. '[S]incere intercivilizational dialogues are needed', as Onuma Yasuaki argues, 'if ever human rights are to be truly globalized'.[55]

International human rights laws do, in fact, reflect this situation in a number of ways. 'Universalist' treaties such as the Universal Declaration of Human Rights (in article 28)[56] and both the International Covenant on Civil and Political Rights[57] and the International Covenant on Economic, Social and Cultural Rights[58] (in article 1 of each) explicitly provide for cultural difference: the rights to cultural participation and self-determination, respectively. These and other treaties also provide scope for culturally contingent limitations on certain rights, typically in the form of legitimate reasons based on public morals, public interest, public health and national security.[59] These provisions have given rise to a considerable body of jurisprudence (developed, in particular, by the European Court of Human Rights), on the limits of those limitations.[60] Reservations and declarations are another legally sanctioned vehicle for the legitimate expression of cultural particularities.[61]

Human rights universalism therefore has a necessary, if limited, embrace of cultural differences in the origin, interpretation and implementation of human rights standards.[62] The significance in the present context of this manifestation of what David Forsythe refers to as 'weak cultural relativism'[63] is that it exposes the intricate complexity of the relationship between the global and the local; between their respective imports and exports of the constituents of universal human rights standards; and ultimately between their ownership of normative human rights claims. Precisely where international human rights are on the Santos chart of globalization 'isms' is genuinely open to debate.

Prosperity and human capabilities

There are two fundamental perspectives of how economic globalization does, and will, impact global prosperity. One perspective is the essentially utilitarian claim that economic globalization – in particular, the elemental role played by globalized free markets – will increase the size of the economic pie. Therefore, all will be better off to some appreciable degree.[64] The fact that a few will benefit enormously is acknowledged both as an incentive as well as a necessary price to be paid for an overall increase in prosperity.[65]

The alternative perspective rejects such a utilitarian rationale by first questioning whether the size of the pie increases at all. Even if it is accepted that it does, the very fact that it benefits the few at the expense of the many strips it of any moral or possibly even economic legitimacy. Thus, far from benefiting even marginally, the greatest number would suffer (and some suffer terribly) through economic exploitation, social disintegration and cultural degradation.[66]

Irrespective of the relative merits of these two positions, both rest on the same, largely unspoken premise regarding human rights protection. Namely, that in order to improve the lot of the many, the conditions within which they live must be such that as individuals they are *capable* of, what might be called 'human rights fulfillment': that is, broadly, the state in which the basic object of human rights protection – the upholding of individual dignity – is attained. Within the immediate context we are concerned with economic conditions or needs. John Gray, who belongs to the latter skeptical school argues that in respect of the ongoing globalization of laissez-faire economic policies, 'free markets are creatures of state power, and persist only so long as the state is able to prevent human needs for security and the control of economic risk from finding political expression'.[67]

Such an economic analysis echoes the human rights concerns of those who advocate the so-called 'needs' or 'capabilities' approach to the advancement of human welfare and quality of life. Strictly speaking, as the pioneers of this movement, Martha Nussbaum and Amartya Sen point out, the capabilities and the human rights approaches are distinct.[68] For the capabilities approach, the key lies in the nature of the central question that must be asked in order to determine the gap between the actual and target states of individual well-being. Both authors also insist that the capabilities approach necessarily incorporates within it a focus on human rights protection.[69]

The capabilities and human rights approaches share the same concern of individual well-being, however, what differs is the means by which one conceives the steps to be taken to promote that end. As Nussbaum puts it: '[w]hat is [a person] actually able to do and to be?'[70] If the answer is that the person is unable to reach certain minimum life-states by reason of the conditions in which they live, then the inquiry shifts to identifying what are the individual needs they require to close the gap. For example, in order that a person is able to have good health, they must be provided with adequate nourishment, shelter and health care. To use the senses of imagination, thought, and reason, to create and maintain attachments to people outside one's self and to be able to form a perception of the good, one must be cultivated by adequate education and freedom to associate with other human beings.[71]

This approach impacts upon the argument being developed in this chapter in two important and interrelated respects. First, a focus on needs and capabilities exposes the reality that for the vast majority of the world's population, favorable economic and social conditions are at least as important to the fulfilment of an individual's capabilities as facilitative civil and political conditions. Second, that globalizing economic forces not only have the means and the opportunity to address these needs, but also, perhaps, the obligation by virtue of the capabilities approach's assimilation of international human rights laws.

Common goals

The rhetorically proclaimed opposition of human rights globalization and economic globalization belies a growing body of common goals between the two. Certainly, on the face of it, the growth of this common ground has been exponential over the last few years. On many fronts and for many reasons there now exist a variety of partnerships, cooperative initiatives, forced marriages and mediated settlements between corporate and human rights interests.[72] These arrangements, or their products, include: (i) purely voluntary self-regulation – the conspicuous number of human rights codes of conduct developed by individual corporations or industry peak bodies; (ii) third-party mediated codes, guidelines or compacts – the United Nations' Global Compact, and the Draft Norms on Responsibilities of Transnational Corporations and other Business Enterprises with Regard to Human Rights,[73] and the OECD's Guidelines for Multinational Enterprises;[74] and (iii) the legal obligations and proposals for legislative regulation. For example, the expanding jurisprudence of the United States' federal Alien Tort Claims Act,[75] the mounting willingness of British and Australian courts in particular, to limit protection afforded to corporations by the doctrine of *forum non-conveniens*,[76] the legislative proposals before the US Congress,[77] the Australian Parliament[78] and the UK Parliament[79] to make corporations accountable under domestic law for their actions overseas,[80] and the deliberations of the European Commission.[81] Human rights considerations have also begun to impact the planning and operations of international trade and aid organizations such as the WTO, the IMF, the World Bank and the Asian Development Bank.[82] Therefore, the link between international trade and human rights is now well established,[83] even if its implications are yet to be fully realized.[84] The argument against recognizing that trade *necessarily* affects human rights is no longer sustainable (if it ever was and even if some still hold to it); rather the debate has now shifted to the issue of the extent to which free trade is compromised by any link between human rights protectionism.[85]

These developments are symptomatic of an apparent shift in corporate culture, especially in large multinational corporations. The commercial context in which they operate is changing.[86] Increasingly, institutional as well as individual shareholders are guided by principles of ethical investment. Many of the largest corporations are now subject (or subject themselves) to social audits undertaken by a variety of auditors, importantly including some of the large accounting firms such as Klynveld Peat Marwick Goerdeler (KPMG) and PricewaterhouseCoopers. Furthermore, there has been an explosion in the provision of advice on corporate social responsibility, whether as part of the standard portfolio of management consultancy or by way of firms specifically focused on providing advice on corporate reputations and responsibilities. There are a host of influential, non-aligned, watch-dog organizations which scrutinize the social responsibility performances of corporations, including for example, Business for Social Responsibility in the United States, Corporate Social Responsibility in Europe and specialized units within Amnesty International and the US-based Lawyers' Committee for Human Rights.

There is considerable potential for corporate impact, beneficial as well as detrimental, on human rights generally, but in particular on economic, social and cultural rights standards. One has little difficulty cataloguing a host of potential scenarios that violate existing international human rights treaties (both global and regional) and domestic laws that protect or can be read to protect economic, social and cultural rights.[87] On the positive side of the ledger, clearly any prevention or reversal of such infringements aids human rights protection. But there are other more proactive avenues that can be pursued. It has, for instance, been pointed out that the protection of economic, social and cultural rights 'will be most important for businesses that carry out apparent state functions [particularly in developing countries], perhaps providing schools or health clinics in a "company town".'[88] And there is further, the fact of pressure being brought to bear indirectly on corporations to conform to the obligations of the International Covenant on Economic Social and Cultural Rights (ICESCR), by way of the demands of the Covenant made directly by the signatory states in which the corporations operate or reside.[89]

The role of the rule of law

The fact of this demonstrated overlap between the phenomena of human rights globalization and commercial/corporate globalization, brings with it a blurring of their respective rule of law claims articulated earlier. As foreshadowed, the classification of the latter's rule of law interests being largely formal and those of the former being largely substantive is too simplistic. Corporate and commercial concerns are now at least more conversant with the social content of laws. In addition, human rights protagonists accept qualifications to their normative assertions, and they accept that in the articulation, substantiation and implementation of human rights, the formal conception of the rule of law has been of enormous importance. These points notwithstanding, perhaps the most revealing conclusion that can be drawn from the preceding analysis is the fact that the rule of law may have only a relatively limited part to play in determining the nature and effect of the globalization of human rights.

Thus, the identification, under 'challenges to human rights universality', of a dimension of cultural relativity in the conception and application of universal human rights, further attenuates the certainty and predictability of the law that backs them. In 'prosperity and human capabilities', though the rule of law plays a part in providing the regulatory framework within which greater wealth may be created through the global expansion of commerce and free trade, 'legal rights and legal systems' do little (though not nothing) to ensure anything like an equitable division of the spoils as needs demand. Also, the bulk of the developments discussed under 'common goals' are non-binding or are not yet in force. The many and various codes of conduct, alliances, compacts and guidelines are indicative of some degree of corporate cultural enlightenment, but they are nevertheless voluntary and inspirational, with no or very little legal backing. It is only under 'human rights categorization' that there exists the prospect of a significant place for the rule of law, but only if one is able to overcome the fact that economic, social and cultural rights are jurisprudentially maligned. Pointing out the analytical shortcomings of the claims that such rights are policy considerations and therefore not amenable to curial decision-making, does not change the fact that economic and social rights are infrequently accorded the same level of legal significance (if expressly articulated as legal rights at all) as civil and political rights.

Notwithstanding these limited opportunities, I must reiterate that I do not see the notion of the rule of law as irrelevant to the notion of human rights. It could not be so, not least for the reasons that I have pointed out in this chapter. First, the two constructs share a number of important precepts, and second, as I have stressed throughout, the legalization of human rights aided their standardization. Instead, my conclusion is that the rule of law on its own is not and will not be sufficient to provide even for minimal human rights protection. Still less can it be sufficient so long as the concept of human rights remains essentially contested in terms of nature, content and implementation, and so long as human rights share the globalization stage with economic actors. Where rules proclaiming human rights are supported by a broad social, political and economic determination to promote them, rather than pulling themselves up by their own bootstraps, as it were, then the rule of law would truly facilitate their global promotion and protection. The necessity of this relationship is as true at any one instant, as it is across time when the form, nature and circumstance of these supporting structures change. For the notion of the rule of law is, as Philip Selznick puts it,

> a governing ideal, not a specific set of injunctions. This ideal is to be realized in history and not outside it. . . . Even when we know the meaning of legality we must work out the relation between general principles [including human rights] and the changing structure of society. New circumstances do not necessarily alter principles, but they may and do require that new rules of law be formulated and old ones changed.[90]

It is true that in circumstances of extreme political, economic and social upheaval the contingencies of the rule of law may be of a different order. As Ruti Teitel argues, there exists

> a tension between the rule of law as backward-looking and forward-looking, as settled versus dynamic. In this dilemma, the rule of law is ultimately contingent; rather than grounding legal order, it serves to mediate the normative shifts in justice that characterize these extraordinary periods.[91]

But this perspective overplays the stability or 'settledness' of legal order not in hyper-transition. It fails to recognize the fact that the rule of law is nevertheless and always contingent on political circumstance in more ordinary times – the difference is simply one of degree, not kind. The system by which a legal order is maintained continues to mediate change in society, to varying levels of efficacy, whether such change is big or small, sudden or gradual.

The reality is that the state of human rights protection just about everywhere at the present time can be fairly said to be somewhere in between the poles of empty proclamation and proclamation with punch.

A pluralist implementation of human rights?

In terms of the future implementation of human rights, it may be asked: whither the rule of law? From the standpoint of the concerns of the present context, there are at least two lines of inquiry that flow from this question – one general, the other specific.

The first, more general analysis, is to reconceive the role we assign to the notion of the rule of law, and move it away from the conception of it as providing the framework for, or instrument of, human rights protection, *sine qua non*. It is more realistic to sidestep, or at least stand back from this doctrinaire, 'access to justice' model. To do so would have the salutary effect of expanding the interests and expertise of those involved in human rights discourse, action and enforcement beyond the traditional dominance of lawyers (especially), diplomats, secretariat officials of international organizations and non-government organization representatives.[92] The traditional dominance of such groups has arisen out of the essentially legal-based means by which they execute their mandates to promote human rights protection.

However, as many have pointed out, these techniques are especially ill-suited to handling, for example, the pressing issues that lie at the heart of economic, social and cultural rights.[93] Law, lawyers and legal apparatus are important, but they are not alone sufficient. Broader economic policy and social welfare strategies are of equal, if not more profound, importance. In this regard, Craig Scott warns in his critique of the dominance of the legal perspective within human rights discourse generally that, '[e]specially after fifty years of gradually building up a body of juridical human rights doctrine, there is a risk that rights analysis could lose touch with the basic rationales for human rights protection. Legal doctrine can all too easily come to develop a legal logic all of its own, to the point that the tail (of doctrinal analysis) begins to wag the dog (of human rights)'.[94] At the very least, this highlights the need to accept and adopts a pluralist approach if we are fully to understand, let alone effectively promote, human rights standards.

The second, specific line of inquiry, stems from the possibility of corporate/ commercial globalization throwing up a supplementary vehicle for the protection of human rights. If the arena of human rights is to be broadened as suggested earlier, then that must include the prospect of domestic and international corporations as well as global economic regulatory bodies taking on active roles as human rights guardians, parallel to the guardianship responsibilities of States. Just as States, at one and the same time, are capable of breaching human rights standards and are charged with the responsibility of upholding those standards, so corporations and other global commercial actors are equally capable and can be expected to shoulder the same or similar responsibility. They may, in any case, be doing so 'voluntarily' – that is, where ultimately they see it as in their own economic interests.[95] Or, they may be doing so in response to perceived or actual legal duress.[96] In reality, the extent of the current coalition of global commercial and human rights interests is a result of a combination of pro-action and reaction on the part of corporate and economic regulators. Still, their concern to protect human rights interests stretches only so far as such protection is seen as instrumental in promoting key commercial interests.

The question is whether this is desirable, legitimate and above all, enough. Certainly, I think it can be said that it is desirable if only because expecting anything more altruistic of the globalized corporate/commercial axis would be unrealistic and quite possibly counterproductive. The legal legitimacy of such responsibility is not yet firmly established, but it seems inevitable that it will to some extent be put in place.[97] Clearly, the current level of human rights protection by these means is not, nor will it ever be enough, if only because whatever may be expected of the human rights responsibilities of global economic actors, it can never replace the overriding obligations of state actors.[98]

Conclusion

This chapter has sought to explore the relationship between the rule of law and the protection and promotion of human rights within the context of globalization, especially economic globalization. I have used the notion of the rule of law mainly as an analytical tool to help to understand the significance of global expansion along the commercial/corporate axis and globalization of human rights standards, both as regards their separate development and their overlap and limited merger. In so doing, the role of the rule of law itself has been thrown into relief. It transpires that its significance has not been as great as might be supposed and that what role it has played is of more historical, rather than future, importance.

Most certainly, the rule of law has been and is part of the facilitative framework upon which the global expansion of both corporate and commercial enterprise and the promotion of human rights have been built – albeit that they use different parts of the framework. Yet, it remains the case that favorable economic conditions are what principally lie behind the designs and successes of globalizing corporate enterprise,[99] rather than the presence of stable, rule-bound legal systems.[100]

In regards to the international expansion of human rights' acceptance, application and enforcement, the legal imperative that they be backed by effective sanction remains ultimately at the mercy of political will. It is accepted that the notion and practice of the rule of law necessarily forms part of these economic and political determinants, but it is in fact this very exposure of the rule of law as merely a subordinate part that is crucial.

In terms of the continuing global promotion and observance of human rights, it is with the reconciliation of the economic with the political, broadly conceived, that so much hangs in the balance. The approach, ideas and propositions here sketched out are intended to provide some limited grounds for consideration as to how this reconciliation might be done for the protection of human rights in general, and economic, social and cultural rights in particular.

Acknowledgements

This chapter is an updated version of an article originally published in the *University of California Journal of International Law and Foreign Affairs (7 U.C.L.A. J. Int'l. L. & For. Aff. 239 (2002–03))*, under the title 'Human Rights, Globalization and the Rule of Law: friends, foes or family?' The author and editor would like to thank the Editor-in-Chief and Board of the *University of California Journal of International Law and Foreign Affairs* for assenting to the reproduction of the article in this updated form.

Notes

* Professor of Law and Director, Castan Centre for Human Rights Law, Monash University Law School. The origins of this article lie in a paper delivered at *Globalizing the Rule of Law*, Vice-Chancellor's Symposium, Griffith University, Queensland, September 2000. I would like to thank Becky Batagol, Hilary Charlesworth, Kay Tucker and Spencer Zifcak and the anonymous editors of the *UCLA Journal of International Law and Foreign Affairs* for their help in thought and deed in the preparation of this piece.

1 Thereby, perhaps, providing an exception to what Philip Alston criticizes as the myopia of (some) international lawyers having not 'devote[d] more explicit attention to the process [of globalization] and its consequences and to explore more systematically the implications for international norms, institutions and processes that follow therefrom'. Alston, P. 'The Myopia of the Handmaidens: international lawyers and globalization', *European Journal of International Law*, vol. 8, no. 3, 1997, pp. 435–47. See also: Gunther Teubner's lament as to the 'astonishing[ly] . . . poor' theoretical foundations of the debate over what he styles 'global law', (Teubner, G. 'Global Bukowina: legal pluralism in the world society', in G. Teubner (ed.) *Global Law Without a State*, Aldershot: Dartmouth, 1997).

2 No more so than since the fall of the Berlin Wall with the incorporation – with varying degrees of eagerness and success – of the notion of the rule of law into the governmental architecture of former Eastern Bloc countries. See generally: Krygier, M. and Czarnota A. (eds) *The Rule of Law after Communism*, Brookfield, VT: Ashgate/Dartmouth

Publishing Co., 1999; and for a more general, philosophical account, Teitel, R. 'Transitional Jurisprudence: the role of law in political transformation', *Yale Law Journal*, vol. 106, issue 7, May 1997, pp. 2011–72.

3 It can be argued that other means by which the same ends as human rights are sought – liberty, equality, dignity – have been swamped (inadvertently, as well as by design) by the tsunami of human rights ideology. See: Kennedy, D. 'The International Human Rights Movement: part of the problem?' *European Human Rights Law Review*, vol. 6, issue 3, 2001. A slightly different angle on the same point is to stress the fact that although the legal dimension of human rights is both necessary and important, it is but one dimension and is not alone sufficient either to understand them or to secure their protection. See generally: Kinley, D. 'The Legal Dimension of Human Rights', in D. Kinley (ed.) *Human Rights in Australian Law: principles, practice and potential*, Leichardt, NSW: The Federation Press, 1998.

4 See generally: Scott, C. 'Multinational Enterprises and Emergent Jurisprudence on Violations of Economic, Social and Cultural Rights', in A. Eide, C. Krause and A. Rosas (eds) *Economic, Social and Cultural Rights: a textbook*, 2nd edn, Boston: Martinus Nijhoff, 2001.

5 Which include even intimacies of personal identity such that, as Anthony Giddens strikingly puts it, 'the image of Nelson Mandela maybe is more familiar to us than the face of our next door neighbour'. Giddens, A. *Lecture 1: Globalization*, in BBC Reith Lectures, 1999, available at: http://www.lse.ac.uk/Giddens/reith_99/week1/week1.htm (accessed 30 March 2004).

6 Giddens, A. *The Consequences of Modernity*, Cambridge, UK: Polity Press in association with Basil Blackwell, Oxford, UK, 1990, p. 64.

7 Santos, B. de Sousa, *Toward a New Common Sense: law, science and politics in the paradigmatic transition*, New York: Routledge, 1995, p. 263.

8 Ibid.

9 Ibid.

10 Ibid., p. 262.

11 Teubner, *Global Law Without a State*, p. 5.

12 To adopt Ehrlich's terminology, see: Ehrlich, E. *Fundamental Principles of the Sociology of Law*, Russell & Russell, New York, 1962, p. 493.

13 Teubner, *Global Law Without a State*, pp. 5–6.

14 Robé, J-P. 'Multinational Enterprises: the constitution of a pluralistic legal order', in Teubner, *Global Law Without a State*, p. 45.

15 Ibid., p. 49.

16 Ibid.

17 Twining, W. *Globalisation and Legal Theory*, Evanston, Ill.: Northwestern University Press, 2000, pp. 224–39.

18 Ibid., pp. 226–27.

19 See: Buckley, R.P. 'The Essential Flaw in the Globalisation of Capital Markets: its impact on human rights in developing countries', *California Western International Law Journal*, vol. 32, no. 1, Fall 2001, pp. 119–20.

20 As of 18 December 2001, the numbers of ratifications of the United Nations' six principal human rights treaties were as follows: International Covenant on Civil and Political Rights, 19 December 1966, 999 UNTS 171 (*entered into force* 23 March 1976) (hereinafter ICCPR) – 147 parties; International Covenant on Economic, Social and Cultural Rights 1966, 16 December 1966, 993 UNTS 3 (*entered into force* 3 January 1976) (hereinafter ICESCR) – 145 parties; Convention on the Elimination of All Forms of Racial Discrimination, 7 March 1966, 660 UNTS 195 (*entered into force* 12 March 1969) (hereinafter ICERD) – 160 parties; International Convention on the Elimination of all forms of Discrimination Against Women, 18 December 1979, 1249 UNTS 13 (*entered into force* 3 September 1981) (hereinafter CEDAW) – 170 parties; Convention Against Torture and Other Cruel, Inhuman or Degrading Treatment or Punishment,

10 December 1984, 1465 UNTS 85 (*entered into force* 26 June 1987) (hereinafter CAT) – 127 parties; Convention on the Rights of the Child, 20 November 1989, 1577 UNTS 3, (*entered into force* 2 September 1990) (hereinafter CRC) – 191 parties; See: Office of the United Nations High Commissioner for Human Rights, Status of Ratification of the Principal Human Rights Treaties as of 18 December 2001 (2001) available at: http://www.unhchr.ch/pdf/report.pdf (accessed 30 March 2004).

Significantly, two of the most recent international UN human rights instruments have attracted the widest (almost universal) support: the CRC (with 191 parties) and the Rome Statute of the International Criminal Court, 17 July 1998, U.N. Doc. A/CONF.183/9 of 17 July 1998 has been signed by 147 countries and as of January 2002 it has been ratified by 48 countries (60 ratifications are required for the Court to come into being).

21 The Council of Europe's Convention for the Protection of Human Rights and Fundamental Freedoms, *opened for signature* 4 November 1950, (ETS No. 5), 213 UNTS 222, (*entered into force* 3 September 1953) (hereinafter ECHR) has 44 ratifications, available at: http://conventions.coe.int/treaty/en/searchsig.asp?NT=005&CM=&DF= (accessed 30 March 2004).

22 The Organisation of American States' American Declaration of the Rights and Duties of Man, O.A.S. Res. XXX, *adopted by* the Ninth International Conference of American States (1948) *reprinted in* Basic Documents Pertaining to Human Rights in the Inter-American System, OEA/Ser.L.V/II.82 doc.6 rev.1 p. 17 (1992) and the American Convention on Human Rights, 22 November 1969, O.A.S.Treaty Series No. 36, 1144 U.N.T.S. 123, (*entered into force* 27 August 1979) (hereinafter the American Convention) (25 ratifications), available at: http://www.oas.org/ (accessed 30 March 2004).

23 *African (Banjul) Charter on Human and Peoples' Rights*, OAU, OAU Doc. CAB/LEG/67/3 rev. 5, 21 I.L.M. 58 (1982), (*entered into force* 21 October 1986). Fifty-three states have ratified the Charter. In 2002, the OAU was succeeded by the African Union under *Constitutive Act of the African Union 2001* which entered into force on 26 May, 2001, see http://www.africa–union.org/home/Welcome.htm (accessed 30 March 2004).

24 *Arab Charter of Human Rights*, Res. 5437, Council of the League of Arab States, 102nd Sess., (1994) reprinted in *Human Rights Law Journal*, vol. 18, 1997, available at: http://www1.umn.edu/humanrts//instree/arabhrcharter.html (accessed 30 March 2004).

25 The Bangkok Declaration, 29 March – 2 April 1993, available at http://www.thinkcentre.org/article.cfm?ArticleID=830 (accessed 30 March 2004), was signed by 40 Asian States as part of the region's preparations for the Vienna World Conference on Human Rights, 1993. However, the instrument was heavily laced with references to the supremacy of national sovereignty over any claims of universal human rights standards. A parallel document signed by 110 Asian NGOs, also entitled the Bangkok Declaration on Human Rights 1993, unequivocally supported the universality and indivisibility of human rights. The latter document has since been followed by another NGO-inspired initiative: the Asian Human Rights Charter 1997, 17 May 1998, available at: http://www.ahrchk.net/charter/index.php (accessed 30 March 2004).

26 Wade, R. 'Global Inequality: winners and losers', *The Economist*, 28 April 2001, pp. 72–4; See also: Tay, A. Erh–Soon 'The New Century, Globalisation and Human Rights', *Asia Pacific Law Review*, 8, 2000, pp. 139–52.

27 See Wade, 'Global Inequality'.

28 Hirst, P. and Thompson, G. *Globalization in Question: the international economy and the possibilities of governance*, 2nd edn, Cambridge, UK; Malden, MA: Polity Press; Blackwell Publishers, 1999, pp. 76, 94–96.

29 Fuller, L.L. *The Morality of Law*, New Haven; London: Yale University Press, 1964, p. 117.

30 See for example: the philosophical analyses of the notion of various authors in Nomos XXXVI (Shapiro, I. (ed.) *The Rule of Law*, New York: New York University Press, 1994) and the more critical approach adopted by those contributors to A.C. Hutchinson and P. Monahan (eds.) *The Rule of Law: ideal or ideology*, Toronto: Carswell, 1987. See also: Margaret Jane Radin's five-part categorization of the components of the notion in Radin, M.J. 'Reconsidering the Rule of Law', *Boston University Law Review*, vol. 69, 1989, p. 792.
31 See: Robé, 'Multinational Enterprises'.
32 See: classically, Dicey, A.V. *Introduction to the Study of Law of the Constitution*, 8th edn, London: MacMillan, 1926, pp. 198–9; Raz, J. 'The Rule of Law and its Virtue', *Law Quarterly Review*, vol. 93, 1977, p. 195; see also: Kinley, D. 'Constitutional Brokerage in Australia: constitutions and the doctrines of parliamentary supremacy and the rule of law', *Federal Law Review*, vol. 22, no. 1, 1994, pp. 201.
33 Hayek, F.A. *The Road to Serfdom*, Chicago: University of Chicago Press, 1944, 1976, p. 72.
34 Krygier, M. The Quality of Civility: post-anti-communist thoughts on civil society and the rule of law, in A. Sajó, (ed.) *In and Out of Authoritarian Law*, The Hague: Kluwer Law International, 2002.
35 Cotterrell, R. *The Politics of Jurisprudence: a critical introduction to legal philosophy*, London: Butterworths, 1989, p. 229.
36 Consider for example, the Asian Development Bank's contention that 'the traditional concept of the rule of law [and] the existence of a stable and predictable legal system . . . [are] essential for the development of all DMCs [developing member countries]', which reflects a widely held view among these constituencies. 'Legal Frameworks in The Asian Development Bank, Governance: sound development management', WP No. 1–95, p. 30 (of 34), (1995), available at: http://www.adb.org/documents/policies/governance/govpolicy.pdf (accessed 30 March 2004).
37 Though a Western bias in their philosophical roots as well as the history of their modern expression in the international instruments is frequently claimed; see: under (b) that follows. Certainly, an appreciation of the origins of contemporary human rights standards is important. See generally: Waltz, S. 'Universalizing Human Rights: the role of small states in the construction of the universal declaration of human rights', *Human Rights Quarterly*, vol. 23, issue 1, February 2001, p. 44. But the more significant issue is whether they are, despite their roots, universally applicable and on that point arguments of cultural relativism are of elemental importance. For an especially insightful relativist critique amongst the many (both insightful and less so), see Yasuaki, O. 'Toward an Intercivilizational Approach to Human Rights', in J.R. Bauer and D.A. Bell (eds) *The East Asian Challenge for Human Rights*, Cambridge, UK: Cambridge University Press, 1999, p. 103.
38 Referring specifically to the Universal Declaration of Human Rights, G.A. Res. 217 (III) art.18, UN. GAOR, 3rd Sess., at 138, U.N. Doc. A/810 (1948) [hereinafter UDHR], Waltz concludes her comprehensive study of its global origins by declaring that 'the UDHR is a legacy that all of us can rightfully claim' (Waltz, 'Universalizing Human Rights', p. 72.
39 The Preamble to the UDHR, para. 3, pronounces that 'human rights should be protected by the rule of law'.
40 See generally: Craig, P. 'Formal and Substantive Conceptions of the Rule of Law: an analytical framework', *Public Law*, 1997, p. 467.
41 Selznick, P. *The Moral Commonwealth: social theory and the promise of community*, Berkeley: University of California Press, 1992, p. 464.
42 Raz, J. *Ethics in the Public Domain: essays in the morality of law and politics*, Oxford: Oxford University Press, 1994, p. 360. For an earlier account of the same consideration in respect the French, American and British legal traditions, see: Marsh, N.S. 'The Rule

of Law as a Supra-National Concept', in A.G. Guest (ed.) *Oxford Essays in Jurisprudence: a collaborative work*, London: Oxford University Press, 1961, pp. 232–4.

43 See: Dworkin, R. *A Matter of Principle*, Cambridge: Harvard University Press, 1985, pp. 11–12.

44 It was in this sense that the noted socialist commentator E.P. Thompson infamously, if with a touch of hyperbole, referred to the rule of law as an 'unqualified human good', and got into a great deal of rhetorical trouble for doing so (Thomson, E.P. *Whigs and Hunters: the origin of the black act*, London: Penguin, 1990, p. 266).

45 Consider the following high-minded statement of the *Vienna Declaration and Programme of Action* UN World Conference on Human Rights, 14–25 June 1993 Part I at para. 5, UN Doc A/Conf.157/23 (1993):

> All human rights are universal, indivisible and interdependent and interrelated. The international community must treat human rights globally in a fair and equal manner, on the same footing, and with the same emphasis. While the significance of national and regional particularities and various historical, cultural and religious backgrounds must be borne in mind, it is the duty of States, regardless of their political, economic and cultural systems, to promote and protect all human rights and fundamental freedoms.

46 ICESCR, *supra* note 20 and ICCPR, *supra* note 20.

47 See, generally: Dijk, P. van and Hoof, G.J.H. Van, *Theory and Practice of the European Convention on Human Rights*, 3rd edn, The Hague; Boston: Kluwer Law International, 1998.

48 See generally: Joseph, S., Schultz, J. and Castan M. *The International Covenant on Civil and Political Rights: cases, materials and commentary*, Oxford; New York: Oxford University Press, 2000.

49 See generally: Harris, D.J. and Livingstone, S. (eds) *The Inter-American System of Human Rights*, Aldershot, UK; Brookfield, VT: Ashgate Publishing Company, 1997. Though the American Convention, *supra* note 22, expressly provides protection for economic, social and cultural rights (in article 26) the vast bulk of the jurisprudence of the inter-American Court focuses on civil and political rights.

50 The Committee's General Comments and Resolutions in common with those of all six of the main UN human rights committees are more in the style of policy statements than legally binding proclamations.

51 For a collection of arguments for and against justiciability of economic, social and cultural rights, see: Steiner, H.J. and Alston, P. *International Human Rights in Context: law, politics, morals: text and materials*, 2nd edn, Oxford; New York: Clarendon Press; Oxford University Press, 2000, pp. 275–300.

52 Craven, M.C.R. *The International Covenant on Economic, Social and Cultural Rights: a perspective on its development*, Oxford: New York: Clarendon Press; Oxford University Press, 1995, p. 26.

53 The developing bodies of law concerning the protection of economic, social and cultural rights emanating from the Indian Supreme Court and (more recently and therefore to a lessor extent) from the South African Constitutional Court are notable exceptions to this predominance. Regarding the former, see: Hunt, P. *Reclaiming Social Rights: international and comparative perspectives*, Aldershot; Brookfield, Vt.: Dartmouth, 1996, p. 153, and in respect to the latter see specifically: the case of Grootboom v. Government of the Republic of South Africa, CCT38/00.

54 See: An-Na'im, A.A. 'Toward an Islamic Reformation: civil liberties', *Human Rights, and International Law*, 1990, pp. 162–70, for both his articulation of this general problem and how he sees it being overcome in the context of Islamic traditions.

55 Yasuaki, Toward an Intercivilizational Approach to Human Rights', p. 120. The objects of Yasuaki's insistence on the sincerity of such dialogue are equally the West

and the East (as he refers to them), such that it is incumbent on both to recognize 'that scrutiny of the tension between predominant local cultures, ethics or religions, with the aim to provide 'enlightened interpretations' compatible with international human rights standards, is needed . . .' ibid., p. 121.

56 UDHR, *supra* note 38.

57 ICCPR, *supra* note 20.

58 ICESCR, *supra* note 20.

59 As provided most clearly by the European Convention on Human Rights, 1950, 4 November 213 UNTS 221 (entered into force 3 September 1953), the ICCPR, *supra* note 20, and the American Convention, *supra* note 22, typically, in respect of rights to free speech, assembly, movement and association as well as freedom of religion, and implicitly in respect of rights to liberty and privacy.

60 By way of the continuing development of the doctrine of the 'margin of appreciation', allowing state parties a degree of scope or 'elbow room' in their implementation of the rights in question. See: Yourow, H.C. *The Margin of Appreciation Doctrine in the Dynamics of European Human Rights Jurisprudence*, London, New York, The Hague: Martinus Nijhoff Publishers, Kluwer Press, 1995.

61 See generally: Gardner, J.P. (ed.) *Human Rights as General Norms and a State's Right to Opt Out: reservations and objections to human rights conventions*, British Institute of International and Comparative Law, London, 1997. On the difficulties in determining the legality of reservations, see generally: Baratta, R. 'Should Invalid Reservations to Human Rights Treaties be Disregarded?', *European Journal of International Law*, vol. 11, issue 2, 2000, pp. 413–25.

62 But only where the claimed reasons for qualifying the universal is actually based on cultural difference rather than merely a front for political expediency or economic gain. See: Ghai, Y. 'Human Rights and Asian Values', *Public Law Review*, vol. 9, 1998, p. 168–82.

63 Forsythe, D.P. *The Internationalization of Human Rights*, Lexington, MA: Lexington Books, 1991, p. 5.

64 'Fighting Back', in A. Giddens and W. Hutton (eds) *On the Edge: living with global capitalism*, London: Vintage, 2001, p. 213.

65 Friedman, T.L. *The Lexus and the Olive Tree*, New York: Anchor Books, 2000, pp. 444–50; and on the argument as to the inevitability of such disparity within a viable liberal democracy, see: Fukuyama, F. *The End of History and the Last Man*, New York; London: Avon Books; Penguin, 1992, pp. 314–16.

66 Gray, J. *False Dawn: the delusions of global capitalism*, New York: New Press: Distributed by W.W. Norton, 1998, pp. 87–92. See also: John Rawls' objection to the utilitarian argument on the ground that it treats people as means rather than ends in Rawls, J. *A Theory of Justice*, MA: Harvard University Press, 1971, pp. 179–83.

67 Gray, *False Dawn*, p. 17.

68 Nussbaum, M. and Sen, A. 'The Quality of Life', in M. Nussbaum and A. Sen (eds) *The Quality of Life*, Oxford: Clarendon Press; New York: Oxford University Press, 1993. See also: Sen, A. 'Capability and Well-Being', in ibid., pp. 30–1.

69 Nussbaum, M. 'Capabilities and Human Rights', *Fordham Law Review*, vol. 66, 1997, pp. 292–7; Sen, A. 'Freedoms and Needs', *New Republic*, 10 and 17 January 1994, p. 38.

70 Nussbaum, 'Capabilities and Human Rights', p. 285.

71 I have drawn these examples from what Nussbaum refers to as a working list of central human capabilities; see: Nussbaum, 'Capabilities and Human Rights', pp. 285–8.

72 For an overview and further discussion of the developments here listed, see: Kinley, D. 'Human Rights as Legally Binding or Merely Relevant?' in S. Bottomley and D. Kinley (eds) *Commercial Law and Human Rights*, Aldershot: Ashgate, 2002, and International Council on Human Rights Policy, *Business Wrongs and Rights: human rights and the developing international legal obligations of companies* 35 (Draft report for consultation), January 2001, available at: http://www.ichrp.org (accessed 30 March 2004).

73 As formulated by a working group of the UN Sub-Commission on the Promotion and Protection of Human Rights. See: U.N. ESCOR, Hum. Rts. Comm., Sub-Commission on the Promotion and Protection of Hum. Rts., 54th Sess. Annex, Agenda Item 4 at 15, U.N. Doc. E/CN.4/Sub.2/2002/13 (15 August 2002), available at: http://www. unhchr.ch/Huridocda/Huridoca.nsf/0/971d73502dd31b7bc1256c1e00533042/$FILE/G0215007.pdf(accessed 30 March 2004). At the present time of writing (late March 2004), the Norms are being considered by the UN Commission on Human Rights in its 60th session in Geneva (March–April 2004). For an excellent analysis of the nature, form and possible impact of the Norms, see: Muchlinski, P. 'The Development of Human Rights Responsibilities for Multinational Enterprises', in Sullivan, R (ed.), *Business and Human Rights: dilemmas and solutions*, Sheffield: Greenleaf, 2003, pp. 33–51)

74 For a compendium that includes both the OECD Guidelines and the UN Norms, along with all the other major international codes, see: Leipziger, D. *The Corporate Responsibility Code Book*, Sheffield: Greenleaf, 2003.

75 See for example: Ratner, S.B. 'Corporations and Human Rights: a theory of legal responsibility', *Yale Law Journal*, vol. 111, issue 3, December 2001, p. 443 and 'Development in the Laws, International Criminal Law: corporate liability for violations of international human rights law', *Harvard Law Review*, vol. 114, pp. 2025–48. See also: Joseph, S. *Transnational Human Rights Litigation against Corporations* (forthcoming, Hart Publications, Oxford, 2004).

76 Rogge, M.J. 'Towards Transnational Corporate Accountability in the Global Economy: challenging the doctrine of forum non conveniens, in re: Union Carbide, Alfaro, Sequihua and Aguinda', *Texas International Law Journal*, vol. 36, issue 2, Spring 2001, pp. 299–318.

77 *The Corporate Code of Conduct Act of 2000*, H.R. 4596, 107th Cong. (2000).

78 *The Corporate Code of Conduct Bill of 2000*, (available at: http://scaleplus.law.gov.au/html/bills/0/2000/0/ 0642452180.htm (accessed 30 March 2004)) a Private Member's Bill sponsored by Senator Vicki Bourne (introduced in September 2000); the bill lapsed with the 2001 general election.

79 This (Private Members') Bill lapsed in November 2003.

80 For a detailed account of these legislative initiatives, see: McBeth, A. *A Look at Corporate Code of Conduct Legislation*, Common Law World Review (forthcoming 2004).

81 Promoting a European Framework for Corporate Social Responsibility: Green Paper (July 2001) and Communication From the Commission Concerning Corporate Social Responsibility: A Business Contribution to Sustainable Development, COM(02)547 final. See generally: Kamminga, M.T. 'Holding Multinational Corporations Accountable for Human Rights Abuses: a challenge for the EC', in Alston, P. (ed.) *The EU and Human Rights*, Oxford, England; New York: Oxford University Press, 1995, pp. 65–7.

82 See for example: Darrow, M. *Between Shadow and Light: the world bank, the international monetary fund and international human rights law*, Oxford; Portland, Or.: Hart, 2003.

83 See for example: Blackett, A. 'Whither the Social Clause? Human Rights, Trade Theory and Treaty Interpretation', *Columbian Human Rights Law Review*, vol. 31, 1999, pp. 1–80.

84 See: Dommen, C. 'Raising Human Rights Concerns in the World Trade Organization: actors, processes and possible strategies', *Human Rights Quarterly*, vol. 24, issue 1, February 2002, pp. 1–50 and Orford, A. 'Globalization and the Right to Development', in Alston, P. (ed.) *Peoples' Rights*, Oxford; New York: Oxford University Press, 2001, p. 147.

85 See for example: Kinley, D. and McBeth, A. 'Human Rights, Trade and Multinational Corporations', in Sullivan, *Business and Human Rights*, pp. 52–68.

86 See for example: the array of material that evidences this, accessible at *Business and Human Rights: a resource website*, available at: http://www.business–humanrights.org

87 See for example: Scott, Multinational Enterprises and Emergent Jurisprudence on Violations of Economic, Social and Cultural Rights', pp. 563–8.

88 International Council for Human Rights Policy, *supra* note 72, p. 117.

89 As Matthew Craven points out regarding the UN Committee on Economic, Social and Cultural Rights, it now sees that 'the realm of State responsibility extends not only to the acts of agents of the State but also those of third parties over whom the State has or should have control.' Craven, *The International Covenant on Economic, Social and Cultural Rights*, p. 113.

90 Selznick, P. 'Sociology and Natural Law', *Natural Law Forum*, vol. 6, 1961, p. 103. Or, as Martin Krygier says in answer to his own question as to how much does context make a difference to the instantiation of the rule of law in post-communist, Eastern European states (the subject of his particular interest), it matters 'much, but not *so* much', Krygier, M. *Transitional Questions About the Rule of Law: why, what and how?* East Central Europe/L'Europe du Centre Est. Eine wissenschaftliche Zeitschrift, vol. 28, part 1 (2001).

91 Teitel, 'Transitional Jurisprudence', p. 2016.

92 Alston, P. 'Economic and Social Rights', in L. Henkin and J.L. Hargrove (eds) *Human Rights: an agenda for the next century*, American Society of International Law, Washington, D.C, 1994, pp. 152–53. On the restrictions of an overly legal conception of economic and social rights, see generally: Scott, C. 'Reaching Beyond (Without Abandoning) the Category of "Economic, Social and Cultural Rights" ', *Human Rights Quarterly*, vol. 21, issue 3, 1999, pp. 633–60.

93 See for example: Alton, 'Economic and Social Rights', pp.152–53.

94 Scott, 'Reaching Beyond (Without Abandoning) the Category of Economic, Social and Cultural Rights', p. 637.

95 As the relatively long-standing protection of core labor rights, at least in the West, classically demonstrates.

96 As discussed under (c) earlier.

97 See for example: Kinley, D. and Tadaki, J. 'From Talk to Walk: the emergence of human rights responsibilities for corporations at international law', *Virginia Journal of International Law*, vol. 44 issue 4, (2003–04; forthcoming), and the collection of essays in M.T. Kamminga and S. Zia–Zarifi (eds) *Liability of Multinational Corporations Under International Law*, The Hague: Kluwer Law International, 2000.

98 See: Kamminga and Zia–Zafiri 'Liability of Multinational Corporations Under International Law: an introduction', in Kamminga and Zia–Zarifi, *Liability of Multinational Corporations*, p. 6, and generally, in respect of the necessity of the system of state responsibility for rights protection (despite its flaws), see: Kingsbury, B. 'Sovereignty and Inequality', *European Journal of International Law*, vol. 9, issue 4, 1998, pp. 599–625.

99 See: Muchlinski, P. *Multinational Enterprises and the Law*, Oxford; Cambridge, MA: Blackwell Publishers, 1999, pp. 44–5.

100 Thus, for example, Amanda Perry has found – somewhat counter-intuitively – that in her case-study of the corporate users of the courts in Sri Lanka, most were satisfied with the 'flexibility' of judicial behavior, as distinct from the more rigid (i.e. predictable) expectations of rule of law orthodoxy; Perry, A. 'An Ideal Legal System for Attracting Foreign Direct Investment? Some Theory and Reality', *American University International Law Review*, vol. 15, no. 6, October 2000, pp. 1627–57.

Part III

International commerce and the rule of law

6 The rule of law and international economic transactions

The Hon. Sir Anthony Mason AC, KBE

The emergence of the global economy

International commerce has existed since time immemorial. Trade between the Middle East and China along the old Silk Road, the sea-borne trade between Arabia and China, the international circulation of currency dating back to Roman times and the extensive financial activities of the Italian Renaissance bankers demonstrate that international commerce and finance have been alive and well for a long time.

In more recent times (*c.*1910–1950), the expansion of world trade was impeded by the growth of protectionism as governments of nation states sought to protect home production against competition from cheaper imported products. Tariff protection was a device to which industrialized nations resorted in order to protect their high cost, labor-intensive industries against imports from nations with a lower labor cost structure.

In the twentieth century, the advocates of free trade, who saw the opening of world trade as an avenue to greater prosperity, became influential. Since 1948, the General Agreement on Tariffs and Trade (GATT) has secured important reductions in customs duties, quotas and other protectionist devices which impeded cross-border trade. In 1994, following the Uruguay Round of multilateral trade negotiations, GATT was replaced by the World Trade Organization (WTO) which, despite significant weaknesses, is a more effective organization than GATT. During the operation of GATT, regional agreements and trade blocs were successful in dismantling trade barriers between participating nations. This success resulted in an expansion of cross-border trade at an annual rate of more than six per cent between 1950 and 1994.[1] Cross-border money flows, facilitated by electronic commerce and floating exchange rates, have expanded at a remarkable rate.

Another factor has been the phenomenal increase in the number of bilateral investment treaties (BITs), the primary purpose of which has been to encourage foreign investment in developing countries. The protection given to foreign investors by BITs has resulted in restrictions on the capacity of the host state to protect its interests.

These developments in turn have led to an increase in both foreign direct investment and portfolio investment across borders. Likewise, the number of multinational corporations (MNCs) or transnational corporations (TNCs) has greatly increased, as has the scale of their activities.

The vast expansion which has occurred in cross-border trade and finance has seen the emergence of what has been described as 'the global economy' or 'the global market', an economy in which territorial borders are becoming increasingly irrelevant. Prices for commodities, goods, even shares, are influenced by price movements elsewhere. And no economy, not even that of the United States, is completely insulated from developments in other economies.

There are many influences driving the liberalization of international trade and the rise of the global economy. A major influence has been the ideology of economic rationalism which suited the spirit of the times and gave emphasis to the paramountcy of economic outcomes. At the same time, the advances in communications and information technology facilitated entry into international transactions, making national borders irrelevant.

Economic rationalism led to the downsizing of the welfare state. Privatization resulted in the withdrawal of the state from government-owned enterprises which were acquired and operated by the private sector. Other government activities have been outsourced. Labor standards and conditions have been exposed to increased competition by exposing the labor market to individual contracts in place of union negotiated industrial awards. Corporations, particularly MNCs and their activities, have prospered.

Recent experience has shown that the unrestrained pursuit of world trade liberalization is inconsistent with domestic commitments to the maintenance of a system of laws and policies aimed at underpinning a welfare state. Effective surrender of sovereignty (as Multilateral Agreement on Investment (MAI) appeared to contemplate) or mutual exchange of sovereignty (as WTO appears to contemplate) can scarcely be reconciled with the capacity of the nation to maintain the welfare state. The welfare state, unless it is very restrictively defined, needs to protect its people, its economy and its industries, to some extent at least, against competition from imported goods and services which threaten the continued existence of the way of life which it offers.

There is no obvious solution to the dilemma: does a nation opt for liberalization of world trade or opt to preserve its capacity to maintain a welfare state economy? So far, the choice presented is a stark choice between the two, in which event one is inside the world trade tent or left outside in the cold. It is, however, possible that antagonism to MAI and WTO will result in a greater willingness to protect the economy of the nation state in return for wider negotiated access to markets and continued international review of protectionist stratagems masquerading under health and environmental precautions.

It is important not to overstate what has happened. The developments that have occurred are uneven across the world. For one thing, there is a substantial residue of protectionism. The trade wars between the United States and Europe, the Tasmanian insistence or retaining quarantine obstacles to the importation of Canadian salmon and the lower United States quota for Australian and New Zealand lamb are but a few of the many recent disputes which have their origins in continuing protectionism. Protectionism often takes the form of health and quarantine restrictions, ostensibly designed to protect home consumers and home production from the entry of allegedly harmful products. Very recently, the European Union (EU) announced its intention to challenge Australian quarantine restrictions on the ground that they are protectionist devices.

Another development has been the freeing-up of the labor market. Although it varies across jurisdictions, overall the power of trade unions has been eroded substantially.

A powerful popular reaction to the global economy has emerged. Although economic rationalists see the free-world market and unrestricted competition as enhancing the material welfare of the people of the world, the job losses that have accompanied the emphasis on economic efficiency have created the impression that it is the welfare of the rich and powerful that has been enhanced at the expense of those less well off. This impression may be mistaken. Economic statistics appear to show that the expansion of world trade has increased the material welfare of the world. Whether this increase in material welfare has been accompanied by a growing inequality between rich and poor nations is a matter of controversy. The beneficial impact of trade liberalization has, however, come at a cost to the environment, to labor standards, to job security and to the cultural heritage in many countries.

To the economic rationalists, it matters not that the developments which have taken place and are taking place weaken national sovereignty and effectively reduce the capacity of the nation state to protect domestic interests, including domestic production. But the reduction in that capacity, along with the drastic consequences for domestic production and enforcement when it is exposed to the bitter winds of import competition, has stirred up wide-ranging antagonism to the global economy. The consequences of the prevailing philosophy of profit maximization are evidenced by Nike's opening or closing of 55 factories in North America and East Asia in response to changes in the relative costs of production.[2] Some of the antagonism to what has occurred has its roots in a belief, be it right or wrong, that world trade has expanded in areas that suit the economic interests of the United States.

The multilateral agreement on investment ('The MAI')

The MAI was the high watermark of both the attempts to lift investor protection and the adverse reaction to globalization. But it went beyond establishing a simple legal régime for investor protection. It sought to guarantee 'national treatment' to foreign investors, to prevent governments from giving subsidies and advantages to local companies and to prohibit discriminatory treatment of foreign companies. All this was sought to be justified in the name of competition. Ironically, its effect, if implemented, would be to limit the capacity of developing countries to restrict foreign ownership as a step in developing their own national economies and restrict their freedom to decide what is best for those economies. Its effect would be inconsistent with regional trade agreements such as the North American Free Trade Agreement (NAFTA) under which national and local communities exercise some control over foreign investors.[3]

The demise of the MAI came about because the perception was that it failed to adequately balance investor protection against other considerations, including protection of domestic interests and countervailing considerations of international concern, such as protection of the environment. Indeed, the general perception in countries like Canada and Australia was that these matters were being ignored.

The MAI came undone partly because the negotiations in the Organization for Economic Cooperation and Development (OECD) were conducted under a veil of secrecy. Once the veil was penetrated, the imbalance in the protection given to investors as against the host state's incapacity to protect its interests, for example, capital flows (flight of capital), the environment and disadvantaged groups, became legitimate targets of criticism, as did the proposed dispute settlement procedure which was weighted in favor of investors. The MAI episode is a lesson in transparency and accountability. It reinforced suspicions of the agenda of big business and large corporations.

The regulation of the global economy

The regulation of the global economy presents a variety of problems. There is the question whether any regulation is necessary or desirable. Although the advocates of a market economy may wish to deny it, regulation is necessary to prevent distortion of the market, to ensure that residual national and regional protection is eliminated unless it can be justified and to ensure that other legitimate international and national interests, for example, protection of the environment and anticompetitive conduct, are sufficiently accommodated.

In 1995, the collapse of Barings Bank in consequence of the fraudulent activities of a single employee in its Singapore branch office demonstrated not only that the highly leveraged market for derivatives is global but also that effective regulation depends upon adequate domestic frameworks.[4] On the other hand, the mobility of capital makes it difficult for a nation state to control environmentally destructive behavior by corporations.[5] Further, lack of resources prevents poorer nations from maintaining regulatory mechanisms to protect consumers from, for example, the importation of dangerous pharmaceuticals banned in the United States and Europe.

Just what form of regulation will be appropriate, will depend upon the nature of the particular activity with which we are concerned. The form of regulation to be selected will, of course, be closely connected with the applicable legal régime governing the particular activity, whatever that may be.

Although domestic regulation may be necessary or appropriate, the momentum behind financial globalization may render domestic regulation impracticable. The current aversion to any market impediments and the apprehension on the part of capital-importing nations that controls may discourage lenders and investors or alienate the International Monetary Fund (IMF) or the World Bank, which favor complete mobility of capital, results in a reluctance to regulate. In this way, globalization reduces the capacity of the nation state to respond to democratic pressure, thereby constraining the power of the citizens to control their own economic lives.[6] Yet it is unrealistic to think that international regulation will fill the regulatory vacuum created by national reluctance to take appropriate steps.

In the context of foreign investment, there is now a strong emphasis on the need to ensure that nations seeking foreign investment have in place appropriate legal institutions and a sound legal system (sometimes called 'the rule of law') as a secure foundation for the protection of the foreign investor. The World Bank and the Asian Development Bank have exhibited a keen interest in encouraging the development of appropriate legal institutions in developing countries with a view to providing adequate protection to foreign investors and lenders.[7] Unless a sound legal system is in place in the jurisdiction in which the investment is made, the investor cannot be assured that its contractual rights will be protected and that it will have adequate recourse to legal remedies.

The rule of law

The 'rule of law' is a chameleon-like expression used in a variety of senses. Traditionally, the rule of law signified the principle that every person and organization, including the government, is subject to and bound by the law. According to A.V. Dicey, there were at least four aspects to the rule of law. They were (i) government under rules of law as distinct from government under the arbitrary discretion of those exercising power; (ii) the equality of everyone, including government officials, before the law; (iii) the administration of justice, involving the application of the ordinary law of the land, by the ordinary courts consisting of an independent judiciary; and (iv) the doctrine of parliamentary supremacy. The precise content of these elements of the rule of law has been the subject of much debate.

The content of the first three elements of the rule of law embraced at least the following general principles:

1 laws should be prospective;
2 laws should be open;
3 laws should be certain (the principle of legal certainty), though the existence of non-arbitrary discretions did not offend the principle of certainty;
4 the principles of natural justice (due process) should be observed;
5 the independence of the judiciary must be guaranteed;
6 the courts should be readily accessible to litigants seeking a determination of their rights, without access being subject to executive discretion;
7 the decisions of the courts should be reasoned and principled.[8]

These principles identified the characteristics of a domestic legal system which conformed to the ideal of the rule of law. Conformity to the requirements of the rule is a matter of degree.[9] With the exception of principles, 5 and 6, the principles did not seek to prescribe the substantive content of law.

As Joseph Raz correctly pointed out in 1977, the rule of law was 'not to be confused with democracy, justice, equality (before the law or otherwise), human rights of any kind or respect for persons or for the dignity of man'.[10] Since then, the expression 'the rule of law' has often been used in the very sense decried by Raz, so as to comprehend substantive notions on a range of topics, including democratic values and fundamental human rights. This development has come about because the rule of law has been seen as a central element in a modern liberal democracy and there has been a tendency to include within the concept the substantive rights, freedoms and protections that we associate with such a democracy. Spencer Zifcak, in his introduction to this volume, discusses this conception of the rule of law and presents a philosophy to support it. Because this conception remains an ideal, it has gained currency despite the marked expansion in the substantive content which it gives to the rule of law, to the point that it verges on a social philosophy, and despite its lack of precision and its tendency to pick up what are thought to be contemporary democratic values, for example, fairness.[11] There are indications, certainly in England and perhaps in Australia, that the ideal of the rule of law, at least in its traditional sense, is becoming an important source in the development of the common law.[12] Whether this development will extend to the rule of law in its broadest sense is unclear.

In the context of the globalized world, a desirable legal régime means more than Dicey had in mind. It would, for example, include access not only to ordinary courts but also to domestic and international tribunals for the determination of legal rights and obligations. In the minds of many, it would also include principles of substantive law which ensured the equal treatment (especially non-discriminatory treatment) under the law of foreign and local litigants. Regional economic arrangements such as the Treaty of Rome and the NAFTA, as well as international trade agreements, contain provisions prohibiting discriminatory or protectionist treatment against foreign competition.

Another important factor is the capacity of a successful litigant who obtains judgment to execute the judgment against the person or property of the defendant. In some jurisdictions, successful litigants have found that inability to enforce a judgment has effectively deprived them of the benefits of their judgment, rendering recourse to the law and the courts a meaningless exercise.[13] That capacity is an important element in the shaping of a régime of desirable rules to govern transactions falling within the general description of international trade and investment.

In the context of foreign investment, insistence on the rule of law has a substantive as well as an institutional content. First, there is the requirement for the elements of a legal system which guarantees access to independent courts or tribunals which provide objective and neutral adjudication. Then, there is the requirement that the substantive law will give effect to the contractual rights of the parties and provide effective remedies in the event of breach of those rights, along with fair compensation for breach of those rights. To those matters should be added provision for effective execution of judgments. And there is the demand, already mentioned, for non-discriminatory treatment.

Beyond foreign investment

Beyond the context of foreign investment, apart from insistence on the broader aspects of the rule of law which have already been discussed, there is a strong demand for substantive rules which will facilitate the flow of international trade. So, there is a search for a uniform substantive law or uniform substantive rules of law. This is because uniformity or harmonization of rules, is thought to lead to greater certainty and predictability of outcomes and in turn to facilitate international trade. The trend towards uniformity or harmonization of substantive rules has seen many international and regional developments, such as the UN Convention on Contracts for the International Sale of Goods (the Vienna Sales Convention) and the Hague-Visby Rules. Accompanying this trend has been the development of common forms of contract and standard terms of trade.

The legal régime: national and supra-national law

In the past, we were accustomed to a legal régime consisting of national laws as the governing legal framework within which international transactions were conducted, recognizing that the parties could to a significant extent protect themselves by shaping their contract as they saw fit. Any sophisticated system of national law incorporated choice of law or conflict of law provisions applicable to transnational and international transactions. International law had little part to play in that legal régime.

But that legal régime was not concerned with the expansion of world trade. Nor was it directed to curtailing the power of sovereign states to erect barriers to the conduct of world trade, whether by means of tariffs, quotas or otherwise. It was a 'private law' legal régime which regulated the rights and obligations of the parties to a contract, subject to such other statute laws as might be enacted by the legislature of the sovereign state.

That framework is still in existence. In large measure, it still provides the rules of substantive law which govern international transactions. It is, however, now supplemented by a new corpus of substantive law (often incorporated in statute law), contained in such instruments as the Vienna Sales Convention and the Hague Rules. Some instruments – the Vienna Sales Convention is an example – embody rules which are applicable at the option of the contracting parties. It is possible for the contracting parties to exclude the application of the Convention to any particular contract and to provide that the law to be applied shall be the domestic law of a nominated country. A principal purpose of the Convention was to overcome the problem of identifying the proper law of the contract and the difficulty of encountering a proper law which is unfamiliar or unacceptable.[14]

Beyond the régime of private law there is now a substantial corpus of law arising from international and regional agreements. It is sufficient to mention three examples – the Uruguay Round Agreement in 1994 which took effect on 1 January 1995 and set up the WTO, the Treaty of Rome and NAFTA. These instruments operate as agreements to which nation states are parties. The Treaty of

Rome appears to operate as if it were a constitutional instrument. In this respect, it differs from other free-trade agreements. These agreements impose obligations on the party to bring its law into conformity with the agreement, though in a number of jurisdictions, such as the United States and European nations, the provisions of the agreement form part of the law of the land without the need, as there is in Australia, the United Kingdom, Canada and New Zealand, for legislation to transform the provisions into law.

Globalization challenges the rule of law

Globalization presents a challenge to the rule of law. The challenge arises partly from the traditional characteristics of international law. International law was a body of law governing the conduct, obligations, privileges and immunities of sovereign states. In conformity with that conception of international law, it followed that breaches of international law were actionable by states against states. There was no scope, generally speaking, for individuals to bring actions in international tribunals for violations of international law, though a state could take up a matter on behalf of a citizen or corporation.

In this respect, international law is in process of change. This process is partly driven by regional trade agreements, such as NAFTA and the Inter-America Trade Agreement, which enable a person or an organization to bring proceedings against a state which is a party to such an agreement. In other respects, however, agreements between governments are generally actionable by governments. So there is a problem of justiciability and also of access on the part of non-government parties. This problem is illustrated by the way in which the WTO tribunals operate. There is also a problem with openness in terms of the way in which these tribunals operate. These problems are accentuated by the lack of access to domestic courts and tribunals for violation of international law and international agreements, for international law is not part of the ordinary law of the land in many common law countries like Australia unless it is implemented by legislation.

The WTO

In the light of this challenge to the rule of law, it is convenient to look at WTO and the part that it plays in dispute resolution. WTO has a broader range of responsibilities than GATT. Unlike GATT, it is not merely an international secretariat. It is an international organization of which the members are the nation states themselves. Because it is a member organization, its structure provides a vehicle for negotiations between members. Meetings of members are held biennially.

To some extent, its structure seems to have been based on that of the EU. Certainly, the idea of pooling sovereignty is similar to the EU, as was the idea of locking in agreements on a range of topics. But, membership of WTO does not involve the same general conjunction of economic and geopolitical interests as binds the members of the EU. So WTO may not make the same onward progress as the EU. It would be a mistake to assume that pooling of sovereignty will necessarily replace the nation-state system of sovereignty.

The Uruguay Round Agreement's 29 separate accords extended GATT rules to agriculture, services, intellectual property and foreign investment. It reduced tariffs on manufactured goods to a low level and provided for the elimination or reduction of import quotas and subsidies.

The WTO is intended to play a stronger and more influential role in liberalizing world trade than GATT did. To that end, it has more extensive rules which may enable it to bring about a situation in which multilateral rules, rather than unilateral actions and bilateral negotiations, govern world trade. Whether the WTO will succeed in bringing this about remains to be seen. Australia, for example, has continued since 1995 to give emphasis to the desirability of bi-lateral trade arrangements, exemplified most recently by its entry into a free-trade agreement with the United States. The WTO, however, has an important trade policy review function, the purpose of which is to review members' actions.

There are some troublesome matters that await resolution by the WTO. First and foremost is agriculture. Although progress has been made by bringing agriculture within the purview of the WTO, by moving from non-transparent non-tariff barriers to transparent tariff barriers and curtailing export subsidies, the agriculture programs of the major industrial nations, especially the EU, remain substantially in place. That the inherent problems remain is evidenced by a continuation of the trade disputes between the United States and the EU. The textile and clothing agreement, part of the Uruguay Round, is yet to be implemented. Protection of intellectual property rights, though mandated by The Agreement on Trade Related aspects of Intellectual Property Rights (TRIPS) continues to be a source of conflict between developed and developing countries. And the demise of the MAI leaves foreign direct investment with the WTO, unless the OECD takes the matter up again. Another problem which might end up with the WTO is genetically modified products.

Constraints on funding and personnel as well as its unwieldy structure present a problem for the WTO. Already, major economic powers have resorted to *ad hoc* extralegal processes outside the WTO. It was intended that the WTO would cooperate with the IMF, the World Bank and other international organizations with a view to providing an institutional framework for dealing with complex issues involving linkages among trade, monetary and other features of the interdependent world economy. Robert Gilpin does not think that the effort will succeed. He says:

> The huge number of trade issues on the table and the large number of players mean that the WTO is already facing an immense challenge to assemble a package for a new round of trade negotiations large enough to permit nations to make trade-offs among sectors and issues. If the WTO fails in this task, the fundamental concept of general reciprocity will be further undermined, and the tendency towards specific reciprocity and managed trade will intensify.

He goes on to say:

> . . . WTO decisions must be accepted by a member state before they can be applied to that state . . . . Officially, if the United States were found liable for

an infringement of the trade regime, a plaintiff could demand compensation or retaliation against the United States.

However, US power has ensured that such things seldom happen. One can expect, therefore, that (as under the GATT) the normal practice will continue and WTO regulations will tend to be based on consensus. Moreover, although a decision by majority vote is possible, the procedures of the organization are structured in such a way that the big powers can block any significant decision with which they disagree. Therefore, it is more likely that the WTO will be ineffective than that it will threaten the national sovereignty of the United States or any other country.[15]

Criticism of the WTO

The massive protest against the WTO at Seattle drew attention to the deficiencies of an approach which has put trade and economic advantage as the sole or paramount consideration. Seattle emphasized the blinkered nature of such an approach. The consequence may be that the pace of economic reform will be slowed and that any future approach will reflect a balance between economic advantage and the protection of other legitimate interests. Such interests should include not only international interests (the environment) but also national interests (the environment, freedom of domestic competition and, to a lesser extent, protection of satisfactory 'fair trade' labor conditions). Antagonism to the WTO is sharpened by its lack of transparency (the secrecy which attends its decision-making processes) and lack of public participation in those processes.

While the WTO may not be a threat to the sovereignty of the United States, Japan or the members of the EU – it presents a stronger threat to the sovereignty of lesser nations which lack the clout of the major economic powers. Weaker nations who find themselves without majority support may find that they have little alternative but to go along with the dominant view. Although it is reasonable to expect the WTO to engineer some improvement of world trade, that does not mean that the lot of developing countries will be improved as against the major economic powers. The WTO may reinforce the dominance of the major economic powers.

The rise of the WTO and the emergence of the world market has coincided with the propagation by powerful corporations and economic interest groups, sometimes masquerading under independent public interest names, of the economic advantages of the free-market economy. This approach is now coming under sustained attack by an array of opposing forces, including Greenpeace. The environmentalists rightly claim that the WTO has pursued policies and settled disputes without adequate regard to environmental issues. The concern is that '[A]n institution which has few transparent or democratic procedures has the power to strike down multilateral environmental agreements by invoking its internal rules to ensure free trade'.[16]

A focal point of this criticism is the WTO decision in the *Shrimp case*.[17] The United States had banned the import of shrimp caught in a manner adverse to endangered species of sea turtle which were protected under international environment instruments. The bans had been placed on imports of shrimp harvested without the use of turtle excluder devices, these devices being the most environmentally-safe means of harvesting shrimp. The Appellate Body of the Dispute Settlement Panel held that the US legislation was a protectionist measure. The criticism generated by this decision was that the WTO decisions were subject to little democratic accountability, that they had an impact on multilateral environmental agreements without taking into account such environmental principles as sustainable development and the precautionary principle and that the WTO did not take account of expert scientific evidence on the environment.[18] The *Shrimp case* followed a GATT case in which Mexico successfully challenged a US ban on Mexican tuna by reason of the use of excessive dolphin-netting in tuna-fishing.[19]

There is force in the argument that multilateral environmental agreements should not be subordinated to WTO rules. Fortunately, the Cartagena Protocol on Biosafety adopted in Montreal in January 2000 states: 'trade and environment agreements should be mutually supportive with a view to achieving sustainable development', and points out that there is no intention to 'subordinate this protocol to other international agreements'.

Greenpeace does not seek environmental rights as human rights. Instead, Greenpeace advocates the incorporation of the precautionary principle and sustainable development into all decision-making processes, pointing to the Preamble to the Uruguay Round Agreement which calls for 'optimal use of the world's resources in accordance with the principle of sustainable development, seeking to both protect and preserve the environment'.[20]

The Greenpeace recipe for WTO reform echoes other criticisms which are not necessarily confined to environmental concerns. The recipe includes rights for NGOs and citizens, including the right to be heard and participate, and access to the decision-making process. These rights would 'open up' the WTO and make it more transparent and accountable.[21] Moreover, incorporation of the precautionary principle and sustainable development into WTO decision-making processes would adjust the present imbalance with economic factors.

These proposals would require, at least:

- the consideration of environmental information and opinions gathered from relevant stakeholders;
- a scientific evaluations of the adverse impacts and scientific uncertainties involved if the trade measure is allowed; and
- a change in the burden of proof as to whether or not a trade or product is safe for human health and the environment.[22]

There are signs that big business is beginning to take a responsible attitude. In January 2000, the *Financial Times* reported that the Ford Motor Company had withdrawn from the Global Climate Coalition whose primary purpose is to dispute the risk of global warming and resist the imposition of government action to restrict carbon emissions. Earlier, Shell and BP had joined the Business Environmental Leadership Council which includes 21 leading companies pressing the American Congress for action on carbon emissions.[23]

It is difficult to see the WTO becoming a forum in which environmental concerns will play a very important role. The WTO lacks the expertise. Environmentalists distrust it and commercial interests as well as governments are opposed to it venturing into this field. As John Braithwaite and Peter Drahos observe: 'No important actor wants the WTO to take over environmental policy'.[24]

Environmental issues must be dealt by an international body with relevant qualifications and the WTO should be required to give effect to or take account of that body's decisions. The World Bank inspection panels are not a suitable model. Those panels are part of a self-regulatory régime. Their object is simply to monitor compliance with World Bank's own policies and procedures.[25]

The WTO involves a mutual exchange of national sovereignty presided over by the Council of member states. Although it is said that the principle of national sovereignty is in retreat from the trade arena – in the Uruguay Round, states were required to take TRIPS and the General Agreement on Trade in Services (GATS) as a total package without reservations – mutual exchange of sovereignty will only be acceptable if the problems of transparency and public participation in the WTO are resolved.[26]

Under the WTO, member states agreed to the resolution by international panels of disputes relating to transgression of trade rules. This is a sensible approach. In the case of international rules, it is appropriate to give jurisdiction to an international tribunal rather than a domestic tribunal. Impartiality and uniformity of treatment resulting in a coherent corpus of rulings is more likely in an international régime than under a series of diverse national rulings. On the other hand, as we have seen with decisions of UN agencies affecting Australian interests, decisions of international tribunals do not have the same authority as domestic court decisions. Yet, if trade rules are international, there is much to be said for international resolution of disputes arising under those rules.

The WTO adjudication is state-based adjudication. Access on the part of corporations, organizations (including NGOs) and individuals should be available as it is in national tribunals. Failure to provide it is a serious shortfall in the rule of law. The criteria to be applied by an international panel like the WTO panels depend upon how questions already mentioned are to be resolved. Should an international panel have regard to factors other than trade factors, for example, environmental considerations, labor conditions, the economy of a particular state? Is it required to take into account decisions of an environmental authority?

Further progress in dismantling protectionist barriers to increased international economic transactions depends upon the development of adequate institutional protection for environmental interests. Additional economic advances can only be achieved if environmental concerns are satisfied. It is unlikely that these concerns can be adequately addressed in the WTO with the result that an appropriate world environmental organization should be brought into existence by an international convention. Such an organization could collate and assess environmental information and opinions, make scientific evaluations of the adverse impact of particular trade measures including an evaluation of the scientific possibilities and uncertainties.

International agreement on the terms of the precautionary principle, including the burden of proof, should be sought. In this respect, it would now seem appropriate, in the case of a serious threat to the environment, to throw the burden on those who assert that the trade measure will not damage the environment. The WTO should be required to recognize this principle and to respect the decisions of the environmental organization. At the same time, the WTO should be reformed so that its decision-making processes become more accessible and accountable.

Whether it is possible to bring all issues of environmental concern within the purview of one international environmental organization is uncertain, to say the least of it. It may be necessary to formulate particular conventions, for example, the Whaling Convention 1931 and the Convention for the Conservation of Southern Bluefin Tuna 1993. Environmental issues are so numerous and so varied that one organization cannot be expected to deal with them promptly.

Similar comments may apply to labor conditions. Here, it may be possible to formulate a new labor convention, the terms of which could be applied by WTO panels.

Zifcak, in Chapter 2 in this volume, has pointed to the very considerable difficulties that would attach to imposing on the WTO, at every stage of its deliberations, a requirement to take account of the impact of its policies, rules and practices upon economic and social rights protected by international instruments. To add this responsibility to the enormous burdens already placed on WTO would be altogether too oppressive and prejudice its prospects of attaining its present goals.

It is possible that the WTO Charter could be amended so as to require WTO policies to be formulated in the light of relevant international instruments, which would then be applied by the dispute resolution panels and the Appellate Body. It would, however, be unrealistic to think that the panels and the Appellate Body are equipped themselves to formulate the appropriate policies. Indeed, it is extremely doubtful that they could conveniently make useful impact assessments on economic and social rights in the course of dispute resolution. Problems of this kind should be resolved at the political level.

Corporations must continue to take the risk that government policy will change. There will, however, arise particular situations in which a government, in order to encourage foreign investment, will responsibly enter into policy commitments as a condition of the making of that investment. Acceptance of legal liability in such situations may be inevitable. Likewise, acceptance of government legal liability may well be inevitable in a régime like the WTO.

NAFTA

The main aim of NAFTA was to liberalize trade and facilitate foreign direct investment in North America, Mexico being the jurisdiction which expected to attract increased foreign investment. NAFTA also represented a move on the part of the United States away from multilateralism to a multi-track foreign economic policy, increasing its bargaining strength, albeit in limited respects only, as against the EU.

It is too early to assess the effects of NAFTA. Economic movements that have occurred in member countries have largely been the product of other forces such as the Mexican currency crisis. But it is said that NAFTA has given a considerable stimulus to the regionalization of production, especially in automobiles, electronics and textiles.[27] Another effect is the development of cross-border transportation systems.[28] This development should enhance the development of an integrated North American market.

NAFTA has done well by Mexico. NAFTA has accelerated the industrialization of Mexico and facilitated foreign investment in that country. Although NAFTA has accelerated the restructuring of the North American automobile industry, it has not had a substantial impact on American wages and employment.[29]

Yet Robert Gilpin says:

> NAFTA constituted a Pyrrhic victory and a serious defeat for further trade liberalization. The bitter fight over its ratification and the reckless, ill-informed denunciation of the Agreement . . . poisoned the atmosphere with descriptions of the evils of globalization . . . . The bitter controversy over NAFTA turned labor, environmentalists, and many others against trade liberalization and became a major factor in the 1997 defeat of the proposed fast-track legislation. . . . It is difficult to believe that North American regionalism benefited American consumers or the United States as a whole . . .'.[30]

Gilpin's statement brings out the inherent tension between regional and multilateral trade liberalization. NAFTA's dispute resolution mechanism, like that of the WTO, subjects the sovereign state to decision-making by an international tribunal. These tribunals exercise jurisdiction in relation to a complaint that a sovereign state has failed to comply with its treaty obligations.

Genetically modified (GM) foods and crops

Nothing demonstrates popular anxiety about technological advance and globalization of trade more than the GM controversy. On their face, GM food and crops offer extraordinary potential for the development of agriculture in the poor and needy regions of the world. That potential may not be realized because popular anxiety in Europe has spread to other countries, including Australia, thus threatening the very markets in which GM products would be sold. There is no scientific evidence to support the concerns that are expressed by those who oppose GM products. These concerns appear to reflect other unsatisfactory experiences of food products which are the outcome of modern production methods, for example, beef and the Creutzfeldt-Jakob Disease (CJD disease). These days lack of scientific evidence, even expert scientific evidence, discounting the existence of a food health problem, is of no avail. Too often in the past assurances by producers and manufacturers have proved to be flawed.

Australian states are now considering the introduction of compulsory labelling of GM products in line with the EU model, despite Federal opposition to such a requirement.

It is predicted that European and Asian hostility to US-grown GM crops could generate conflicts in WTO and the Convention on Biological Diversity (CBD). Within the WTO, the Sanitary and Phytosanitary (SPS) Agreement allows restrictions on imports in the name of health or environmental protection. Yet to be resolved is the question whether the precautionary principle permits restrictions on imports under conditions of scientific uncertainty. The SPS agreement allows restrictions only on a provisional basis while a government seeks additional information.[31]

The EU is undermining this requirement. In January 2000, it succeeded in inserting the precautionary principle in the new Protocol on Biosafety in the CBD. The Protocol governs trade in transgenic organisms. It states that 'a lack of scientific certainty due to insufficient relevant scientific information and knowledge' should not prevent states from taking precautionary import action. The Protocol requires exporters of living modified organisms (plants or seeds) to give prior notification of relevant biosafety information and to solicit an informed consent agreement from importers.[32]

The interest of the developing countries in growing and marketing GM products is likely to be frustrated by the apprehensions of consumers in the Western world, these apprehensions presently lacking scientific credibility. Be this as it may, the problem requires resolution, WTO being the most likely forum. What is required is the formulation of an appropriate legal rule, for example, an agreed version of the precautionary principle. That version will only emerge out of a process of negotiation within the WTO.

C. Ford Runge and Benjamin Senauer say:

> The GM issue connects agriculture, trade, the environment and food security to form a complex relationship that cries out for a global structure of rules and disciplines. This is precisely what the . . . WTO system can provide. At the same time, these 'Frankenfoods' have become central to the new protectionist case against the world trading system. The only way out of this quagmire is for the WTO to incorporate the successful concession-based approach of the past and tie food security and GM issues into a broader framework of regulations for trade, intellectual property and the environment. The global problem posed by food security is inextricably linked to the development of the rules and agreements that operate at a level higher than the nation state. Food security is a problem of national action that can be pursued only through multinational policies, just like international commerce or environmental issues.[33]

Food security, hitherto a matter falling exclusively within national regulation, is now seen as a matter which, like many others, is to be regulated on a multilateral basis.

To achieve this, the authors advocate the development of new fora or the development of existing institutions to maintain the necessary multinational infrastructure. This would require in agriculture, increased market access and reduced export subsidies in the next round of WTO multilateral negotiations.[34] It would also require the creation of a WTO-like environmental authority 'to address the need for rules on ecological independence'.[35] Such an organization could assess the environmental implications of the market for GM foods, including the need for labelling which will meet consumer resistance.

MNCs

MNCs are now in a position of great strength, such is the desire of most nations for foreign investment. Throughout the world nations are offering extravagant incentives to entice foreign investment, whether in the form of subsidies or tax advantages. MNCs can drive a very hard bargain. But national governments should not agree to accept legal liability at the hands of MNCs for alterations in policy that affect such corporations adversely.

Corporations have always and must continue to take the risk that government policy will change. There will, however, arise particular situations in which a government, in order to encourage foreign investment, will responsibly enter into policy commitments as a condition of the making of that investment. Acceptance of legal liability in such situations may be inevitable. Likewise, acceptance of government legal liability may well be inevitable in a régime like the WTO.

Regulation of the activities of MNCs is a thorny problem. The only basis on which the activities of TNCs can be made subject to an international rule of law is by formulating appropriate rules by means of an international convention or conventions. Two areas in which this might be achieved are the environment and competition law. I leave out of account intellectual property which is a separate and developing régime. Rules so formulated must be enforceable. That means not only conferring jurisdiction on tribunals but also providing sanctions. That in turn means translating the convention rules into domestic rules and imposing sanctions directly on TNCs or on nation states which can then take consequential action, whether for recovery of compensation or otherwise against infringing TNCs.

Regulating the policies of the World Bank and the IMF

In an ideal world it might be possible to structure the World Bank and the IMF so that their policies are subject to an international legal régime administered by independent international authorities, vague and uncertain though this proposal is. But the world we know is far from ideal and the provision of financial assistance through the World Bank and the IMF depends upon the participation of wealthy and powerful states, most notably the United States. As the Asian economic meltdown exacted its toll on the funds of the IMF, it became necessary to seek further funding from the United States. That meant persuading Congress. What hope would there be of securing additional commitments from the United States and other wealthy nations if policies were to be determined otherwise than by their shareholders, whether in their own interests or otherwise?

The way forward

There is an inherent tension between liberalization of world trade and the formation of regional trading blocs which lock outsiders out. Regional trading blocs such as the EU and NAFTA are here to stay. Indeed, they will tend to expand. So the liberalization of world trade must proceed despite the difficulties presented by the existence of regional trading blocs.

Domestic trade law must harmonize with international trade law. If it does not do so, the nation state will be the economic loser, as Vietnam found to its cost. Whether the same comment should be made about competition law is another question. International competition law may leave a nation's valuable assets in the hands of foreign interests. Take, for example, the struggle for control of North Broken Hill Ltd (Australia) between two foreign companies, one of which Anglo-American was supported by the Japanese buyers of our iron ore, and the efforts by Royal Dutch Shell to gain control of Woodside Petroleum Ltd. Foreign ownership and control of the media is a perennial illustration of the problems, though media ownership may constitute a recognized exception in favor of national control. A failure by a nation state to conform to international competition law standards may result in retaliatory economic action like the recent trade wars between the EU and the United States. There are signs that national competition watchdogs are harmonizing their approaches to common problems. Much depends on decisions taken by United States and EU authorities.

In an ideal world, it would be desirable to make international decision-making with respect to world trade and finance more democratic. We can dismiss immediately any idea that it is feasible to set up a world democracy along the lines of a national democracy. It is simply not a practical or achievable goal.[36] Democracy, as we know it, is a matter for attention at national and sub-national level, though there may be a limited role for a regional legislature in systems similar to the EU. Our efforts should therefore be directed at making governments, which are the main participating players in international fora, more responsive and more accountable to their constituents. That means adopting and enforcing models of good governance, providing information, consulting and shaping policies in public, before entering into international commitments.

Correspondingly, international fora should be much more open in their processes and accountable. The traditional confidentiality that has surrounded diplomatic negotiation must give way to democratic transparency. In addition, international fora must become more open to participation by NGOs and others. There are, of course, limits to openness and open participation, particularly where confidential financial matters are being negotiated.

The protection and development of international economic transactions, including direct foreign investment, require the establishment of appropriate domestic legal infrastructures which will protect the rights and legitimate interests of foreign traders and investors. Such infrastructures should make provision for access to independent courts or tribunals for the adjudication of rights of contracting parties, according to a body of substantive law which is internationally recognized and also makes provision for the execution of judgments against a party and his or her property. These characteristics would assist in ensuring a rule of law régime applying to international trade and financial transactions.

In order to promote the development of these characteristics in domestic legal systems, appropriate international conventions should be formulated. In the event that a successor to the MAI is proposed, the strong pro-foreign investor approach which brought the MAI down should be modified. In the post-Seattle era, it is unlikely that developing countries or, for that matter, countries such as Canada and Australia, will acquiesce in a complete abdication of capacity to discriminate, to some degree, in favor of local investors.

Whether we can sufficiently secure the guaranteed independence of international trade tribunal membership is problematic, as is access to such tribunals on the part of persons and bodies adversely affected. Likewise, in the sphere of international trade, there may be greater scope for the making of discretionary decisions. It is in these areas, along with the democratic deficit and possible human rights violations, that the rule of law may in its extended sense be vulnerable.

Notes

1 Baylis, J. and Smith, S. (eds) *The Globalization of World Politics: an introduction to international relations*, Oxford, UK: Oxford University Press, 1997, p. 433.
2 Abegglo, J.C. *Sea Change: Pacific Asia as the new world industrial center*, New York; Sydney: Free Press, 1994, p. 26.
3 Mittelman, J.H. *The Globalization Syndrome: transformation and resistance*, Princeton, NJ: Princeton University Press, 2000, p. 229.
4 Ibid., p. 135.
5 Ibid.
6 Ibid.
7 The World Bank, the Asian Development Bank and the Inter-American Development Bank have also set up independent Inspection Panels to investigate the Banks' compliance with their own policies and procedures. See generally: Shihata, I.F.I. *The World Bank Inspection Panel: in practice*, 2nd edn, Oxford: Oxford University Press, 2000. A request may be made for an inspection by the World Bank Panel by an affected party in the territory of the borrower which is not an individual. Before hearing the request, the Panel must satisfy itself that the Bank Management has failed to demonstrate that it has followed or is taking adequate steps to follow the Bank's policies and procedures and that the alleged violation is of a serious character. After deciding to investigate, the Panel submits its report to the Executive Directors and the President. The report considers all relevant facts and makes findings. Management then submits to the Executive Directors its recommendations in response to the findings. The Bank then informs the affected party of the results of the investigation and the action taken, if any.
8 For similar lists of principles, see: Fuller, L. *The Morality of Law* (revised edn), New Haven; London: Yale University Press, 1969, chapter 2; Raz, J. 'The Rule of Law and its Virtue', *Law Quarterly Review*, vol. 93, April 1977, pp. 198–202.
9 Ibid.
10 Ibid., 196.
11 While fairness may be described as an ideal democratic value and procedural fairness is a common law legal doctrine, substantive fairness is not a criterion of administrative or judicial decision-making in Australia.

12 *R. v Secretary of State for Home Department; ex parte Pierson* [1998] AC 539 at 587–591, per Lord Steyn; cf Mason, K. 'The Rule of Law', in P.D. Finn (ed.) *Essays in Law and Government*, vol. 1, Sydney: Law Book Co., 1995, pp. 125–6.
13 See for example: the discussion by Clarke, D.C. 'The Execution of Civil Judgments in China', in S. Lubman (ed.) *China's Legal Reforms*, Oxford; New York: Oxford University Press, 1996, p. 65.
14 For a discussion of the Convention, see: Nicholas, B. 'The Vienna Convention', *Law Quarterly Review*, vol. 105, 1989, p. 201.
15 Gilpin, R. *The Challenge of Global Capitalism: the world economy in the 21st century*, Princeton, NJ: Princeton University Press, 2000, pp. 111–2.
16 Tripley, D. 'Safe Trade and the WTO', *Amicus Curiae*, issue 28, 2000, p. 9.
17 World Trade Organization: Report of Panel on the United States Import Prohibition of certain Shrimp and Shrimp Products, (1998) 37 ILM 832.
18 Tripley, 'Safe Trade and the WTO', p. 9.
19 Thomas and Tereposky, 'The Evolving Relationship between Trade and Environmental Regulation', *Journal of World Trade*, vol. 27, no. 4, 1993, pp. 30–1.
20 The principle that where there are threats of serious environmental damage, lack of scientific certainty is not a reason for refusing to take action which, on the balance of probabilities, would present the damage.
21 Tripley, 'Safe Trade and the WTO', p. 9. Note that the European Court of Human Rights has rejected arguments that the European Convention on Human Rights protects such rights or a right to environmental information (*Guerra v. Haly* (1998) 26 EHRR 357; *Balmer-Shafroth v. Switzerland* (1998) 25 EHRR 598).
22 Tripley, 'Safe Trade and the WTO', p. 12.
23 Polden, M. 'The Law, the Environment and the Mosquito', *Amicus Curiae*, issue 28, June 2000, p. 7. The author makes the point that the companies see this not only as ethical thinking but also as good economics. He says there is the beginning of a ground swell in favor of corporate activity with greater responsibility.
24 Braithwaite, J. and Drahos, P. *Global Business Regulation*, Cambridge: Cambridge University Press, 2000, p. 260.
25 See generally: Shihata, *The World Bank Inspection Panel.*
26 Ibid., p. 211.
27 Gilpin, *The Challenge of Global Capitalism*, p. 245.
28 Ibid.
29 Ibid., p. 246.
30 Ibid., pp. 246–7.
31 See Paarlberg, R. 'The Global Food Fight', *Foreign Affairs*, vol. 79, issue 3, May–June 2000, p. 29 (where the author reviews the problem generally).
32 Ibid., pp. 30–1.
33 Rung, C.F. and Senauer, B. 'A Removable Feast', *Foreign Affairs*, vol. 79, issue 3, May–June 2000, pp. 47–8.
34 Ibid., p. 48.
35 Ibid., p. 49.
36 For a contrary view, see: Falk, R. and Strauss, A. 'Toward Global Parliament', *Foreign Affairs*, vol. 80, issue 1, January–February 2001, pp. 216–20.

7 The role of the rule of law in the regulation of global capital flows

Ross P. Buckley

The global economy has changed profoundly in the past 30 years. In 1970, the capital that moved around the globe to support trade in goods and services far exceeded that which moved to support direct and portfolio investment. Today, capital flows outweigh trade flows by a factor of over 60 to 1.[1]

This extraordinary statistic tells only part of the story of the profound, unprecedented changes in the world in which we live. Financial globalization currently is yet to reach the heights reached between 1870 and 1913. And it is true that the capital exports of the world's then capital-exporting countries – Britain, The Netherlands, France and Germany – were a larger proportion of their GDP than capital exports are today of the Gross Domestic Product (GDP) of capital-exporting countries. However, these statistics tell only one-half of the story. For in the last years of the nineteenth century and the first of the twentieth, capital flows were all in the direction one would expect – from the capital-rich to the capital-poor countries (such as Australia, Argentina, Canada and New Zealand).

The truly surprising thing, and the reason the current globalization of capital flows is without historical precedent, is that today there are major capital flows from poor to rich countries (as rich individuals and companies in poor countries invest in developed countries), as well as from rich countries to poor countries.

It is generally accepted that excessive inflows of foreign capital, particularly short-term capital, into East Asian economies from 1993 to early 1997 was one of the principal causes of the Asian economic crisis. However, these economies are capital exporters, with some of the highest savings rates in the world. Capital inflows as a crisis cause should have been surprising. All that had to be done for Korea, Malaysia or Thailand to have all the capital they needed to fund their own development was for impervious barriers to the outflow of capital to be erected around those countries or for impervious barriers to the entry of this capital to be erected around developed countries.[2] Now this is a very difficult task; contemporary capital is too fluid. And even if it were achievable, the side effects of such barriers are distinctly unpleasant. Nonetheless, we do live in a most unusual world, a world in which the poor lend money to the rich[3] and money sloshes around the globe looking for a productive use. All in all, it is a world that might be usefully compared to an upturned garbage bin lid filled with water – the lid is the international financial system, the water is capital. Holding such a lid steady is no easy task. However, steadiness is imperative for the slightest tilting will see a considerable volume of water splashed onto the floor and lost; precisely the effect of the African and Latin American debt crisis of 1982, the Mexican peso crisis of 1995, Asia's economic crisis of 1997, Russia's economic meltdown in 1998 and Argentina's ongoing crisis.

Who should work to keep the lid steady and its precious water within it, and the role of the rule of law in achieving this stability, is the topic of this chapter.[4] This topic demands an understanding of the rule of law and of globalized capital flows. So let me begin with definitions and descriptions of each.

The rule of law

The rule of law operates in a society when the great majority of its people abide by its laws. In such a society, disputes are resolved principally by resort to the laws, not to personal authority or force. For the rule of law to thrive, the legal system needs a number of characteristics:[5]

- the laws need to be relatively clear, accessible and prospective in their operation;
- the laws need to be seen to be legitimate and enjoy a broad measure of community support; this legitimacy and support usually derives from the laws being considered to be generally just; and
- the laws need to be interpreted and applied openly by an independent judiciary which itself enjoys a broad measure of community acceptance.

The rule of law in this sense operates in many, though certainly not most, nations in the world.

In their seminal work, *Global Business Regulation*,[6] John Braithwaite and Peter Drahos identify a major departure from the rule of law in the global arena. In their words,

> the globalization of regulation has ushered in the rule of principles . . . (meaning that regulatory contests are fought at the level of principles). . . . The rule of principles is the . . . empirical reality of global business regulation.[7]

Complex multi-party negotiations lend themselves to negotiation over principles; negotiation over specific rules is too cumbersome, difficult and slow. This is a major departure from the rule of law.

A useful analogy exists with the global contest over the existence and enforceability of intellectual property rights. When the developing countries gained the ascendancy in the United Nations Conference on Trade and Development (UNCTAD) and the World Intellectual Property Organization (WIPO), the US and European Commission (EC) moved the debate over intellectual property into the General Agreement on Tariffs and Trade (GATT)/World Trade Organization (WTO). The US and EC simply changed the game to a forum more likely to value and uphold their priorities.

Similarly, because the nature of principles better suits the aims and ends of the powerful actors, they have become the ground upon which all now fight their battles. In the words of Braithwaite and Drahos:

> Principles do not provide a neutral framework in which autonomous actors pursue their interests [as does the rule of law]. Rather, they are operational tools that serve to entrench or defend the goals of actors. Principles need not be enacted by states, they need not be recognized by law in order to be part of a regulatory contest and to influence conduct. . . . So . . . we have a disjunction between what ought to be (the rule of law) and what is (the rule of principles as we have described it).[8]

One might question whether the rule of law provides a neutral framework. The rule of law certainly provides a framework of rules that are generally accepted, but are these rules always 'neutral' in the sense of not favoring certain parties over others? The identification of the power of the rule of principles is critical. The consequences of this for the regulation of global capital flows will be explored after we consider these flows, and the strategic options for their regulation.

Global capital flows

Globalization finds its fullest contemporary expression in global capital flows and capital markets. The level of financial integration within, and across, the international economy is high and increasing because capital, intangible and moving in response to information, is almost perfectly suited to a single global market.[9] The globalization of capital flows and markets includes the following phenomena and trends:[10]

1 Massive transnational capital flows are a fact of life and foreign investors in particular are opportunists. Foreign investors will move money into an economy quickly, and in large quantities in good times, and seek to remove it even more quickly when trouble looms.
2 The nature and management of investors changed radically in the 1990s. The proportion of capital controlled by large institutional investors (mutual funds, pension funds, insurance companies etc.) increased substantially.[11] Hedge funds brought aggressive new investment techniques to bear. More significantly, but with less publicity, virtually all major commercial and investment banks and securities firms established departments that function virtually as hedge funds, making extensive use of leverage and derivatives and the capacity to move in to and out of markets swiftly. Indeed, the entire

money-management industry has become far more performance-driven, less risk-averse and more inclined to use leverage heavily.[12]

3 Access up to the minute information facilitates investment decisions at great distances and foreign investors receive relatively homogenized information. Before the communications revolution, long-term investment was often the only sensible approach to foreign investment. Today, an investment portfolio in Brazil can be managed as aggressively and intensively as if it is one's own country. Yet the sources of information for such investment decisions will be far less diverse than if it was in one's own country, with volatility-enhancing consequences for investor behavior.

4 Modern financial derivatives provide tremendous opportunities for hedging risks, but are perhaps more often used to facilitate speculation and as integral elements of volatility inducing activities.

5 Liquidity is often illusory but temptingly easy to believe in. Capital markets that are deep and efficient in good times can rapidly become thin, volatile and illiquid in bad times. This is especially true of secondary markets in debt and of access to new money through debt issues.

6 Owing to the preceding factors, capital markets in the debt and equity of developed and developing nations are integrated and interdependent today to an unprecedented degree.[13]

Each of these aspects of globalization increases the volume of capital flows to emerging market nations and the volatility of such flows. The question for this chapter is how such capital flows can be regulated and the role of the rule of law in achieving this end.

Global regulatory options for capital flows

The strategic options for the regulation of globalized capital flows that require reform of the international financial architecture include:[14]

1 a global bankruptcy court;
2 a global central bank;
3 a global lender of last resort; or
4 some form of tax on international financial flows, the so-called 'Tobintax'.

Each of these options will be considered.

A global bankruptcy court

In domestic legal systems, the prospect of debtor bankruptcy serves to focus the mind of lenders and diminish their appetite for risk. This critical discipline is mostly absent in the international context. Sovereign debtors cannot go bankrupt in the legal sense, and corporate debtors in debtor countries are subject to the often underdeveloped local bankruptcy laws. Accordingly, many writers have advocated the establishment of a global bankruptcy court as a way of allocating losses more fairly between lenders and borrowers and of improving the efficiency of the system.[15]

The comprehensive approach would be to establish a sovereign bankruptcy court (or an *ad hoc* tribunal for each case) applying a highly developed body of rules and procedures, very much like the International Criminal Court that commenced on 1 July 2002.[16] Such a court/tribunal and rules may require years of planning and negotiations to be implemented by a treaty between nations.[17]

The proposal which is closest to the law in most countries is that developed by the Jubilee framework.[18] This envisages a bankruptcy procedure based on Chapter 9 of the US Bankruptcy Code (which deals with municipal bankruptcies) and enforced by an *ad hoc* independent panel of experts convened for a specific proceeding. The best long-term model for any sovereign bankruptcy regime is undoubtedly Chapter 9 of the US Code[19] which has worked effectively and efficiently in the bankruptcy of local municipalities within the US and already deals with the issues peculiar to the bankruptcy of governments.

The principal reason we do not have a global sovereign bankruptcy regime is because the creditors believe its absence works in their favor. The banks have argued vociferously against a bankruptcy regime internationally when they accept, and indeed welcome, bankruptcy regimes nationally. Why? In the words of William Rhodes, Senior Vice-Chairman of Citibank:

> the existence of a formal bankruptcy mechanism, whether invoked or not, would cause uncertainty in the markets, deter potential lenders and investors, and drive up the countries' borrowing costs.[20]

This is nonsense. National bankruptcy regimes greatly enhance certainty and this serves generally to attract lenders and investors and thus diminish borrowing costs and there is no reason it would be any different internationally.[21] On the other hand, there is no formal structure for the resolution of sovereign debt crises and each crisis typically casts a pall for many years on debtor country prospects and bank profits. Debtor countries suffer with no new capital and ever-increasing debt loads and banks suffer because, in most cases, they have to keep advancing new funds for years to enable the debtors to keep paying interest.[22]

William Rhodes is the world's most experienced banker in sovereign debt restructurings. He must know he is speaking nonsense, but does so presumably because he can't admit the truth – that the banks like the present arrangement under which, when a crisis hits, the poor in developing countries are consigned to the debtors' prisons of poverty, ill-health and ignorance[23] so that the loans made by the banks can be repaid.

The history of the past 50 years tells us that debtor nations usually continue to service their debts even when, as nations, they are functionally bankrupt and can do so only by borrowing ever more debt.[24] Countries can always repay loans precisely because they can always increase taxes and reduce spending on health, education and nutrition – and at some point with poor countries such reductions in spending lead to unconscionable hardship. The most impoverished nations today spend four times more repaying debt than on health, education, sanitation and other basic needs. The total external indebtedness of developing countries is almost $2.5 trillion.[25]

National bankruptcy regimes seek to ensure the maximum return to creditors while ensuring the debtors have food, housing and the capacity to work. Humane nations tolerate nothing less. We rejected debtors' prisons centuries ago.[26] The absence of an international bankruptcy regime means people starve, and live without adequate shelter, healthcare and education, while their country's wealth goes to service loans. Why is it that what is considered unacceptable within any developed nation, is considered acceptable by the international financial community when it applies in other, poorer, borrowing countries?

The International Monetary Fund (IMF), since late 2001, has put forward the idea of a Sovereign Debt Restructuring Mechanism (SDRM) as an effective approach to sovereign bankruptcy. The IMF's proposal, as developed and modified of late, has four principal elements:[27]

1 Majority restructuring so as to circumvent the collective action problems that are particularly prevalent with bond financing and to remove the free-riding and rogue creditor problems.
2 Deterrence of disruptive litigation – by providing for any amounts recovered to be deducted from any eventual residual claims.
3 Protection of creditor interests by a restraint on the debtor paying non-priority creditors and by an IMF assurance of good economic conduct by the debtor to give the creditors an assurance the debtor will pursue policies that protect asset values and restore growth.
4 Seniority for new lending, so as to attract it to the country.

The SDRM would also involve the appointment of a Sovereign Debt Dispute Resolution Forum, which is described as independent even though its members would be nominated and endorsed by the Fund. The Forum would have the power to decide disputes between creditors and between creditors and debtors. However its role falls far short of that of a bankruptcy court and the SDRM falls far short of the bankruptcy regimes that are an essential part of all national economic systems.[28] Specifically there are six problems with the SDRM initiative:

1 The determination of whether a nation qualifies for debt restructuring is to be made not by the Sovereign Debt Dispute Resolution Forum, as one would expect, but by the IMF.
2 The determination of a nation's level of debt sustainability, from which the necessary amount of debt reduction will follow as a matter of logic, is to be made not by the Sovereign Debt Dispute Resolution Forum, as one would expect, but by the IMF.[29]
3 The IMF will discharge these two critical functions while compromised by its status as a major creditor of the debtor, and presumably with one eye upon the

recoverability of its own loans. That one should never be a judge in one's own cause is a fundamental principle of natural justice that the SDRM proposal ignores.

4 The SDRM applies only to commercial bank debt and leaves Paris Club debt[30] and IMF and World Bank loans out of the equation. This means that even considerable debt reductions granted by commercial creditors may be insufficient to return the debtor nation to viability as the overall debt burden on the nation will be insufficiently reduced.

5 In a recent about-face, the stay on enforcement of claims that is a feature of all domestic bankruptcy regimes has been dropped from the SDRM proposal and replaced by the less effective 'Hotchpot rule' under which any amounts recovered by a creditor are deducted from the creditor's eventual entitlements.[31]

6 The laws and rules that the Forum would apply are yet to be drafted – so the IMF is in effect requesting support for a process, the final form of which is completely uncertain.

Perhaps unsurprisingly, given it is a creation of the IMF, the SDRM serves to entrench the IMF in its role of international debt and economic crisis policeman by increasing the legal basis for that role – a role it has conspicuously failed to discharge well ever since it took it on in late 1982. The nations in Sub-Saharan Africa that ignored or only paid lip service to IMF structural adjustment programmes in the 1980s and 1990s enjoyed consistently higher rates of economic growth than those that applied such IMF programmes strictly. Likewise, the IMF's initial policy prescription of budgetary austerity for the nations most affected by the Asian economic crisis in 1997 was wrong, as the Chief Economist of the World Bank identified at the time and as the Fund itself subsequently tacitly admitted by endorsing expansionary policy-settings in those nations. Similarly, and finally, Argentina was a model IMF pupil in the decade up to its catastrophic debt default in late 2001 – and is today suffering through an economic meltdown that was in many ways promoted and facilitated by IMF-endorsed policies.[32]

The SDRM proposal seeks to render more efficient the current, haphazard debt restructuring process without addressing any of the inequities or power imbalances of the present system. In the IMF's words, 'We are not proposing a bankruptcy mechanism for countries, but simply a mechanism to facilitate debt workout negotiations between a debtor and its creditors'.[33] Yet a bankruptcy mechanism is precisely what is needed. One purpose of a rules-based system is to redress power imbalances by the application of fair and just rules – to replace the law of the jungle under which the most powerful party wins. The SDRM fails this test. The rules it will administer are yet to be formulated, but the critical issues in those rules will be determined and applied not by an independent court, but by an interested party, the IMF itself. Furthermore, in seeking to render the current system more efficient, it appears to seek to do no more than entrench and enhance the power of the creditors.

Applying the three factors identified earlier as being critical to the rule of law to the SDRM proposal,[34] we discover that the SDRM proposal:

- will presumably satisfy the first requirement of rules being clear, accessible and prospective in their operation;
- fails the second requirement of being seen to be legitimate and fair; and
- fails the third requirement of being interpreted and applied openly by an independent judiciary (at least for as long as the two central issues are left for determination by the IMF).

In the lyrics of the old Meatloaf song, 'Two Out of Three Ain't Bad', but one out of three ain't good. Certainly it is difficult to see why developing nations would support the SDRM initiative. Developing nations, and the international financial system, would be far better served by a carefully crafted set of bankruptcy rules, based on Chapter 9 of the US Bankruptcy Law, and applied and enforced by a truly independent tribunal, than it will be increasing the role of the IMF in areas in which it has already proven itself repeatedly to be less than competent.

A global central bank

Within national financial systems, central banks often discharge a number of functions including those of financial regulator and lender of last resort (LoLR). This section deals with a central bank as financial regulator. The next will deal with the LoLR function.

Today, global financial regulation is handled by bodies such as the Bank for International Settlements and other affiliations of central banks and nations that issue non-binding edicts or recommendations, the implementation of which is left to national authorities. This flexible system provides a great deal of guidance in the form of model laws and regulations and know-how for national authorities that seek to implement effective regulation. It has, however, no direct authority to require such behavior from uninterested national authorities.

As capital flows are now global, and the operations of capital markets are global, financial regulation needs to be global. The problem of transnational capital flows and transnational markets governed by national regulation is obvious.[35] However, the establishment of a global financial regulator with enforcement powers poses a massive challenge to the sovereignty of nations. Furthermore, no existing supranational institution has such general credibility that it is a plausible candidate for the role, and there is almost no appetite, particularly within the United States, to create yet another supranational institution. The decisions of such a regulator would have far-reaching consequences for each nation's financial system as, almost inevitably, many of such decisions would have the effects of favoring one nation's financial system over another. As strong as the need is, for these reasons, the prospects of a global financial regulator are extremely slight.

A global lender of last resort

Banking is an inherently unstable business as it typically involves banks holding illiquid assets (such as long-term mortgages) and highly liquid liabilities (such as short-term deposits).

A LoLR provides stability to each national banking system by committing in advance to lend funds to banks freely and quickly, on good security and at high interest rates in times of need (according to the classic nineteenth century prescription of Walter Bagehot). The provision of large amounts of funds quickly and freely discourages runs on banks by depositors as they are assured the bank will have funds to meet their claims. The requirements of good security and high interest rates discourages banks from relying on the lender of last resort's services and avoids the moral hazard that would otherwise flow from the provision of such a service.[36]

There is no LoLR in the international system. The IMF conditions its loans and the bailouts it orchestrates upon economic reform in the recipient countries, so these commitments to lend do not have the unconditional nature required to quell the fears of creditors and investors. Furthermore, the IMF typically disburses these funds slowly over time as compliance with the required reforms is proven by the recipients – the funds are not disbursed quickly as required by Bagehot's prescription. Finally, especially in the wake of the Asian economic crisis that commenced in 1997 and the IMF's difficulties in securing subscriptions from some member countries, it simply does not have resources of the magnitude required to serve as a credible LoLR to sovereign entities.

There is a clear need for a global LoLR. No domestic banking system would be stable without such a backstop so it is no surprise that the international system is not particularly stable. The challenges in implementing an international LoLR are three-fold: (i) the fears of some sovereigns that the establishment of such an entity will result in some loss of sovereignty; (ii) the difficulty of ensuring that the LoLR lends only on adequate enforceable security, so that exceptional moral hazard is not engendered by its activities;[37] and (iii) the difficulty of providing the LoLR with the resources to do the job.

The sovereignty fears should be far less with a LoLR than with a global financial regulator. Indeed, a LoLR detracts less from national sovereignty than even a global bankruptcy court. After all, the LoLR would merely be serving as a lender to a troubled country – its loans need not be accepted and its existence would not require any reduction in the freedom to act of the country or its judicial system.

However, the provision of adequate security poses very real difficulties indeed. Oil exporting nations such as Mexico can charge future oil revenues to serve as collateral for such a facility, however non-oil exporters may well lack adequate realizable security on the scale required and it may be necessary to structure some sort of escrow arrangement under which, upon a loan being made by the LoLR, a set proportion of the nation's subsequent export earnings are redirected to a trusted third party to use to secure the loan(s). The difficulty is that in troubled times, which by definition will be the period after a LoLR has been called upon, developing nations invariably need all of their foreign exchange earnings to service existing debt and to acquire imports needed by their domestic industries. To redirect a substantial proportion of foreign exchange from export earnings into repaying the loans of the LoLR would typically be unsustainable. Accordingly, most countries are going to find the provision of adequate security for the amounts of loans likely to be needed from a LoLR to be extremely problematic, if not downright impossible. For this reason, and the associated moral hazard if adequate security is not provided, it is difficult to conceive of an effective global LoLR.

However, setting aside that issue for the time being, the resources challenge may be less steep than is commonly considered, and leads us to the next strategic option.

A tax on international capital flows

This proposal is for a minute tax to be levied on each international capital flow. Such a tax was the brainchild of the Nobel laureate in economics, James Tobin, and it is often referred to as a Tobin tax. He conceived of the tax not to raise revenue but to serve as sand in the cogs of international financial flows to reduce short-term flows in particular and thus reduce volatility in such flows. One of the clear lessons of each of the Mexican peso crisis of late 1994, the Asian economic crisis of 1997 and Russia's economic meltdown in 1998, is that short-term capital flows are destabilizing and debtor countries are served by minimizing the proportion of capital inflows that are short-term in duration.[38] Accordingly, such a tax may well make a distinct contribution to the stability of the international financial system.

Furthermore, taxes raise revenue and this proposal is often seized upon gratefully by proponents of changes to the international financial architecture as a means to fund such changes. Certainly the proceeds of such a tax could most usefully fund an international LoLR. The proceeds are at times also suggested as an autonomous source of revenue for the activities of the IMF (and to a lesser extent the World Bank) but few countries so trust the IMF that they would be willing to cut it free from the control they wield over its purse strings – and this applies in particular to its major financier, the United States.

Interim conclusion on global regulatory options

In summary, there currently appears to be little prospect of a global financial regulator and regulatory system. The reason is the actual or perceived loss of national sovereignty. This is the view of virtually all commentators. The research of Braithwaite and Drahos explains why it is so.

Once global regulation is seen to be the product of a contest of principles rather than rules, and national sovereignty is seen to be the operative principle, it is clear why such a principle will trump any desire to attempt to avoid or ameliorate future financial crises: sovereignty is simply too close to the hearts of most governments, and too significant politically. This is particularly so because the loss of control over one's national economy is immediate upon the inception of a global central bank or global financial regulator, whereas the benefits of having such a bank or regulator are at that stage mere potentialities, benefits that may or may not be realized over time.

Accordingly, the only achievable major structural reforms of the international financial architecture are those that leave national sovereignty largely untouched: a global bankruptcy court or the establishment of a global LoLR funded by some form of Tobin tax.

The problem for any global bankruptcy court or tribunal is that it would almost certainly have to be created by international treaty among the affected nations – the home jurisdictions of the creditors and the debtor nations (this is assuming, as seems utterly safe, that the commercial bank creditors as a whole, and the debtors, decline to agree voluntarily to such a court or tribunal). And law reform by international treaty is usually grindingly slow. The International Criminal Court was some 55 years in the making. The WTO came into being 50 years after it was first proposed as the third of the Bretton Woods institutions in 1945. Even the Uniform Customs and Practice for Documentary Credits, which is only a set of standard terms for letters of credit, was in existence for some 40 years, and went through three revisions before gaining widespread usage and acceptance globally. History is not on the side of expeditious reforms of this type. There is one cause for optimism – the Basle Accord of the Bank for International Settlements was promulgated to regulate the capital adequacy of banks only some six or so years after the Latin American and African debt crisis of 1982 which prompted it.

However, the Basle Accord sought to achieve what the international creditor community knew was essential for systemic stability. A global bankruptcy regime seeks to achieve what is essential in terms of justice and fairness for the people of the debtor nations and for the efficiency and stability of the international financial system – and while this would most definitely enhance global prosperity in the long term, it will not necessarily enhance the bottom line for international banks in the short term. The international banks have a major interest in an efficient, stable international financial system and their long-term self-interest would be best served, as it is domestically, by an efficient global bankruptcy regime. However, more research, and a major educative effort, will be required to prove this to the banks and until they accept and understand it, a global bankruptcy regime is unlikely.

The problem for a global LoLR funded by some form of Tobin tax is that it is difficult to see how debtor nations can provide adequate security for the LoLR's loans, and thus how massive moral hazard can be avoided.

In summary, the future is not bright for any of the global reforms to the international financial architecture – which brings us to the national regulatory options.

National regulatory options for capital flows

The principal options for the regulation of capital flows by sovereign states are:

1 Capital controls
2 Exchange rate policy

3 Effective Prudential Regulation
4 Debt policy
5 Access to liquidity.

I have considered these elsewhere[39], but will nevertheless offer a brief summary here.

Capital controls

Capital controls broadly take two forms: inflow controls and outflow controls. The most successful and widely cited example of the former were implemented by Chile between 1991 and 1998. Chile's controls consisted of requiring a specified fraction of most capital inflows to be put on non-interest-bearing deposit with the Central Bank for a year. This served as a proportionally small tax on long-term flows, and a proportionally major impost on short-term flows. The experiences of Chile in the 1990s suggest that carefully structured and transparently applied controls on capital inflows can serve to decrease the proportion of incoming capital which is short term, while maintaining access to needed long-term capital.

Outflow controls work to restrict capital already in a nation from leaving. In 1998 and 1999, Malaysia implemented a raft of controls which served to suspend foreign trading in the ringgit and restrict withdrawal of foreign capital from the country. Because outflow controls represent a change in the rules while the game is in progress, they are particularly disliked by investors. Outflow controls are more readily circumvented than inflow controls – over-invoicing of imports and under-invoicing of exports to related companies works a treat and is next to impossible to prevent. Furthermore, the imperative to circumvent these controls is stronger because the controls keep a corporation apart from its profits.

Nonetheless, the experience of Malaysia in 1998–99 suggests that carefully structured and transparently applied controls on capital outflows can serve effectively as a barrier behind which a nation can reflate its economy in times of recession and/or make needed changes to its financial system without such actions leading to destabilizing capital flight.[40]

Exchange rate policy

One of the clearest lessons of the past decade for developing countries is that fixed exchange rates increase the prospects of financial crises.[41]

A floating exchange rate is a major avenue of economic adjustment for an economy. For instance, if an economy is strong, the demand for capital, and hence interest rates, will increase. At the same time, direct and portfolio investment will become more attractive to foreigners who will buy local currency with which to invest. The increase in demand for local currency, plus the higher interest rates, will each tend to strengthen the currency. The higher currency will, in turn, tend to reduce exports, as they become relatively more expensive, and increase correspondingly cheaper imports, thus moving the economy towards an equilibrium state. Likewise, when the economy turns down, its lower priced currency will tend to promote exports and reduce imports. A floating exchange rate regime thus tends to move an economy towards equilibrium.

Fixed exchange rates appeal to developing countries in particular, because they offer lower costs of credit and lower rates of inflation and provide discipline against monetary or fiscal excesses by government.[42] Fixed exchange rates have proven critical in breaking wage-price-currency spirals that led to ruinous inflation in nations such as Argentina and in promoting exports (through slightly undervalued exchange rates) and a stable external environment in times of export-led growth in Asia.[43] The cost of credit is lower with fixed exchange rates as borrowers will typically trust to the peg and borrow in foreign currency (at rates invariably lower than local currency rates).[44]

However, fixed exchange rates pose their own political and economic problems. When the economy of a nation with a fixed exchange rate is performing less strongly than that of the nation(s) to whose currency its currency is fixed, the peg requires adjustment or the fixed currency will become overvalued. Choosing to devalue the nation's currency is often difficult for politicians as it risks inflation and may well be seen domestically as evidence of a failure in economic leadership.

It is very easy, with a fixed rate regime, for a nation's currency to become overvalued. It happened in Mexico in 1993 and 1994, in Thailand and Indonesia in 1996–97, in Russia in 1997–98 and in Argentina from 1997 to 2001. And smaller economies lack the resources to defend the value of their currency against speculative attack.[45]

The other problem with fixed exchange rates is that they encourage excessive borrowing in foreign currency. Borrowers, like most people, believe what they want to believe, and so choose to take the lower interest rates that are usually on offer abroad and trust to the fixed exchange rate to deal with the currency risk. Exchange rate uncertainty, healthily, tends to keep borrowers at home.[46]

An overvalued fixed exchange rate was at the heart of each of the Mexican peso crisis of late 1994, the Asian crisis of 1997, the Russian collapse of 1998, Brazil's devaluation of early 1999 and Argentina's current crisis.[47] While a floating exchange rate is no insurance against a currency crisis (as Korea learned in 1997), the overwhelming policy lesson of the past five years is that flexible exchange rates provide some protection against such crises and the accompanying economic problems.[48] A pure floating exchange rate may not be strictly necessary, a managed flexible rate, provided it is managed in a sensible and market responsive manner, may be enough.[49] However a fixed rate, in the contemporary world of massive capital flows, is an invitation to trouble.

Effective prudential regulation

Effective regulation of the financial services sector is a difficult challenge for many developing countries for two reasons: (i) it is expensive; and (ii) it requires a highly developed rule of law. Each aspect will be considered.

Prudential regulation is expensive because it is labor-intensive and people with the relevant skills are in short supply and high demand, particularly in developing countries. Regulation generally tends to be better accomplished in the more developed economies of this world with larger tax bases from which to fund it. This is particularly so of prudential regulation due to the marked skills shortage in financial services in virtually all developing countries.

Second, and more significantly, prudential regulation requires a high degree of adherence to the rule of law. The product of banking is money, and most stability-inducing prudential regulations are also, in the short term, profit-reducing regulations, so the temptation to circumvent them is tremendous.

In East Asia, the local financial sectors were insufficiently sophisticated to intermediate efficiently the increased inflow of capital from 1993 onwards and disclosure and regulatory standards were inadequate across the region.[50] Faced with a steep yield curve,[51] local banks succumbed to the dangerous temptation to borrow short and lend long and did so, in the main, without hedging their foreign exchange exposures. This lack of sophistication in, and adequate prudential regulation of, local financial sectors was compounded by the moral hazard engendered by the crony capitalism prevalent in many countries in the region. Local banks were often owned and controlled by people with strong connections to the ruling political party and their frequent choice of highly risky, highly lucrative funding strategies was doubtless influenced by the prospect of a local bailout should the risks result in losses.

Indiscriminate international borrowing and domestic lending had been common throughout the region, and when the bubble burst domestic banks were in crisis in many countries, particularly Indonesia, Korea and Thailand.[52] A major lesson from the Asian economic crisis is that effective regulation of a nation's financial services sector must precede its liberalization – opening one's financial sector to the rest of the world without first ensuring its adequate supervision is an invitation to disaster and adequate prudential regulation is probably only achievable when capital markets understand how their own self-interest is advanced by their regulation.

Debt policy

A further lesson from the Asian crisis is that debtor countries need to manage the composition of their overall indebtedness so as to limit the proportion of short-term indebtedness and of unhedged foreign-currency-denominated indebtedness. Increasing levels of short-term indebtedness (typically sovereign and corporate bonds and bank credits of one, two or three months duration) were a predictor of incipient crisis in Mexico in late 1994, Asia in 1997 and Russia in 1998 – in part because in times of increasing uncertainty and decreasing creditworthiness this is the principal type of debt financing on offer. Nonetheless, high levels of short-term indebtedness can be most damaging. The expectation underpinning such short-term credits is that they will be rolled over upon maturity. However, at the first signs of serious trouble, the creditors will no longer renew these credits which leads to a potentially damaging capital outflow.

At the same time as severely limiting their appetite for short-term debt, nations need to develop and deepen their local capital markets and support the initiatives of the World Bank and other supranational agencies in issuing long-term debt denominated in emerging market currencies.[53] Local capital markets and longer term local currency debt are the sustainable and stable alternatives to short-term and foreign-currency-denominated indebtedness.

Access to liquidity

Access to sufficient liquidity has been promoted by Martin Feldstein and others[54] as the best defence for developing nations against currency crises.[55] Nations have two options to improve their liquidity: accumulate foreign exchange reserves or arrange long-term standby loan facilities.

The accumulation of foreign exchange reserves is difficult – it requires the promotion of exports, the deferral of pleasure in the guise of imports and considerable time. However, the experience of each of the People's Republic of China and the Republic of China in the Asian economic crisis bears testament to the resilience that large foreign exchange reserves bring to an economy. Accordingly, much like the parental admonition to save for a rainy day, it is worth repeating that substantial foreign exchange reserves offer considerable stability to an economy and a substantial degree of insurance against speculative currency attacks.

The short-term route to increase national liquidity is to arrange substantial long-term loan facilities with international banks and keep them in reserve to be used at times extra liquidity is required and this is the path advocated by Feldstein and others. Such facilities are best arranged in good times, for then their pricing will be at its finest. In arranging such a facility, a nation is facilitating its acting as its own LoLR for its foreign borrowing. One can have no quibble with this policy measure, except that the scale of such facilities is limited both by the willingness of the major banks to extend them and the capacity of the nations to afford them. Accordingly, such standby loan facilities can only serve as one aspect of a multifaceted approach to the problem of developing country financial instability.

Conclusion

There is much evidence that capital markets discharge critical functions in the efficient allocation of capital[56] and that capital markets promote economic growth.[57] Effective financial systems and access to foreign capital are critical to development.

However, there currently appears to be very little prospect of the global regulation of global capital flows. Braithwaite and Drahos' formulation of the 'rule of principles' casts much light on why this is so. The 'rule of principles' explains global business regulation as the product of contests of principles, not rules, and the principle of sovereignty will almost always take precedence over the search for a more stable international financial system given how much sovereignty nations would need to cede to a global financial regulator for it to be able effectively to discharge its role.

The regulation of globalized capital flows will, in all probability, continue to fall to nation states aided, as is proper and appropriate, by the standard setting activities of international bodies such as the Basle Committee of the Bank for International Settlements. This is achievable and there is no evidence to date that national regulation of capital flows, handled properly, is inadequate for the task – although there is much evidence of poor national prudential regulation coupled to some poorly considered interventions by supranational agencies such as the IMF. The challenge before the international community is to assist national regulators to discharge their duties effectively. The international community is doing much good work in this regard in terms of the preparation of appropriate international standards and otherwise making available expertise and information. However, regulation is labor intensive and expensive. This is particularly so in developing countries in which skilled capital markets professionals are rare. And it is on this front – resources – that the international community's contribution is far from adequate.

In the immediate aftermath of the Asian economic crisis, it was striking that the IMF identified poor local prudential regulation and underdeveloped local capital markets as two of the principal contributing causes to the crisis and yet the IMF-orchestrated bailouts contained not one dollar to put right these weaknesses. The international community has done well on the knowledge side of the ledger in tackling the prudential issues required to make the world financial order more stable. It is now time for the community to address the resource side of the ledger and put money in behind their good ideas so as to help make them a reality. As has been identified, in financial regulation the rule of law operates principally at the national level and this is the level at which the world's efforts and resources should be directed.

In particular, resources are needed for three functions:

1 to formulate appropriate laws and rules;
2 to enforce those laws and rules effectively; and
3 to educate participants in the capital markets as to the need for, and their self-interest in, a well-regulated system.

The easiest and least expensive of these functions is the first, and so it is unsurprising that it is the area in which the most, and best, work has been done. Promulgating laws on statute books is relatively easy and inexpensive. Enforcing those laws is much more difficult – enforcement requires ongoing substantial funding and a long-term commitment to invest in the skills development of the regulatory staff. Nonetheless, it is essentially a matter of resources and priorities and it is silly for the IMF, quite correctly, to identify inadequate local regulation as a major cause of global financial instability and then to not provide long-term resources to address this deficiency.

Finally, there is the need for education. Capital market participants in developing countries need education as to (a) the need for stringent regulation of their markets; (b) the need for a rigorous application of the rule of law to those markets; and (c) how such regulation will in the long-term benefit them enormously. One of the reasons the US economy is such a magnet for foreign capital is that its highly regulated financial markets protect investors and investors like this. The local capital markets in developing countries will only grow dramatically with large infusions of local investor funds when those investors perceive them to be orderly and fair markets for their money – a change from which local capital market participants can only benefit.

In the interests of a more stable international financial system, the laws and the rule of law regarding capital flows and capital market activity needs to be strengthened. As these laws operate principally at the national level, it is incumbent upon the international bodies to work at that level in strengthening the relevant laws and the rule of law.

Acknowledgments

An earlier version of this chapter was presented to the Vice-Chancellor's Symposium, Parliament House, Brisbane, August, 2001. Thanks to Dr Haig Patapan for his most helpful comments on one section of this chapter and to the Australian Research Council for a grant which, among other things, supported this research. All responsibility is mine.

Notes

1 Sutherland, P. *Managing the International Economy in an Age of Globalization*, The 1998 Per Jacobsson Lecture, the Annual meeting of the IMF and the World Bank.
2 Espinosa-Vega, M.A., Smith, B.D. and Yip, C.K. *Barriers to International Capital Flows: who should erect them and how big should they be?* Federal Reserve Bank of Atlanta Working Paper 99–6, July 1999.
3 Or, at least, rich individuals and companies in poor countries invest in and lend to entities in rich countries.
4 Or, in the more formal words of Sebastian Edwards, 'Economists have long recognized that cross-border capital movements pose a difficult policy issue. In the absence of strong financial supervision in either lending or borrowing countries, unregulated capital flows may . . . be misallocated, . . . generating waves of major disruptions in the receiving nations': Edwards, S. *How Effective Are Capital Controls?*, NBER Working Paper No. W7413, November 1999, available at: http://www.nber.org/papers/w7413 (accessed 25 February 2004).
5 Drawn from the Introduction to this book.
6 Braithwaite, J. and Drahos, P. *Global Business Regulation*, Cambridge: Cambridge University Press, 2000.
7 Ibid., p. 531; see also: p. 30.
8 Ibid., p. 531.
9 Jones, R.J.B. *The World Turned Upside Down?: globalization and the future of the state*, Manchester, UK; New York: Manchester University Press, 2000, p. 36.
10 The following factors owe much to Kaufman, H. 'Protecting Against the Next Financial Crisis: the need to reform global financial oversight, the IMF, and monetary policy goals', *Business Economics*, July 1999, available at: http://www.findarticles.com/m1094/3_34/issue.jhtml (accessed 16 March 2004).
11 For instance, US mutual funds assets increased over four times between 1990 and 1997 from US$1067 billion to US$4490 billion: US Dept of Commerce, *Statistical Abstract of the United States*, 1998 (118th edn) 533.
12 Makin, C. 'Doesn't Anybody Remember Risk?' *Institutional Investor*, April 1994, p. 41.

13 Ayuso, J. and Blanco, R. 'Has Financial Market Integration Increased During the 1990s?', Paper presented at International Financial Markets and the Implications for Monetary and Financial Stability, a Conference of the Bank for International Settlements, 25–26 October 1999, available at: http://www.bis.org/publ/confer08.htm (accessed 26 February 2004). As one example, Russia's economic troubles in August 1998 sent yields on the US long bond to unprecedented lows and affected even US municipal bonds.

14 For more on these strategic options, see: *Reports on the International Financial Architecture by the G22 Working Group on Transparency and Accountability, Strengthening Financial Systems, and International Financial Crises*, October, 1998, http://www.imf.org/external/np/g22/index/htm (accessed 17 March 2000); Buiter, W. and Sibert, A. *UDROP: a small contribution to the international financial architecture 1999*, Discussion Paper 0425, http://cep.lse.ac.uk/ papers/discussion/table.html (accessed 26 February 2004); Eichengreen, B. *Toward A New International Financial Architecture: a practical post-Asia agenda*, Institute for International Economics, 1999; *Safeguarding Prosperity in a Global Financial System: the future international financial architecture*, Report of an Independent Task Force Sponsored by the Council on Foreign Relations, September 1999; Garten J.E. 'Lessons for the Next Financial Crisis', *Foreign Affairs*, vol. 78, issue 2, March–April 1999, p. 76; Goldstein, M. 'The Future of the International Financial Architecture; a council on foreign relations taskforce', *Foreign Affairs*, vol. 78, no. 6, November–December, 1999, p. 169; Dorn, J.A. *A New Global Financial Architecture*, Center for Trade Policy Studies http://www.freetrade.org/pubs/articles/jd–11–04–98.html (accessed 17 March 2000); Neiss, H. 'Blueprint for a Bold New Financial Architecture: A Commentary', *Sydney Morning Herald*, 9 November 1998; Singh, K. '*Restructuring the International Financial Architecture*', Asia–Europe Dialogue Articles, 1999, http://www.ased.org (accessed 5 March 2004); Blinder, A.S. 'Eight Steps to a New Financial Order', *Foreign Affairs*, vol. 78, issue 5, September–October 1999, p. 50. For a very good analysis of the supranational options, see: Rogoff, K. *International Institutions for Reducing Global Financial Instability*, NBER Working Paper No. W7265, 1999, http://www.nber.org/papers/w7265 (accessed 26 February 2004).

15 Raffer, K. 'Applying Chapter 9 Insolvency to International Debts: an economically efficient solution with a human face', *World Development*, vol. 18, issue 2, February 1990, p. 301; Raffer, K. 'International Debts; a crisis for whom?', in H.W. Singer and S. Sharma (eds) *Economic Development and World Debt*, London: Macmillan, 1989, p. 51; and see: the research referred to in Rogoff, K. and Zettelmeyer, J. *Early Ideas on Sovereign Bankruptcy Reorganization: a survey*, IMF Working Paper WP/02/57, 2002 available at: http://www.imf.org/external/pubs/ft/wp/2002/wp0257.pdf (accessed 5 March 2004).

16 Presently, no court has jurisdiction over disputes between a sovereign state and citizens (such as banks or bondholders) of another sovereign state – the International Court of Justice deals only with disputes between sovereign states (White, M., 'Sovereigns in Distress: do they need bankruptcy?', *Brookings Paper on Economic Activity*, Spring 2002, pp. 287–320). Arbitral tribunals, such as those under the auspices of the International Centre for the Settlement of Investment Disputes (ICSID), do deal with such disputes, but are, of course, not courts. For more on ICSID, see: Buckley, R.P. 'Now We Have Come to the 'ICSID' Party: are its awards final and enforceable?' *Sydney Law Review*, vol. 14, 1992, pp. 358–72.

17 The two principal models widely discussed for any such transnational law are Chapters 9 and 11 of the US Bankruptcy Code. Professor Kunibert Raffer has made a very strong case for why Chapter 9 provides the best available precedent for international sovereign bankruptcies: see: Raffer, K. 'Solving Sovereign Debt Overhang by Internationalizing Chapter 9 Procedures', *Studien von Zeitfragen*, 2002, available at http://www.jahrbuch2002. studien-von-zeitfragen.net/Weltfinanz/RAFFER_1/raffer_1.HTM (accessed 5 March 2004).

18 Pettifor, A. 'Resolving International Debt Crises – the Jubilee Framework for International Insolvency', January 2002, available at: www.jubileeplus.org/analysis/reports/jubilee_framework.html (accessed 26 February 2004).

19 Pettifor, ibid.; and Rasche, P.W. 'Argentina: test case for a new approach to insolvency?' *Studien von Zeitfragen*, 5 January 2002.

20 Quoted in Peter Hartcher, 'US Reigns in IMF with Tough Debt Rules', *Australian Financial Review*, 22 April 2002.

21 In the IMF's words, 'In the domestic context, the existence of a bankruptcy law makes debt markets more efficient. . . . The same principle should hold for international capital markets'. See: IMF, 'Proposals for a Sovereign Debt Restructuring Mechanism (SDRM) A Factsheet', January 2003, D.5, available at: http://www.imf.org/external/np/exr/facts/sdrm.htm (accessed 26 February 2004).

22 Buckley, R. *Emerging Markets Debt*, Kluwer Law International, London, 1999, pp. 33–4.

23 In developmental terms, virtually everyone agrees that the 1980s was a lost decade in Latin America due to the Debt Crisis. Even Anne Krueger agrees. See: Krueger, A. *A New Approach to Sovereign Debt Restructuring*, 2002, available at: http://www.imf.org/external/pubs/ft/exrp/sdrm/eng/index.htm (accessed 26 February 2004). No progress was made between 1982 and 1989 on debt relief or meaningful ways forward for debtor nations, and so the continent's poor went hungry, its young poor went uneducated, and its infrastructure crumbled, as nations continued to service an overwhelming debt burden (usually through new loans which simply increased the total indebtedness). The debt gridlock of the 1980s was in no one's long-term interests but damaged the debtors far more than the creditors. See: Marichal, C.A. *Century of Debt Crises in Latin America: from independence to the great depression 1820–1930*, Princeton NJ: Princeton University Press, 1989, p. 237; and Buckley, *Emerging Markets Debt*, pp. 34–6.

24 See: Buchheit L.C. and Mitu Gulati, G. 'Sovereign Bonds and the Collective Will', *Emory Law Journal*, vol. 51, no. 4, Fall 2002, 1317–64.

25 The total external indebtedness of developing countries in 2000 was $2492 billion, see World Bank, *2002 World Development Indicators*, p. 198, available at: www.worldbank.org/data/wdi2002/economy.pdf (accessed 26 February 2004).

26 An excellent analysis of the history of the early common law remedies against debtors, including imprisonment for debt, can be found in Rose, D. (ed.) *Lewis Australian Bankruptcy Law*, Sydney: Law Book Co., 1994, pp. 7–10.

27 These are drawn from the IMF publication, 'Proposals for a Sovereign Debt Restructuring Mechanism (SDRM) A Factsheet', and also from Krueger, *New Approach to Sovereign Debt Restructuring*.

28 Pettifor, A. and Raffer, K. *Report on the IMF's Conference on the SDRM*, 22 January 2003', unpublished report on file with author.

29 Raffer, K. 'The IMF's SDRM – Another Form of Simply Disastrous Rescheduling Management?', in C. Jochnick and F. Preston (eds) *Sovereign Debts at the Crossroads*, Oxford University Press, forthcoming, 2004.

30 Official inter-governmental loans are rescheduled through a process known as the Paris Club.

31 See: Raffer, K. 'To Stay or Not to Stay – A Short Note on Differing Versions of the SDRM', 31 January 2003, available at: http://www.jubilee2000uk.org/latest/raffer310103.htm (accessed 26 February 2004).

32 Buckley, R. 'Do Cry for the Argentines: an analysis of their crisis', *Banking and Finance Law Review*, vol. 17, 2003, pp. 373–93.

33 IMF, 'Proposals for a Sovereign Debt Restructuring Mechanism (SDRM) A Factsheet', B.6.

34 The SDRM is, after all, no more than a body of laws and an interpretation and enforcement mechanism for them.

35 On the need to reconceive our liberal and social democratic values as genuinely global values and then frame the institutions that will sustain and advance them,

see Sampford, C. 'Challenges to the Concepts of "Sovereignty" and "Intervention" ', in B. Leiser and T. Campbell (eds) *Human Rights in Philosophy and Practice*, London: Ashgate, 2001, chapter 16.

36 Moral hazard arises whenever a financial actor does not bear, or anticipate bearing, the full risk attached to its actions.

37 Jones, R.J.B. *The World Turned Upside Down? globalization and the future of the state*, Manchester, UK; New York: Manchester University Press, 2000, n 9, p. 255.

38 Buckley, R. 'Strategic Options for Asian Nations in the Era of Hot Money', in C. Sampford, S. Condlln, M. Palmer and T. Round (eds) *Asia Pacific Governance: from crisis to reform*, Aldershot: Ashgate, 2002; and Buckley, R. 'Six Lessons for Banking Regulators from the Asian Economic Crisis', in W. Weerasooria (ed.) *Perspectives on Banking, Finance and Credit Law*, St Leonards, NSW: Prospect Media, 1999, p. 67.

39 Buckley, 'National Sovereignty in the Era of Hot Money: Strategic Options for Asian Nations'; and Buckley 'Six Lessons for Banking Regulators from the Asian Economic Crisis', p. 67.

40 For more on this see: Buckley, R. 'The Role of Capital Controls in International Financial Crises', *Bond Law Review*, vol. 11, no. 2, December 1999, p. 231; and Ariyoshi, A., Habermeier, K., Laurens, B., Otker-Robe, I., Canales-Kriljenko J.I. and Kirilenko, A. *Country Experiences with the Use and Liberalization of Capital Controls*, IMF Paper, January 2000, available at: http://www.imf.org/external/pubs/ft/op/op190/ (accessed 26 February 2004). These findings are made the more compelling and authoritative by their appearance in an IMF publication by IMF staff so soon after the IMF had led the international criticism of Malaysia for introducing outflow controls. (As a consistent critic of many IMF policy prescriptions, the appearance of these findings in an IMF publication compels me to commend the institution for its commitment to free debate and the pursuit of the truth.)

41 Sachs, J.D. 'Alternative Approaches to Financial Crises in Emerging Markets', in M. Kahler (ed.) *Capital Flows and Financial Crises*, Ithaca, NY: Cornell University Press, 1998, p. 250. See also: Reinhart, C.M. and Reinhart, V.R. 'Some Lessons for Policy Makers Who Deal with the Mixed Blessing of Capital Inflows', in M. Kahler (ed.) *Capital Flows and Financial Crises*, pp. 110–15 and Buckley, 'Do Cry for the Argentines: an analysis of their crisis'.

42 Feldstein, M. 'A Self-Help Guide for Emerging Markets', *Foreign Affairs*, vol. 78, issue 2, March–April 1999, p. 93.

43 Viscio, I. 'The Recent Experience with Capital Flows to Emerging Market Economies', *OECD Economic Outlook*, vol. 65, June 1999, pp. 177–95.

44 Ibid., p. 5; See also: Bustelo, P., Garcia, C. and Olivié, I. *Global and Domestic Factors of Financial Crises in Emerging Economies: lessons from the East Asian episodes (1997–1999)*, ICEI Working Paper No. 16, Instituto Complutense De Estudios Internacionales, Madrid, 1999, p. 78. As the Asian crisis demonstrated conclusively, this behavior is highly risky and masks the real cost of borrowing in a foreign currency: the currency risk doesn't go away merely because one's domestic currency is pegged to the foreign currency.

45 To understand speculative attacks on currencies, it is necessary to understand that speculators can sell currency they do not own. Now, of course, if you or I try that with a car or boat the local constabulary will soon be a calling. However, investors can simply borrow a currency such as baht or rupiah, sell it for a hard currency, such as US dollars, and then trust to a fall in the value of the baht or rupiah before they have to repurchase it to repay the borrowing (Blinder, 'Eight Steps to a New Financial Order'). Accordingly, there can, in the short term, be waves of currency sales that are not preceded by currency purchases and such is the mechanism of speculative attacks.

46 'Keeping the hot money out', *The Economist*, vol. 346, no. 8052, 24 January 1998.

47 Blinder, 'Eight Steps to a New Financial Order'.

48 Viscio, 'The Recent Experience with Capital Flows to Emerging Market Economies', p. 5; Bustelo, Garcia and Olivié, *Global and Domestic Factors of Financial Crises in Emerging*

Economies, n 44, p. 78; and Meyer, L.H. *Lessons from the Asian Crisis: a central banker's perspective*, Levy Economics Institute Working Paper No. 276, 1999.

49 Such management of exchange rates, however, has proven a difficult task: Meyer, ibid.

50 The World Bank, *Global Development Finance 1998*, vol. 1, 1998, p. 4.

51 A yield curve is a graph which plots yield of fixed interest securities against their time to maturity. A steep yield curve means yields on longer term securities are much higher than on shorter term securities.

52 Dornbusch, R. 'A Bail-out Won't Do the Trick in Korea', *Business Week*, 8 December 1997, p. 26; and Garran, R. 'Korea Crisis', *The Australian*, 19 November 1997, p. 36, col. 1.

53 Blinder, 'Eight Steps to a New Financial Order'; and Rubin, R. Treasury Secretary Robert E. Rubin Remarks on Reform of the International Financial Architecture to the School of Advanced International Studies, (21 April 1999).

54 Feldstein, 'A Self-Help Guide for Emerging Markets'; Eichengreen, B. 'Bailing in the Private Sector: burden sharing in international financial crisis management', *The Fletcher Forum of World Affairs*, vol. 23, no. 1, Winter–Spring 1999, p. 59; and Viscio, 'The Recent Experience with Capital Flows to Emerging Market Economies', p. 177.

55 Currency crises are only one of the types of financial crises that can afflict such nations, so this policy measure is not a general remedy.

56 Wurgler, J. 'Financial Markets and the Allocation of Capital' (unpublished manuscript), 2000. Wurgler found the efficiency of capital allocation to be positively correlated with the amount of firm-specific information in local stock markets and with the legal protection of minority shareholders.

57 King, R.G. and Levine, R. 'Finance and Growth: Schumpeter might be right', *The Quarterly Journal of Economics*, vol. 108, issue 3, August 1993, pp. 717–38; King, R.G. and Levine, R. 'Finance, Entrepreneurship and Growth', *Journal of Monetary Economics*, vol. 32, issue 3, December 1993, pp. 513–42; and Levine, R. and Zervos, S. 'Stock Markets, Banks, and Economic Growth', *The American Economic Review*, vol. 88, issue 1, June 1998, pp. 537–59. Indeed, an innovative and effective financial system was central to the growth and modernization of history's most successful 'emerging market', the United States of America in the first half of the nineteenth century. See: Rousseau, P.L. and Sylla, R. *Emerging Financial Markets and Early U.S. Growth*, Cambridge, MA: National Bureau of Economic Research, 1999.

Part IV

International security and the rule of law

8 Sovereignty, international law and global cooperation

The Rt. Hon. Malcolm Fraser AC, CH

The desire to establish an effective international order is not new. After the horrors of the World War I, United States President Woodrow Wilson played a lead role in the establishment of the League of Nations. The fact that the US Congress refused to join the League is rumored to have contributed to his death.

The failure of the League was not only in large part because the United States did not join, but also because there was no real will from world leaders to make the League work. The Treaty of Versailles had set the stage for hostilities that, combined with the Great Depression, set the scene for rising fascism in Europe and ultimately the World War II.

Two world wars within a quarter of a century brought home the clear necessity for the formation of an organization dedicated to 'maintaining international peace and security',[1] and to 'developing friendly relations among nations based on respect for the principle of equal rights and self-determination of peoples'.[2] In 1944, even before the war had ended, the allies were meeting in San Francisco drafting the Charter of a new international organization – the United Nations – whose primary purpose would be to promote peace and security throughout the world. The Charter of the United Nations opened for signature on 26 June 1945 and entered into force 24 October 1945. Its preamble is worth quoting here as it demonstrates great depth of feeling and commitment:

> We the peoples of the United Nations determined
>
> - to save succeeding generations from the scourge of war, which twice in our lifetime has brought untold sorrow to mankind, and
> - to reaffirm faith in fundamental human rights, in the dignity and worth of the human person, in the equal rights of men and women and of nations large and small, and . . .
>
> And for these ends
>
> - To practice tolerance and live together in peace with one another as good neighbors . . .

This was an organization that had a baptism of fire. The failure to capitalize on opportunities which presented themselves after World War I was to be avoided a second time. But it was not long after the end of the war that tensions between the Soviet bloc and the West began to emerge. Ideological differences were acute, there was little room for middle ground. The world was soon split in two camps: the East and the West and this schism dominated world politics for the next 40 years.

During this time, given the structure of the Security Council, the United Nations was severely limited in its capacity to act as a keeper of the peace. The veto held by the five major powers (United States, United Kingdom, France, China, USSR) meant that the Council was unable to act independently of the ideological factions – East or West. The extraordinary exception to this was when a UN resolution was passed while the Soviet delegation was absent, establishing a force to fight with South Korea against the North. Needless to say, the Soviet chair was never empty from that time on.

The end of the Cold War presented the world with opportunities unlike any since those heady days of allied victory in 1945 when the UN Charter was drafted. President George Bush talked of a New World Order and America lead the United Nations to war against Iraq in the Gulf in 1991. But the New World Order was not only founded on war but on the increased capacity of the Security Council to act on behalf of humanity. Operation Restore Hope, the UN humanitarian intervention in Somalia 1992–95, was the first time the United Nations had used Chapter VII powers and the use of force to fulfil a truly humanitarian mandate. Over 100,000 people had starved to death, aid agencies were overwhelmed and the Horn of Africa was no longer a plaything of the two major superpowers.

In September 2000, I made a speech in Osaka which discussed the Security Council and the use of its Chapter VII powers. Since those early days of the post-cold-war era we have seen increasing discretion and inconsistency in the way that the Security Council wields power. What encourages it to act in some instances and turn aside in others?

At the same time the United States, the only remaining superpower in the world, is becoming increasingly and, in my view, dangerously unilateralist. International law, established to make sense of the manner in which nation states relate to each other and to their own citizens, is largely of voluntary competence. Without the consent of states it is unenforceable, and even decisions made before the International Court of Justice are not binding. Where then does this lead a New World Order? Does it allow the possibility of a just world? And what role is there for the application and enforcement of international law?

Security and international humanitarian law

Since the end of the Cold War, international security and humanitarianism have become more complex than ever before. We have seen international action, which a decade ago would have been unimaginable. The international community, with the sanction of the UN Security Council, went to war against an aggressor State. Shortly afterwards the international community mobilized as never before to assist a desperate nation. The Gulf War and Somalia's Restore Hope operations heralded a 'New World Order'. It was anticipated that peace and justice would prevail, that illegal and inhumane acts would no longer be tolerated. The United Nations was no longer a lion with no roar but had the capacity and the mettle to defend and protect its member States in the manner its Charter envisioned.

But it was not long before there was widespread disillusionment with the United Nations: while the famine abated, anarchy continued in Somalia placing at risk aid workers and the UN and American forces on the ground. The war in Bosnia was raging and reports of appalling war crimes were emerging. Shortly afterwards, in 1994, the United Nations made an ignominious retreat from Rwanda where an estimated 500,000 Tutsis were slaughtered by the Interahamwe Militias. The international community rightly began to ask, was this the vision for the New World Order?

Ultimately, security and humanitarianism is important because of those people that policies and actions are designed to protect. The United Nations has a key role to play as the world lurches into the twenty-first century with industrial, technological and social changes more rapid than ever before. While there have been valid criticisms of the United Nations, we must bear in mind that the United Nations is limited by what its major States are prepared to do. The United Nations is often blamed unjustly where its Members have denied action. Still the United Nations must be prepared to learn and apply the lessons of the past.

The UN Security Council was established under the UN Charter to ensure a mechanism for quick and decisive action concerning matters of global peace and security. Yet there are many problems.

John Foster Dulles noted,[3] as early as 1950 that:

> The Security Council is not a body that merely enforces agreed law. It is a law unto itself. If it considers any situation as a threat to the peace it may decide what measures shall be taken. No principles of law are laid down to guide it; it can decide in accordance with what it thinks is expedient. It could be a tool enabling certain powers to advance their selfish interests at the expense of another power.

What would he think of action the Security Council has taken over the last 10 years?

Article 2(4) of the UN Charter clearly defines a universally accepted principle of international law. That 'All Members shall refrain in their international relations from the threat or use of force against the territorial integrity or political independence of any state, or in any other manner inconsistent with the Purposes of the UN'.

An exception to this principle of non-intervention is laid out in Article 2(7) which iterates that 'nothing . . . in the . . . Charter shall authorise the UN to intervene in matters which are essentially within the domestic jurisdiction of any state . . . but this principle *shall not prejudice the application of enforcement measures under Chapter VII*' (my emphasis).

Chapter VII refers to the powers of the Security Council – which having determined that there is either a threat to the peace, a breach of the peace, or an act of aggression – can institute enforcement measures. These measures, such as economic sanctions or the use of military force, can be binding on member States in an effort to 'maintain or restore international peace and security'.

Where it is reasonably easy to determine a breach of the peace, or an act of aggression, the Security Council's determination of what constitutes a 'threat to the peace' has been shown to be highly subjective and has, in recent times, been used in somewhat 'creative' circumstances.

One of the Security Council's first controversial undertakings was Resolution 687 of April 1991 which put an end to the Gulf war and determined the conditions for the ceasefire between Iraq and Kuwait and other states. This resolution, and later ones relating to the payment of compensation by Iraq for the damage and costs caused by its occupation of Kuwait, included compulsory measures laid down by the Security Council under Chapter VII.

Given that the war was over,. and there was no current 'breach of the peace', it can only be assumed that the nature of Saddam Hussein's Government, or the failure to pay compensation for war damages, constituted a threat to the peace. Otherwise Chapter VII compulsory measures could not have been instituted. This had grave consequences for the children and people of Iraq. UNICEF has estimated that, prior to the recent war, the sanctions contributed to the deaths of some 500,000 children under the age of five.

The other interpretation of the Chapter VII measures against Iraq is that where there has been a threat to the peace (or in this instance an act of aggression), the Security Council is prepared to extend Chapter VII measures even *after* that threat or act of aggression is over.

In the final analysis, the embargo on Iraq and the appalling humanitarian consequences it generated presented two issues. First, if a country violated the Chapter VII compulsory embargo in order to assist the population of Iraq, would its action be considered by the Security Council to constitute a 'threat to the peace' and thereby possibly find itself to be the subject of Chapter VII measures?

Second, the Iraqi situation at that time demonstrated the lack of sufficient debate and accountability of Security Council policies regarding Iraq, and the consequences of those policies both for the people of Iraq and for the achievement of the UN' objective.

By continuing to impose sanctions in Iraq, the United Nations (led strongly in this instance by the United States) said to the disenfranchised of Iraq 'rise up and change your leader and then you'll have a future'. It was demanding the impossible. The Iraqi people had no influence and no power, and unthinking application of a harsh-sanctions regime served only to cause almost intolerable human suffering.

In fact, the suffering in Iraq directly caused by UN sanctions rivalled and probably exceeded the human suffering in the Balkans – does this constitute a crime against humanity? Can the Security Council's capacity to determine that a threat to the peace and thereby institute Chapter VII measures at enormous human cost go unchecked?

In a domestic context such as Australia, the government is accountable to the people. If the government appoints bad judges then it is still accountable. How can we make an international institution accountable? At the moment, the only sanction that has been applied to the United Nations has been the withholding of US dues. The purpose of this, however, has not been to establish a better international system but to compel the United Nations to adopt policies acceptable to the United States. At the moment there is no way of holding the United Nations accountable.

For the development of a stable and just world, the application of law and punitive measures needs to be seen to be applied equitably and impartially without fear or favor. We have one major example where this has not happened.

Following the bombing of Pan Am flight over Lockerbie, the Security Council determined that Libya's support for terrorist activity and its failure to extradite the two suspects constituted a threat to the peace.[4] Security Council Resolution 748 (1992) imposed an embargo on the supply of weapons and aircraft to Libya. Yet on the other side of the world, another terrorist act took place with the knowledge and support of its government. I refer to France's bombing of Greenpeace's 'Rainbow Warrior' in New Zealand.[5]

Geoffrey Granville-Wood, a distinguished international lawyer from Canada, was highly critical of the decision to impose Chapter VII measures on Libya. He noted: 'Did France's refusal a few years ago to hand over to New Zealand their secret service agents who bombed the Greenpeace ship the "Rainbow Warrior" also constitute a threat to international peace and security?'[6] He warned of a dangerous precedent being set and questioned whether the UN Security Council was in danger of becoming the 'plaything of a few Western Powers'.[7]

The quality of these terrorist actions is similar although the scale of the disaster was incomparable. Yet, New Zealand had no adequate redress against France because of France's reputation and the fact that it is a permanent member of the Security Council. On the other hand, Libya, regarded by members of the Security Council as a 'rogue state', received the application of maximum penalty.

Following Iraq and Libya, a third example of Security Council 'flexibility and discretion' in the determination of what constitutes a threat to international peace and security is the establishment of the *ad hoc* Tribunals for the Prosecution of War Crimes committed in the Territory of the Former Yugoslavia and Rwanda. While no one would deny that the perpetrators of such violations should be brought to trial, the evolution of the tribunals themselves is interesting in the context of the use of Security Council Powers.

Normally such tribunals would be established through a treaty between the parties to the dispute. In 1993 the Secretary-General Boutros Boutros-Ghali suggested that this process would be too cumbersome and lengthy and that the Security Council could institute the Tribunals under Chapter VII. One interpretation, therefore, is that the Members of the Security Council were prepared to concede that allowing the people who had perpetrated war crimes to remain at large was a threat to the peace. What could happen if other international law is violated? Could that also constitute a threat to the peace if it served the purpose of the Security Council?

The other interpretation from the establishment of the *ad hoc* Tribunals is that the Security Council is prepared to pervert the Charter, and the principles laid down in Chapter VII, to achieve its aims. The powerful members have decided that a 'threat to the peace' is not an essential ingredient for the application of compulsory measures but instead that the façade of a threat is sufficient. This interpretation can only result in a totally unpredictable system of international law run on *ad hocery* and the power of a privileged few. (I return to this theme presently in the context of the recent war in Iraq.) Ultimately though, the determination of a threat to the peace is left to the discretion of the Security Council. Such discretion has, in some instances, enabled quick and decisive action on behalf of the United Nations where none of the permanent members have applied the veto.

Where a traditional perspective on what might constitute a 'threat to the peace' may have involved some form of military activity between sovereign states, the Security Council has not been constrained by such traditional views. Failure to pay compensation for war damages, failure to extradite suspected terrorists, and grave breaches of the Geneva Conventions and violations of international humanitarian law have all been deemed to be a threat to the peace. Secretary-General Boutros Boutros-Ghali also suggested that poverty, disease and famine may constitute a threat to the peace.

The decade prior to Kosovo had been extraordinary in the history of the United Nations in terms of Security Council cooperation. When the Soviet Union disintegrated, Mikhail Gorbachev, and later Boris Yeltsin, needed the moral and financial support of the West and were therefore more enthusiastic about Western initiatives.[8] This is the only thing that made the Gulf War possible.

While the veto is widely criticized, it is clearly important in light of the extraordinary powers held by the Security Council. The United Nations' founders foresaw the need for a mechanism to be established to enable the Security Council to be effective, but at the same time prevent it from becoming tyrannical. When there were two superpowers, in a strange way there was a measure of balance in global politics. Each power restrained the other from excesses that could jeopardize world peace. Now that the world has just one superpower, such restraint is not necessarily there.

A problem arises then, if that one superpower and some other countries wish to take action which is unlikely to be condoned by the Security Council. If, as a result, those powers circumvent the United Nations and act within the scope of a regional organization, it may occur contrary to international law. Such action would not have been possible when there was more than one superpower but the dominance of the United States has lead to a real crisis for the United Nations and the international community. I am speaking, of course, of the examples of Kosovo, September 11 and Iraq.

Kosovo

To bomb Yugoslavia without the consent of the UN Security Council was undoubtedly military aggression in violation of international law. The question that remains, then, is what should the international community do when there is a deadlock in the Security Council, and the internal situation in a State is judged to violate the human rights of a minority within that State?

This is an old conflict between two principles of international law: that of sovereign integrity and universal human rights. This conflict was perceived by the United Nations' founders who wrote into the Charter the requirement for enforcement action to be authorized by the Security Council. This was intended to be one, and perhaps the principal legal justification for the use of force.

In addition, under Article 5 of its own Charter, the North Atlantic Treaty Organisation, (NATO) is forbidden to go to war against any State other than to defend a member under attack. NATO's action, then, was doubly contentious – it had no support from the Security Council and the United Nations, and it perverted its own Charter.

In Kosovo, the situation was not as clear as the United States would have us believe. For several years, a guerrilla war had been waged with the explicit goal, on behalf of the Kosovo Liberation Army (KLA), to liberate the Albanian-dominated areas of Macedonia, Montenegro and Serbia in order to create a unified Albanian State.

The talks at Rambouillet can be interpreted as an effort by the West to force the secession of a minority-dominated territory in a sovereign State.[9] This could set a precedent with far-reaching consequences. While the right to self-determination is widely recognized, in no human rights, or international law instrument, is the right to secession outside the principle of uti possidetis juris, upheld.[10]

Negotiations in Rambouillet came to a head with NATO threatening to bomb Serbia if they failed to sign the agreement. The Rambouillet demands, and the result at the conclusion at the end of the war were critically different. At Rambouillet, the occupying force to keep the peace in Kosovo was to be NATO. At the end of the war it was agreed the force should be from the United Nations. At Rambouillet, the NATO force was to have free access to any part of Yugoslavia. At the end of the war the UN force is restricted within the borders of Kosovo. At Rambouillet, the proposal contained a vote after 3 years to determine the future status of Kosovo. At the end of the war Kosovo is recognized by the international community as an integral part of Yugoslavia. Slobodan Milosevic had a major victory on all three counts.[11]

NATO argued that Kosovo was a 'humanitarian intervention'. That gross violations of human rights were being perpetrated in Kosovo that were unacceptable to the international community. They also argued that it was a legal intervention under the universal principle of self-defence. The facts and the law do not measure up to the position of the United States and its NATO allies. The mass graves of tens of thousands of people supposed to have been killed by Serb forces in Kosovo failed to materialise. The post-war revised estimates of the numbers killed in the guerrilla war before the NATO bombing began is at about 2500. This increase in fatalities only occurred after the Dayton Accords when it became clear that an independent Kosovo would not be part of the Bosnian peace settlement.[12] As a result, the KLA took up arms against the Serbian forces in Kosovo. This is comparable to other civil strife in Africa, and possibly Chechnya and Turkey where no international action has been taken. The humanitarian intervention argument in defence of action against Serbia, therefore, was arguably partisan and spurious.

Unlike the Organization of African Unity's (OAU) intervention in Sierre Leone, NATO had no Security Council authority for intervention in Kosovo directly in breach of Article 2(4) of the Charter respecting the sovereign integrity of Member States.[13] The rules of engagement and other relevant instructions have not been revealed to major human rights bodies such as Amnesty International for determination as to whether they complied with international humanitarian law. Amnesty International has concerns as to whether NATO took sufficient precautions in selecting targets and executing its attacks to minimize civilian casualties. Several attacks, such as the bombing of the Serbian State television building in Belgrade killing 15 civilians, and the missile attack on a train carrying civilians, were particularly questionable in terms of international humanitarian law.

In the final analysis NATO's arguments regarding the legality of its actions are weak at best. While it acted against its own Charter, it is also questionable whether sufficient human rights violations were being perpetrated by the Serbian army on the civilian Albanian population of Kosovo or whether casualties were those of a civil war. The argument NATO put forward pertaining to European collective self-defence is weak on geopolitical grounds, and the grounds for aggressive action against another State. Security Council approval under Chapter VII had not been granted.

In addition to the legal question, the political question at the heart of the conflict remained unsettled. In *Foreign Affairs*, the most highly respected American journal dealing with international issues, Michael Mandelbaum noted that the Albanians were fighting for the right to independence based on the right to national self-determination. The Serbs fought to keep Kosovo part of Yugoslavia. While insisting that Kosovo have autonomy, it also asserted it must remain part of Yugoslavia. Mandelbaum goes on to note that 'The alliance had therefore intervened in a civil war and defeated one side, but embraced the position of the party it had defeated on the issue over which the war had been fought'.[14] The position of the Americans and NATO after the war was very different to the proposition brought to the table at Rambouillet.

Madeleine Albright seemed to have believed that three to four days of bombing would bring the Serbs to heel.[15] How often have the Americans believed that bombing alone would bring an enemy into line, and how often have they been wrong? It is also worth noting that to try to end centuries old problems with a surgical stroke – such as a military action – would be difficult at best.

The West's views of responsibility and culpability in the Balkans have been, from the first, highly partisan. CARE Australia has been working with 500,000 Serbian refugees who were ethnically cleansed from Tudjman's Croatia[16] – a forced movement that was essentially condoned by the Dayton accords. But the real problems in the Balkans go back long before the current crises – expectations of a quick solution are fallacious.

While the bombing of Serbia continued, Prime Minister Blair made a speech in Chicago as part of the 50th Anniversary of NATO. He said he viewed the action in the Balkans to be an example of NATO ethical actions in this century. If he really meant it, the consequences are alarming. It is frightening enough for a leader of a major State to make such a statement without understanding its consequences. If ever such an idea came about, it would re-establish wars of ideology as a major disruptive facet of this century.

Three important questions come out of the Kosovo experience:

1 Is it possible to wage war on humanitarian grounds?
2 Is the rule of law compatible with the use of force?
3 What should the rule of law mean in an international setting?

Humanitarian intervention

There are quite a few examples of humanitarian intervention being used as an excuse to invade a neighboring country. In such instances the legal tension emerges between the universal acceptance and regard for human rights, and the basis of the international system – that of protection and respect for the territorial integrity of States.

History shows us the world's reluctance to accept humanitarian intervention as a reason for aggression against another State. Tanzania was widely condemned as it moved in to Uganda to oust the invidious regime of Idi Amin.[17] An even more potent example of the refusal to accept humanitarian intervention as a reasonable justification for aggression was the international community's response to the invasion of Kampuchea by Vietnam. After four years from year zero, Pol Pot had succeeded in killing between one and two million people. The Vietnamese put a halt to the killings in 1979 when they invaded and liberated Phnom Penh. Pol Pot and his Khmer Rouge fled into the mountains and into neighboring Thailand.

Geopolitical considerations (particularly the United States' position towards Vietnam following the Vietnam war and the unresolved issue of American servicemen Missing in Action) meant that Vietnam was not hailed as a liberator of the persecuted peoples of Kampuchea, but as an aggressive invader. The Khmer Rouge, despite the extraordinary and un-humanitarian nature of its regime, maintained the Kampuchean seat at the General Assembly for many years after the brutality of the regime was widely known and understood. In addition, Cambodia was the victim of a trade embargo, which was not lifted until 1991.

We now know that the major humanitarian problems in relation to Kosovo occurred after the bombing started. The United States is enthusiastic about the effectiveness of bombing from afar as a means of humanitarian intervention. Yet in relation to Kosovo, a number of NATO advisers suggested that if the Serb forces were unable to come into direct contact with the enemy – NATO – that the humanitarian crisis would be expanded many times. Their frustration would be carried out in Kosovo itself. This analysis proved to be true.

The mass exodus of refugees from Kosovo was predictable, and foreseen. Why, in a so-called humanitarian war, was there no preparation, and no provision made for those people in the first instance? In addition, why, in a humanitarian war, were there, according to independent reports, up to 500 civilians killed by questionable NATO targeting?

Somalia is an example, perhaps, of a truly humanitarian intervention, at least at the outset. Over 100,000 Somalis had died of starvation. The internal security situation had deteriorated into a state of anarchy and aid workers were under threat. There were no jobs, no administration, no judiciary or government or police force, there was no rule of law.

With the end of the Cold War there was no real political reason motivating the intervention of the international community, but the harrowing scenes of starving children demanded action. For the *first time* a Security Council decision was made under Chapter VII to allow for an international humanitarian force to enter Somalia, and establish an environment enabling the satisfactory distribution of aid to the civilian population.

The fact that a political solution to the problem was not a part of the original UN mandate is an omission made by the United Nations and United States for which the Somalis are still paying today. It is an omission that ultimately led to the failure of the UN rescue plan and is an important lesson to be learned as Somalia continues in anarchy today.

Apart from the desperate need to feed the starving there was a major and urgent need for someone to be appointed to Somalia as Special Envoy with the authority to bring the three factions together in order to establish a Government of National Reconciliation.

At the beginning of the UN effort this need seemed to be recognized in the appointment of Ambassador Sahnoun, a highly intelligent and committed person, who was never supported by the UN Headquarters in New York.[18] After his resignation, nobody with adequate qualifications to undertake the two-to-three year task of political and social rehabilitation was ever appointed to Somalia. How Secretary-General Boutros Boutros-Ghali and the major states determining UN policy could have permitted such an omission to occur is beyond comprehension. Especially as there was a significant lobbying effort at the time to get such an appointment made. It is also curious in light of the fact that in Cambodia, just such a UN mission was established to enable that country to make the social and political transition required to satisfy the humanitarian needs of returning refugees and a new peace settlement.

The use of war, the terms of 'humanitarian intervention' for alleged humanitarian purposes is, ultimately, an admission of failure. A war will generally result in greater humanitarian problems than existed beforehand, and the world should have the wit and the will to achieve a humanitarian objective by peaceful means.

It is not unreasonable to ask, within a global context, when humanitarian intervention *is* justified. Was Vietnam's invasion of Kampuchea solely humanitarian? Was NATO's war in Kosovo humanitarian at all? Or was Somalia the only true humanitarian intervention the world has seen in recent years even if the intervention did fail to find a political solution? It appears that the jury is still out on this issue. The question remains: how can we move to protect human rights, and ensure humanitarianism prevails?

The history of 'humanitarian intervention' has shown that protection of human rights is really determined on the whim of the 'great powers'. Whose human rights are they prepared to support? At present the geo-political realities and interests of particular States contribute to the determination of whose human rights are, or are not, supported by the international community.

Human rights should exist as was intended in the Universal Declaration and subsequent human rights treaties, as a matter of fact, for all people, 'without distinction of any kind, such as race, color, sex, language, religion, political or other opinion, national or social origin, property, birth or other status' (UDHR Article 2). Signature to the Optional Protocol of the International Covenant on Civil and Political Rights (ICCPR) goes some way towards protecting the rights of individuals and groups in participating States Parties. But until States are prepared to agree to the jurisdiction of an international body, with powers of enforcement, such universal human rights can only remain a utopian dream.

The rule of law and the rule of force

The second question brought about by the Kosovo scenario is whether the rule of law is compatible with the use of force?

Most commentators would agree that it is, and that Chapter VII of the UN Charter, and far-reaching powers of the Security Council thereunder, were expressly inserted to enable the legal use of force against an aggressor nation or rebel State. The requirements for the lawful use of force are generally agreed on: proper authorization, just and achievable political ends, and the employment of appropriate means.

The Gulf War has been heralded as the first legal war. (With the exception of Korea whose Security Council Chapter VII resolution enabling UN forces to go to South Korea was 'slipped through' while the Soviet Union was out of the room). The allied forces had authorization from the Security Council. Their purpose – to rid Kuwait of the Iraqi forces – was just and achievable, and they could possibly have been said to use appropriate means in most instances although some of their targeting was questionable under the Geneva Conventions and Optional Protocols.[19]

The only safe and secure system with regards to the use of force and maintenance of the rule of law is if it is done through and with the support of the United Nations. Any other use of force should be considered illegal unless directly for ones own self-defence, or the defence of an ally under attack.

Middle-ranking States such as Australia have everything to gain by such a regime. And the veto power in the Security Council should be regarded as a protection against the abuse of that power. The greatest danger to global peace has always been the arbitrary use of power by a supreme power.

A global rule of law?

Third, where a war has been fought illegally, such as the NATO bombing of Serbia, what is the legal redress? Can the people of Serbia whose loved ones died seek compensation? Is it possible to hold international institutions accountable when they are found to have committed crimes against humanity of which Amnesty International has argued that NATO is guilty?

At present, the short answer is NO. The United Nations cannot be held responsible for their failure to act to prevent the genocide of Rwanda, and NATO cannot be brought to trial before any international court of justice.

One option open to States is to take the Member States of an international institution to the International Court of Justice (ICJ). Yugoslavia has undertaken just such a case against the individual member states of NATO.

But while there is voluntary competence, combined with a lack of enforcement measures or means of sanction against the guilty party, the international courts have limited power. While there are laws governing the use of force, in an international context it appears there is far too inadequate judicial review or accountability with regard to the application of those rules. The Security Council is not accountable to any institution other than, in a roundabout way, the General Assembly. The ICJ has shown its unwillingness to make judgments regarding the legality of Security Council resolutions.

In this context, the commencement of the International Criminal Court (ICC) is an urgent priority for the progress of international law and international justice. It is important because this Court will have the the capacity, among other things, to bring individuals, not States, to trial for crimes such as genocide, war crimes and crimes against humanity. It is an important landmark for women who find, for the first time, rape categorized as a crime against humanity and, when committed during time of conflict, a war crime. The ICC will have the capacity to act when national courts are unable to unwilling to bring people to trial. Another breakthrough with the Court is that not only States, but also the Court's prosecutors may bring cases before the Court.

The rule of law, if it is to mean anything, must apply to the powerful as well as the weak – to democracies as well as dictatorships. And until we can establish a system of international law, which is universal, we have government by the powerful, government by the wealthy. If that is not checked it will lead to chaos.

The reality of international politics has always relied on the opportunity to do something, as well as the need and a willingness to act. If there was an effective legal regime operating in the international sphere, the need could provide adequate cause for redress in an international court, a court not of voluntary but of compulsory competence. And in many ways we are back where we started for if an international court has compulsory competence then it also has supremacy over the highest courts of its member States. The conflict between international law and domestic sovereignty arises again – and awaits resolution.

How to establish an international system of international law which all countries, even the most powerful will respect, may be the greatest challenge to be faced in this century. But with all its complexities and difficulties, it must be met if we are to get to a civilized community of nations. Clearly, as both the events of September 11 and the war in Iraq demonstrate, there is still a long way to go.

September 11 and its consequences

Regrettably, recent geopolitical events have moved us further away from, rather than towards, a functioning international political and legal system. The terror attacks on the World Trade Centre Towers on 11 September 2001, changed America's attitude substantially. From this point on it was America's view that prevailed. A new unilateralism was born. Here we had the most powerful nation on earth being attacked in a planned, systematic and terrifying way. Terrorism by its very nature has no respect for the international laws of war or for the fate of innocent bystanders, and September 11 demonstrated this fact clearly, dramatically and in a manner totally without mercy or precedent in its scale. The American nation was rocked. The implications and impact of the attack are still only beginning to be understood.

In its response America was swift. The international community condemned the terrorist act and NATO, for the first time in the history of the alliance, invoked its constitution declaring that an ally had been attacked and that NATO would assist in its defence. President George W. Bush made it clear that there were only two sides – good and evil. 'You're either with us, or against us', he said, demanding an allegiance unlike any ever before.

The United Nations had an important role to play immediately after the terror attacks, yet it was sidelined very early on while the United States followed its own course of self-defence and counter-attack. Attacks on the United States would not go unpunished. A war on terror was declared. This war included not only the terrorists but also those who worked with them and the countries that harbored them. A wide, sweeping coalition was formed including America's old enemies, China and the Russian Federation. Still, the United Nations was marginalized.

When Saddam Hussein invaded Kuwait, vital interests for the industrialized world were at stake. First, territorial gain through the use of force could not be tolerated. Second, it was essential for the economies of the West (and particularly that of America) that the oil fields of Kuwait remain in friendly hands. The Desert Storm response was unique as the Security Council invoked Chapter VII and the United Nations force was formed.[20] The UN acted in the manner for which it was formed – a global coalition for the protection and promotion of world peace. While it was led by the United States, it was undoubtedly a global coalition, with the approval of the Security Council.[21]

The approach of President Bush in 1990–91, and President George W. Bush in 2001, just 10 years later, is markedly different. The unilateralism born of September 11 meant that George W. Bush chose a course of action and expects allies to line up behind him. If they do not it will not necessarily affect the manner in which he conducts his war on terrorism.

In the past the power of the American President had been checked by the balance of the Cold War. The practice of consultation was strong. The ideas and views of allies were carefully considered and played an important role in the international arena. Since September 11, the already increasingly unilateralist United States, has to a large extent, decided that what is good for the United States is good for the world. Meaningful consultations appear to be a thing of the past.

President Bush is clearly the most powerful person on earth but he does not want to use that power for his own ends. The exercise of such unlimited power requires a sense of balance and delicacy. Nevertheless, the President's statements with respect to the 'war on terror' have raised significant concerns. One such source of concern is the ultimate impact of any one nation having so much more power than any other. If America chooses its own course of action against all terrorists throughout the world, no one and nothing on earth can stop it.

There are other disturbing tendencies in western nations, especially in the United States, Britain and Australia. Nothing can ever justify what was done to the World Trade Centre and to the Pentagon. These were barbaric acts and certainly deserve the heaviest penalties. A war against terrorism needs to be pursued but the horror of the events and the damage those events caused should not preclude a debate about how the international community should properly go about its business.

One problem is that that people involved in such things are now seen as so terrible, so outside the civilized world, that we no longer need treat them as people and behavior on our part, which we would otherwise condemn, is thus accepted and condoned.

The world has had a long march through some two centuries to try and create civilized behavior. The Geneva Conventions were a landmark. They determined how prisoners of war should be treated. Standards of behavior were set. We in the West have taken the harshest view of countries that breach those standards.

The Geneva Conventions set certain minimum standards. There is no part in the convention which says, 'if my enemy does not treat me decently, I need not treat him decently'. There is nothing in the Geneva Conventions that suggest that condemnation of a particular act provides justification for unreasonable alien or unjust behavior. The Conventions do not allow exceptions on the grounds of necessity or self defence. People detained as war criminals from the last World War, from wars since, the wars in the Balkans, were all treated according to these Conventions.

It would appear that some alleged war criminals in the Balkans were responsible for more deaths than Bin Laden in relation to the World Trade Centre. Nobody has said that therefore justifies that they may be held in unusually harsh conditions or that they do not deserve basic human treatment. But now there is a subtle acceptance in the air: these terrorists are so evil that we ourselves do not need to behave with common humanity. In the minds of many, they are judged guilty without trial, without 'due process'. And so we have individuals from all parts of the world held, beyond the rule of international and national law, at Guantanamo Bay in Cuba.

I also read into this a strong element of racism because it is easier for people to move into that thought mode because the people concerned are principally Iraqis, Afghans and Muslims. If they were Caucasian and Christian, would that alter the judgment?

Terror takes many forms. It has been present in Northern Ireland for decades. It would be interesting to ask President Bush whether his 'war on terror' will include war on those who have funded and supplied arms to the IRA through those decades. We should not forget the Irish Republican Army (IRA) sought to blow up Prime Minister Thatcher and half her government.[22] If there is to be war on terror, it needs to be war on all terrorism, not just terrorism which meets the disapproval of the United States.

There is a golden rule that should govern the behavior of all democracies, indeed all people, if we want a civilized world. That golden rule proclaims that all people, endowed with reason and conscience, must accept a responsibility to each and all, to families and communities, to races, nations and religions in a spirit of solidarity: 'What you do not wish to be done to yourself, do not do to others'. This is the only basis on which there can be civilized behavior within a nation and between nations. If bad behavior justifies bad behavior by another, then there will inevitably be a competition to see who will be toughest, perhaps in the hope that that will deter the opponent. That has never worked; it will not work now.

Great errors, terrible acts, do not justify breaching that rule. We need to act by our own standards and not by lower standards that others may set. By so doing we would hope to move to a world where those higher standards were more widely accepted. A great step forward was made in 1948 with the Proclamation of the Universal Declaration of Human Rights. Steady but slow progress has been made in the years since to advance human rights and decent behavior. The West needs to look closely at its own house, to make sure that what happens in the coming months does not defile those standards. We need future generations to be able to read about what we did in our time, so that they will conclude that we behaved with humanity and with common decency, in accordance with 'due process' and the rule of law. If we do not, we betray ourselves and our futures.

Australia provides a recent, domestic example of the breach of this principle. After September 11, the Australian government drew linkages between terrorists and asylum-seekers, thus justifying its ill-treatment of people seeking refuge on its shores. It is now abundantly clear that Australia is treating asylum-seekers with great inhumanity. People driven through years of desperation have pressures on their minds which most of us cannot comprehend. These pressures are obviously magnified many times when women and children are involved.

The government, however, won an election on defending Australia's borders yet our borders were not under threat; the rhetoric, the suggestion that there were millions queuing up to come to Australia, was never true. Four or five thousand people a year, many of them women and children offer no threat to the sovereignty of Australia. Europe manages a problem of over 400,000 asylum-seekers a year with much greater compassion and humanity than Australia shows to a relatively trivial number.

Australia has denied such people 'due process' under normal protection of the law. The government has put them outside the law and thus sought to justify treatment that would be condemned in any civilized society. Their sin, exercising their right in accordance with the Universal Declaration of Human Rights and the International Refugee Convention, is nothing more than seeking safe haven. Australia has responded harshly. Their periods in prison are often lengthy, running into years.[23] So much for the international rule of law. So much for common humanity.

The war in Iraq

A further, decisive shift away from an international rule of law occurred with the advent of the recent war in Iraq. Nobody doubted that the 'coalition of the willing' would win this war. Nor can there be any argument about the barbarity of Saddam Hussein's regime. But proper debate must now take place about the means used by the coalition and the cost to the world of this 'successful' military intervention.

The reasons given for the war have shifted backwards and forwards between the need to eliminate weapons of mass destruction and the need to provide humanitarian assistance to the Iraqi people. The apparent indifference of wealthy nations to the humanitarian plight of people in many other countries makes it difficult to believe the humanitarian argument. One cannot help but wonder instead whether a desire to remove one of Israel's major enemies and the need to gain control of significant oil supplies were also reasons for the American action. Whatever the reasons, the cost is high and we need to understand how fundamentally this war has altered the world.

Since World War II, major states have sought to make the United Nations the principal vehicle to ensure peace and security and to build a better world based on law and international treaties, rather than on the power of the gun. Again, however, President Bush made it plain from the very outset that if the UN Security Council did not do what America wanted in relation to Iraq, America would act alone, or with the so-called 'coalition of the willing'.

If the world's most powerful nation is not prepared to concede that other states may have a view worth considering and, even before debate is joined, announces that its view must prevail, how can an international, political and legal system work?

The Bush administration also effectively destroyed the Atlantic alliance and has caused deep divisions in NATO. The United States apparently is not concerned about these consequences. It would probably say that the destruction of the international system is a pity, but of little account beside the need to follow the 'right' path– the American path. The hawks in Washington are jubilant, believing America has rightfully exercised its power. Any great power must be persuasive if it wishes to maintain great influence. The Bush administration, however, has demonstrated that, in its view, persuasion is not critical.

We will never know whether the majority view of the UN Security Council would have won the day without a war. However, the argument in the Council that diplomacy needed more time was powerful, especially given that Hans Blix's inspection teams were making progress.[24] In this way, the divisions created by the unilateral action may have been avoided.

The debate here is between those who believe in the development of an international system founded upon law and agreement and those who believe in the exercise of American power by an America that has become impatient with diplomacy. America's patent contempt for alternate points of view has divided Europe, fractured the Atlantic alliance, weakened the Security Council and done grievous damage to the efforts of the last 55 years to establish a system based on international law and treaty-making.

This is a heavy price to pay for a war whose purpose may still fail. At the time of writing, weapons of mass destruction still have not been found. The United States sent its own inspection team into Iraq, saying there was no further role for UN inspection teams. In doing so, it should have known that much of the world would be deeply suspicious of US findings. Even so, the US inspections themselves have turned up no significant new evidence of the existence of such weapons. Indeed, the Chief US weapons inspector has said he does not now believe that such weapons were in existence at the time of the war's commencement. If it is finally demonstrated that there are no weapons of mass destruction in Iraq, it would clearly be deeply disturbing to the United States and the 'coalition of the willing'. The demolition of this argument and weakness of the humanitarian justification would leave its cupboard almost bare.

There have been reports that the United States wishes to punish France because France took a different view regarding the war. Some have tried to suggest that this is a commercial matter alone but that is not really the point. It is another example of the US not being prepared to concede that other nations have points of view that should be taken into account.

How can the UN system work with effect if the US is so determined that its view must prevail? That America holds such a view is likely to result in further global instability. Are countries that disagree to be punished for their temerity? Is the real American purpose to establish a world in which no country or group of countries can challenge America's will? Does the Bush administration believe it is establishing the foundation stones of American dominance through this century and into the next? Consider the frightening prospect that opens up as we move further into this century. Will there be a new, iron definition of democracy, American style. Fortunately, there are some slim signs that this worst-case scenario may not come about. In recent months, the United States has been sobered by its experience in post-war Iraq. The recent Security Council resolution providing a mandate for coalition forces in Iraq was a first, small step towards a longer term solution.

At present the United States maintains de facto political authority in Iraq. Contracts for reconstruction are let by America, mostly to American companies. Iraqis are not participating fully in important decisions affecting the country. Guerilla attacks are better coordinated and increasingly dangerous. The Iraqi Governing Council is beginning to realize that to be effective, it must become increasingly nationalistic. America wants Turkish troops in the country. The Council does not. The US wants an incremental, indirectly democratic transition of power. The leaders of the Shiite majority want direct elections as soon as possible. How can this dangerous situation be turned around?

In these difficult circumstances, the US strategy will need revision if American forces are to avoid further humiliation. Despite earlier bombast, President Bush needs the United Nations. He needs to recognize the high costs of staying in Iraq. The real act of statesmanship available to him is to change course. He may have to trade some loss of face now for what he could later claim to be ultimate success.

This would involve the following steps. Full political control would be ceded to the Security Council but on certain conditions. Major states, including major Islamic states, would need to commit themselves to the process and support an appeal for funds and resources, including troops. President Bush's international coalition of the first Gulf War would re-emerge in a different form. The reconstruction of Iraq would be fully 'internationalized'. Iraqis would increasingly be making decisions regarding the future of their own country.

While the United States presence in Iraq encourages terrorists and Iraqi nationalists in their guerrilla war, the United Nations with a diverse group of states, including Islamic states, could offer the hope of an early and peaceful outcome. Continuing on the present course, however, will divide and destabilize the world and make it increasingly difficult to justify the claim that the war against terror is not a war against Islam. Indeed, to this point, the war in Iraq has set back significantly the war against terror.

Whatever happens, I am hopeful that neither the United States, nor any other country, will embark on further, pre-emptive wars. Nations should, and will, turn back to the United Nations and recognize that the only ultimate security will come through the processes of the Security Council and the incremental development of a truly international rule of law. By putting a post-war resolution to the United Nations seeking sanction for present action, the United States itself appears to have recognized, at least in these circumstances, that even the most powerful and wealthy country in the world needs the rest of the world if a more stable global order is to be established.

It is far better to internationalize the situation now, to return it to the Security Council, on the condition that the international community is involved in devising and implementing steps for Iraq's reconstruction and early political freedom. If undertaken successfully, these initiatives may make a major contribution towards the development of a strategy of humanitarian intervention under international law and towards a more enduring, international security.

Conclusion

Absolute power corrupts absolutely. Not an original thought but, at the end of the day, in international politics the most important thing in my view is due process. Often we think of due process, if we think of it at all, as cumbersome, bureaucratic and a waste of time and resources. But without it everything we know that holds civilized society together will collapse. Due process is that on which the rule of law depends, it ensures that trials are conducted fairly and without discrimination, it protects our human rights and prevents those who are in positions of great power from abusing it. Due process ensures that liberties that have been hard-won and fought for over centuries are maintained and not prejudiced.

I have been in a country where there was no due process, and there was no civilization as we know it. A country racked by violence. A country with no government, no administration, no jobs, no security forces, no police force and no amenities. It was a country of social and cultural sophistication that had gone to rack and ruin. And in that country there was a saying that went like this:

> I am Somali, my country against the world
> I am Somali, my clan against my country
> I am Somali, me and my brother against my clan
> I am Somali, me against my brother.

Somalia remains a global tragedy. An opportunity for great things was lost in the lack of will to effect political change. The United Nations had the opportunity to bring about a lasting peace in Somalia but instead chose to focus on the humanitarian mandate at the peril of the political future of the country. In 1993 two Black Hawk helicopters were shot down over the Green Line of Mogadishu, American soldiers were dragged through the streets and finally American and UN forces pulled out. Somalia was left to its own devices and is still in political turmoil today. The New World Order heralded by George Bush senior collapsed before it really began.

Australia, along with other smaller and medium-sized nations, has a strong interest in ensuring that such an outcome will not be repeated and that there will be a rule of law in the international arena. For so long international law has been dependent on a system of mutual accountability. A sense of mutual interest in upholding international obligations is essential to a system which still largely depends on a symbolic handshake, a system for which there is little recourse to the law.

Globalization means, among other things, that the world is being brought closer together through travel, communication and the internet. The information passed around the world is unprecedented and nations can no longer act within their own domestic jurisdiction and practise their own national sovereign independence without consequences further afield. Some commentators argue that the burgeoning human rights instruments interfere with national sovereignty in the sense that it is no longer possible for a State to do whatever it wants within its own domestic jurisdiction. The world will no longer turn a blind eye and say that is within their jurisdiction and has nothing to do with us. However, by signing on to human rights treaties a State is exercising its own free choice, the free choice of a sovereign nation to be bound by certain international obligations. Such signatures are not imposed from outside. The obligations that result, therefore, are as a result of an exercise of national sovereignty and cannot be said to derogate from such. A parallel analogy exists. Within a state there is a plethora of domestic law which regulates the behavior of companies and individuals to ensure an orderly and peaceful society. In the international arena there is an increasing amount of international law developing with the intent of keeping states in line and well-behaved. Where an individual within a State breaks the law there are mechanisms and sanctions available. In the international arena such sanctions do not, in reality, exist.

The ICC will go some way towards increasing the accountability of leaders and military personnel in time of war. While the ICC will not address all international human rights violations, or the issue of the unilateralism of the United States, it moves towards establishing a system of global accountability. A system where individuals, more and more the subject of international law, fall under the jurisdiction of a court which upholds and implements that same international law.

Ultimately, countries of a like mind should continue to work for an international system and put in place the fabric and structures that are needed. If that means the United States stands aside, so be it. At least the rest of the world would not be held back because the superpower thinks it is an unwarranted and unwelcome intrusion upon its authority. The old Westphalian idea of the sovereign nation state must not be static. While states will always exist, and are the very cornerstone of the international system as it is today, without an accepted and binding international order with the United Nations at its centre we are destined to a future where the powerful nations of the world make the rules but are not necessarily bound by them. The Security Council is structured in a way that on the one hand gives some prospect of world peace through its diversity, and on the other risks being, as Dulles said, 'a plaything of the rich and powerful'. Latterly, as the events of September 11 and the war in Iraq demonstrate clearly, the politics of opportunity has dominated due process and the rule of law in the international arena. It is apparent that there are different rules for different nations, and different responses by the international community to the same problems in different nations.

Some international lawyers have said that we are waiting for Grotius[25]: for an international lawyer who is able to make sense of the new international order, and the new necessities without wholly discarding the old. We can only hope that he or she arrives soon. But whatever the future holds, of one thing I am certain: the world needs due process and the rule of law. A world where the rule of law is as valid and justiciable in the international arena as it is domestically. Where it has equal strength between the rich and the poor, the East and the West, the North and the South, the strong and the weak. A rule of law for all nations and all peoples. A rule of law that is consistent and where human rights violations in one place are treated as harshly as those in another. A rule of law where the 'dignity and worth of the human person, in the equal rights of men and women and of nations large and small' are valued and upheld.[26]

Acknowledgements

This chapter is an updated version of one originally published in Fraser, M. *Common Ground: issues that should bind and not divide us*, Camberwell, Vic.: Viking, 2002, chapter 4. The author and editor would like to thank Penguin Group Australia for assenting to the reproduction of the chapter in this updated form.

Notes

1 UN Chart Article 1(1).
2 UN Charter Article 1(2).

3 John Foster Dulles was requested by President Harry Truman to assist in the concluding of a Peace Treaty with Japan in 1950. Dulles was appointed Secretary of State by President Dwight Eisenhower.
4 On 21 December 1988, a Pan Am Boeing 747 was blown up over the Scottish town of Lockerbie, killing all 259 on board and 11 on the ground. After years of international wrangling, two Libyans were brought to trial, under Scottish law, in Holland.
5 The *Rainbow Warrior* was blown up in Auckland Harbour on 7 July 1985 by two members of the French Security Service, to stop it sailing to French territorial waters to protest against French nuclear testing.
6 Grenville-Wood, G. 'Sanctions Against Libya Set a Questionable Precedent', *Bulletin of the UN Association of Canada* (1993).
7 Ibid.
8 Mikhail Gorbachev was Soviet President from 1990–1991; Boris Yeltsin was President of the Russian Republic from 1991–99.
9 Talks held at Rambouillet, France, in February 1999, to reach an interim agreement for peace and self-government in Kosovo.
10 The term *uti possidetis juris* concerns the principle that international boundaries follow former colonial administrative boundaries.
11 Slobodan Milosevic was President of Serbia 1990–91, and President of Yugoslavia 1997–2000. He is currently on trial for war crimes at the Hague.
12 The Dayton Peace Accords, signed in December 1995, outlined United States President Bill Clinton's negotiations to end the war in Bosnia.
13 In 1995–96, the UN in collaboration with the OAU attempted to negotiate a settlement with the Revolutionary United Front, which has overthrown Sierra Leone's government.
14 Mandelbaum, M. 'A Perfect Failure: NATO's war against Yugoslavia', *Foreign Affairs*, vol. 78, no. 5, September–October 1999, available at: http://www.foreignpolicy2000.org/library/issuebriefs/readingnotes/fa_mandelbaum.html (accessed 18 March 2004).
15 Madeleine Albright was appointed Secretary of State by US President, Bill Clinton in 1996.
16 Franjo Tudjman was elected first President of the State of Croatia in 1990.
17 Idi Amin seized power in a coup in 1971 while President Milton Obote was out of the country. Amin is alleged to have responsible for the deaths of over 300,000 people. He was ousted by invading Tanzanian forces in 1979 and fled the country.
18 Mohammed Sahnoun was appointed joint UN/OUA Special Representative for the Great Lakes Region of Africa in January 1977.
19 The Geneva Conventions of 12 August 1949 (and the additional Protocols of 8 June 1977) are an international agreement outlining the treatment of the sick, the wounded and the prisoners of war.
20 Desert Storm was the military codename for the attack on Iraq by the allied forces.
21 The only other time there has been such a force was during the war between North and South Korea. The vote was whisked through the Security Council while the Russians were out of the room.
22 On 12 October 1984, two explosions damaged the Brighton hotel in which the Conservative Party's annual convention was being held.
23 While the Australian government calls these detention centres, they are in fact prisons, where the inmates have not been tried or convicted before any court of law.
24 Hans Blix was the United Nations' Chief Weapons Inspector immediately prior to the outbreak of war in Iraq.
25 Dutch humanist Hugo Grotius, whose *On the Law of War and Peace* (1625) was a detailed study of international law.
26 UN Charter, Preamble.

9 The role of the military in globalizing the rule of law

Michael Kelly

> God grant that not only the love of liberty but a thorough knowledge of the rights of man may pervade all the nations of the earth, so that a philosopher may set his foot anywhere on its surface and say: 'This is my country'.[1]
>
> (Benjamin Franklin)

Introduction

There are many aspects to the phenomenon of globalization. Much of the impetus for globalization has been generated by technology and to the extent that these technologies are driven by the demands of global capital the benefits that have been drawn from it accrue mostly to the transnational players in the global economy. There are, of course, many spin-offs for the individual, but these have been unevenly distributed in global terms. The world of migratory capital and industry is not one on which I wish to dwell, however, other than to focus on what this has meant to those military forces which are most regularly called upon to serve the international community. Along with the end of the cold war, globalization has added to the forces that have stirred ethnic, communal and religious seismic forces, whose fault lines run through and within national boundaries. Perceptions of or real inequities in competition for resources, the dislocation and trauma caused by the rapid and large-scale movements of capital and industry, the global effects of a degraded environment which in turn feeds the competition for scarce resources and an ever-growing population have exacerbated insecurity and violence. The increasing concentration of populations in the urban environment has also created zones of social dislocation and tension and underworlds full of potential for conflict and the breakdown of law and order.

There has also been a globalization of aspirations. With the increasing reach of global communications, people around the world are seeking the same material and personal freedoms they see portrayed on television. This has fuelled a large-scale flow of refugees and illegal immigrants and the spawning of an industry to exploit them. Where countries have progressed to greater political liberty they have often been plagued by a lack of legal and technical infrastructure to control the excesses of unfettered capital including that controlled by mafia style organizations, which are also increasingly acting globally. The resources that can be controlled by these illegal organizations, such as the drug cartels of South America, rival or surpass those of many States. At the same time, there are significant opponents of what is seen as Western dominance and materialism and some of these opponents are highly organized, well-funded and committed to promoting their message through extreme violence. Often the very instruments of the 'rule of law' in unstable States are the source of major human rights violations or the reason for the generation of insurgent pressure.

No greater challenge faces the world today than reaffirming or establishing the rule of law as the foundation for the regulation of human dispute and interaction.[2] It is a challenge that requires the effort of all men and women who should be 'thinking globally and acting locally'. Non Government Organizations (NGOs) have had much to say and contribute on related aspects of the rule of law in terms of food, health and in some cases development, as well as alerting the world to human rights emergencies. Particular responsibility, however, rests with the organized and resourced instruments of States as the agencies best positioned to act on the larger or more immediate scale in specific rule of law issues that no NGO can address. There are two dimensions to this responsibility – action that should be taken to prevent the slide into anarchy or systemic violation of human rights, and action that should be taken to arrest a situation that has already passed beyond the preventative phase.

At first glance there would be many 'lay' readers who would regard the concept of the role of the military in globalizing the rule of law as contradictory or at least be strongly suspicious of what contribution the military could make to this struggle. That would be an ill-informed impression or opinion based understandably on the image created by the all too common recent phenomenon of unconstrained armed elements or military forces deposing governments and undermining of the rule of law. The well established democracies have mastered this issue through the strong culture of democracy and respect for law that they have built. This is extended to the military serving these States by embedding thoroughly in their ethos the fact that they exist to defend the democratic order and way of life. These forces are typically well aware that they may be called upon to band with other like forces to defend and advance the ideals of liberty, democracy and the rule of law.

What is meant by the phrase 'rule of law' in the international setting? Quite simply, the reliance by the majority in any national society and the community of nations on a formal process to regulate human and State relations, whereby a neutral mandated agency is the only legitimate wielder of force for the common good. Obviously there are degrees in the quality of the rule of law and the highest form is where the formal process itself is commensurate with fundamental standards of equity and justice. What might these standards be? The distillation of general principles of criminal law in the process of creating the International Criminal Court has helped to highlight these as will be discussed later. In addition, there are formal international instruments such as the Universal Declaration of Human Rights, The International Convention on Civil and Political Rights as well as numerous treaties and documents dealing with torture, discrimination and justice standards. Beyond these things, however, the rule of law is not really about laws and institutions, it is about culture. The real issue that faces the international community is how to build a culture of the rule of law. The grafting of formal standards on places like Bosnia[3] and Cambodia[4] has only taken the issue so far, with the effective cultural dimension still largely missing. That is a battle that is not won overnight and takes generations to nurture and perpetual vigilance to maintain.

The tackling of the rule of law issue in this context is a long-term campaign and this campaign is characterized by many phases. The military resources of the international community have a role to play in a number of these.

Until recent times, international action by the armed forces of allied democracies has been directed largely at securing the international legal order by responding to the territorial aggression of States. Contemporary operations are more likely to be driven by the need to redress the aggression of State or even non-State actors against the human rights of individuals.[5] This in itself is part of the phenomenon of the growing status of the individual in international law and politics in a way that is eroding the inviolability of State sovereignty.[6]

Military organizations like the Australian Defence Force (ADF) increasingly find themselves acting as servants of the international community in the struggle to defend human rights and promote the globalization of the rule of law. This role has two dimensions. The most visible is the operational deployment of troops into a situation that has already passed beyond the realms of persuasion, inducement and non-violent coercion. These environments pose complex challenges and have forced major doctrinal, training and force structure analysis. The remedies or responses adopted in these operations are part of a dynamic environment populated with and shaped by various international and local actors, as well as physical, cultural, demographic and threat factors. Evolutionary developments of particular interest in this area currently are the regionalization of security arrangements or responses and the military role in supporting international tribunals. A second dimension that is evolving and receives less attention is constructive engagement in bilateral and multilateral relations amongst military forces as part of the range of preventative strategies. This chapter will address both these aspects of the role of the military organizations of democratic States in globalizing the rule of law. I will first summarize the practical experience and measures adopted by the ADF and its allies in recent complex peace operations and then consider the potential for expanding and institutionalizing constructive engagement. I will also discuss the implications and possible direction of the role of the military in regional security and in the support of the International Criminal Court (ICC).

Bilateral and multilateral engagement

Organizations such as the ADF have always had a role to play in the diplomatic activity or objectives of the State. They are typically engaged on a regular basis in combined exercises, conferences, exchanges, attendance at overseas training institutions or hosting of foreign officers at their own institutions. Significant contact and exchange of views also takes place during operations in coalition or UN deployments. In addition to this contact there are specific programs or activities undertaken by some States designed to tackle the promotion of democracy and the rule of law. There are also activities created by non-government agencies where representatives of different armed forces will meet and engage on these issues.

In the past, many of the opportunities presented by exercises and institutional training have not been exploited. Engagement was often based on the concept that the right attitudes or approach would 'rub off' on foreign contacts or somehow be absorbed through osmosis. No real attempt was made to embed humanitarian or human rights related scenarios or subjects in exercises or curricula. This situation has changed significantly in recent times. Within the key ADF training institutions of the Command and Staff and Australian Defence Colleges, the ADF Warfare Centre and the ADF Peacekeeping Centre officers from many different States are participants. The curricula at these institutions have been significantly overhauled to incorporate humanitarian law and human rights issues. Scenarios reinforcing important teaching points and planning considerations are incorporated into major exercises through the Joint Exercise Planning organization.

There is an increasing number of international forums that provide opportunities for constructive engagement. A longer term operation is the San Remo Institute for Humanitarian Law in Italy. This non-government agency is heavily supported by the International Committee of the Red Cross (ICRC) and takes participants from around the world. To date the emphasis at San Remo has been exclusively on conventional conflict and humanitarian law while it is also limited in terms of numbers of participants and inadequate representation of the Asia-Pacific region. Another example of specifically targeted activity is contained in the United States' International Military Education and Training (IMET) programme. This programme involves teams of US military personnel conducting courses for small numbers of military personnel, hopefully in key positions, in all aspects of international humanitarian law, the role of the military in a democracy and human rights, including appropriate internal disciplinary administration.

The ADF has also recently become more proactive in this regard through the combined efforts of the Strategic International Policy Division within the Defence Department, the Military Law Centre and the Department of Foreign Affairs and Trade. This has also involved collaboration with the ICRC. Examples of this activity include the delivery of training to the PNG Defence Force, the conduct of an ASEAN Regional Forum (ARF) Seminar on International Humanitarian Law (IHL), the conduct of EXERCISE PIRAP/JABIRU with the Royal Thai Armed Forces, and assistance in follow-on activities in IHL and peace operations for the ARF. The ADF has also provided officers to the ICRC to assist in the development of training materials and strategies and the training of foreign forces all over the world including China, Fiji, South Africa, Bosnia, Croatia and Eastern Europe in general.

There is, however, much more that can be done in this sphere and the ADF is exploring ways to better meet regional engagement objectives. This has been identified as a requirement by the Australian government and parliament. This was highlighted in the Joint Standing Committee on Foreign Affairs, Defence and Trade investigation into 'Australia's Regional Dialogue on Human Rights', the report of which was published in June 1998. The Committee recommended in particular that:

> The Australian government review the operations of its defence co-operation program with a view to providing assistance to the governments of regional countries in provision of training for the military in international human rights law (Recommendation 15).[7]

In Australia, a significant new initiative is the Asia Pacific Centre for Military Law (APCML). The aim of the APCML is to provide a facility to generate more engagement with regional forces and promote respect for and adherence to the rule of law at both international and domestic levels. It will do this through collegial activities and courses where professionals, both legal and non-legal, will discuss the practical problems we mutually encounter and attempt to come up with practical solutions. The APCML is a collaborative venture with the University of Melbourne, with participation from organizations such as the Raoul Wallenberg Institute for Human Rights and Humanitarian Law, United Nations High Commissioner for Refugees (UNHCR) and the ICRC among others. It is planned that this Centre will make a substantial contribution to providing practical answers to contemporary challenges to the rule of law in dysfunctional states and societies.

Trends toward regional security

One aspect of the growing role of the military in globalizing the rule of law has been in the evolution towards the use of regional security mechanisms or arrangements to deal with regionally-sensitive rule of law problems. This trend has included organizations within the concept of Chapter VIII of the UN Charter or, as in the case of NATO, transregional organizations not contemplated by the Charter. This has reached a degree of maturity in Europe with the growing role of NATO, NATO Partnership for Peace (PfP) and the Organization for Security and Cooperation in Europe (OSCE). In Africa, we have seen the substantial effort of the Economic Community of West African States (ECOWAS) in dealing with regional internal conflict and its spill-over through its ECOMOG forces and ongoing efforts to have the Organization for African Unity (OAU) take on more responsibility for peace operations in the continent in general. The Organization of American States (OAS) has been involved in various regional rule of law initiatives including Grenada, Panama, Haiti, Columbia and El Salvador. Most recently, a coalition of forces made up principally from the Asia Pacific region and led by Australia was deployed in East Timor under the INTERFET banner.

This kind of involvement has been encouraged by the realization that forces that have had regular contact and who have exercised together have a better chance of working in cohesion which is essential in robust peace enforcement missions.

It also represents the greater investment these nations have in regional stability and perhaps greater familiarity with the context of the problem and with specific cultural sensitivities. The problem for all coalition forces, whether they come from the region or not, is the fact that some members are bound to have a different approach to how far they should become involved in reordering domestic affairs in the State where intervention has occurred. This will be the case in particular where members of the coalition have differing attitudes to the institutionalization of democracy, the rule of law and human rights. This dilemma highlights the critical importance of continuing constructive engagement.

The trend to regionalization of security elsewhere and the INTERFET operation in East Timor has illuminated the need for a regional cooperative arrangement between countries in the Asia-Pacific. There are substantial factors that militate against such an organization but the prospects are brighter than they once were and the time may not be far away when this becomes a reality. Countries like Thailand, the Philippines, India, Malaysia and Fiji have all had recent peace operations experience that has eroded to some degree the previous reluctance to engage in regional collaboration. Certainly, the harnessing of this experience and standardizing the approaches to the key political and legal issues could only advance the globalization of the rule of law.

Military support to international tribunals

A significant role for the military and which may become increasingly important as the ICC commences its work is the support required of the military for international tribunals and investigations. Many activities in Bosnia that relate directly to the needs of the Hague Tribunal for the Former Yugoslavia have been undertaken by military forces. These have included providing security for investigation and forensic personnel at mass graves and other key-related sites, the apprehension of persons indicted for war crimes, the preservation and recording of evidence and the provision of intelligence material to assist in the direction of investigations. This experience has been repeated in Kosovo, East Timor and Iraq.[8]

The provision of military intelligence has been one of some difficulty and requires a balancing of the security preservation of sources and technical matters and the probative needs of the tribunal. The general modus operandi has been that the military will provide material such as to enable investigations to be refined and productive of probative evidence but the intelligence material itself is rarely, if ever, used in court. This is the same approach that has governed the provision of Australian intelligence material to investigators working on the allegations of crimes against humanity in East Timor. Australian forces in East Timor were also required to engage in the preservation of evidence while investigators could be mobilized and our Military Police were tasked in this respect.

Similar tasks may be undertaken for the ICC. The ICC will have jurisdiction to prosecute persons in circumstances where the local justice administration is unable or unwilling to take action in relation to the relevant crimes. For example, in the environment of a collapsed state, the only organizations in a position to facilitate such prosecutions are military forces that may have been interposed there in a peace operation. In addition, should the ICC seek to prosecute an individual who stands at the head of a large armed organization then it may be only the military that has the wherewithal to 'apprehend' that individual.

The tribunals themselves have been adding to the globalization of the rule of law by settling or developing common or international standards of criminal law. One example is the Hague tribunal's survey of international domestic criminal practice to determine whether the principle of *unus testis, nullus testis* (one witness is no witness, i.e. that the testimony of only one witness is insufficient to convict a person) could be described as a 'general principle of international law'. (Having made this survey they concluded that this rule had not attained that status.)[9] Another example is the international process that has accompanied the development of the crimes, elements of the crimes and rules of procedure and evidence as part of the establishment of the jurisdiction of the ICC. The most interesting aspect of this has been the development of these frameworks by merging the common law and code traditions in particular.[10] Many military legal officers have played a part in developing the ICC provisions and standards including those from the ADF.

The military role in restoring the rule of law

A further, important dimension of the military's role in globalizing the rule of law is where it engages in the restoration of the rule of law in the context of complex peace operations. Generally, the military has been reluctant to become involved in such legally related activity, seeing its role principally as one of restoring order. Frequently, however, the two must go hand in hand, at least in the interim. This was the experience of the UNTAET/UNMISET Peacekeeping Force and was starkly highlighted once again in the dilemmas faced by the Coalition Forces in Iraq in 2003. This realization has come in the context of the desire to speed up the drawdown of military forces and the fastest possible handoff to civil authorities. In order to achieve a rapid transition it is important that action is taken in the critical early phases of an intervention to lay a firm foundation on which to build the transition process.

Both the ADF and NATO have recently participated in such blended activities. The first of the deployments where the maintenance of order and the restoration of the rule of law became an issue was in the UNTAC operation in Cambodia in 1992.[11] Here a wide-ranging UN mandate existed but little practical consideration had been given as to how it should be fulfilled. There was an expectation that the civilian administrative dimension of the operation would be able to engage in restoring law and order while the military forces merely acted as interposition and demobilization supervisors of the armed forces. In reality, the civil administration including policing elements took 12 months to deploy and when they did were unable to operate effectively. The military was looked to for the provision of functions that should ordinarily have been the preserve of civil police. The failure adequately to address the establishment of an efficacious system of justice led to a deeply flawed foundation for the new Cambodian polity.

After this experience, the ADF found itself in the coalition operation into Somalia in what was known as OPERATION RESTORE HOPE in 1993. Here there was a total breakdown of law and order and the institutions of state were in disarray. Many loosely organized criminal elements combined with the more formal militia bodies that were heavily armed and intoxicated with a homicidal life style. The Australian contingent had responsibility for a particular area of operations and within that area adopted a proactive approach to the law and order issue. The foundation of the approach was to assert the application of the Fourth Geneva Convention of 1949[12] which provided firm guidance and authority for just such a situation.

Acting under the UN mandate for the operation and the Fourth Convention, the Australian contingent located survivors of the Somali police force and put them back to work. Survivors from the Judiciary, the Criminal Investigation Division and the Prison Staff were also located and put back into operation using as a basis the Somali Penal Code. Copies of the Code and other related laws such as the Criminal Procedure Code were obtained in English so that informed assistance could be rendered at every level. The Army Engineers with the contingent worked to restore court, police and prison facilities while cooperation was obtained from the NGOs to provide work for food in the early days of the operation.

Using the reconstituted system, action was then taken to assist in the prosecution of war criminals or those guilty of crimes against humanity in the area. The courts were also used to help resolve property disputes and bring the social discourse back to one of institutional dispute resolution rather than resort to violence. This strategy was successful in clearing out the militia and bandit elements that had been responsible for conducting a campaign of genocide against the local traditional clan residents. The fault in the long-term success of the operation in Somalia was that this approach was not adopted for the country as a whole. The efforts of the Australia contingent eventually came to naught two years later when armed forces of the Aideed militia sallied from Mogadishu and overran the area.[13]

The ADF was then confronted with similar dilemmas when it led the INTERFET deployment into East Timor in September 1999. The Indonesians had left a total vacuum in administration when they departed, as all official positions had been filled by Indonesian or personnel loyal to Indonesia. In this respect the situation was worse than that faced in Somalia in that there were no surviving personnel to work with to re-establish the judicial system. Issues also arose as to what law should be applied in the circumstances. Because the deployment in this case was with the consent of the Indonesians and Portugal, and undertaken pursuant to formal agreements, it was not considered that the Fourth Convention could be applied as a matter of law. As the mandate authorized the force commander to take all necessary measures to re-establish peace and security, however, the solution was that the Fourth Convention was applied as a matter of policy.

Under this policy approach a Detainee Management Unit (DMU) was established based on military legal officers from Australia and the Philippines. This unit was to operate as a pre-trial capability to enable basic habeas corpus requirements to be met. In other words, people who had been detained in relation to allegations of criminal offences had to be brought before the tribunal to establish whether a prima facie case existed against them. This justified their continuing detention for long enough to enable them to be brought before a properly constituted full trial tribunal. The DMU operated under an ordinance promulgated by the force commander which drew on the serious offences which the force undertook to police based on the Indonesian Criminal Code. The DMU was established in consultation with the ICRC and was open to scrutiny by that organization and Amnesty International.

From the first moment that the mission was undertaken, pressure was applied by Australia on the United Nations and the international community to address the administration of justice as a top priority and in particular to establish a trial capability that the DMU could handover to at the earliest opportunity. Eventually the DMU did handover to the UNTAET administration in January 2000 although the transition was not ideal and there have been ongoing difficulties in attaining a fully functioning justice system.[14]

NATO experience in Bosnia and Kosovo has mirrored many of these issues. The war in Bosnia gave rise to domination by elements and networks that were, and remain, essentially criminal in nature. The former Republic of Yugoslavia had no tradition of acceptable human rights adherence in the first place and this has created a poor basis upon which to attempt to establish an effective system of justice. Added to the fundamental divides in Bosnian society, the corrupted levels of administration established since the deployment of IFOR and the lack of rigorous commitment by the international community to building the rule of law it is not surprising that SFOR is still engaged in supporting law enforcement operations. A report in May 2000 by a US team on the lessons of SFOR concluded that:

> The pre-eminent lesson from the Bosnia experience is that the military may have an indispensable role to play in securing an environment that is conducive to the rule of law. This was essential in Bosnia because each of the three formally warring ethnic communities (Bosnians, Croats and Serbs) is controlled by power structures that obstruct the development of institutions essential to the rule of law as reflected in the Dayton Accord. These power structures consist of nationalist and obstructionist politicians who rely on formal political party structures as well as extra-legal security services (secret intelligence, police and paramilitary) and transnational criminal syndicates to sustain themselves in power . . . . At the moment, only SFOR has the coercive capacity and intelligence assets to combat these power structures; however SFOR certainly cannot shape the environment needed to sustain the rule of law alone.[15]

The experience of NATO forces in Kosovo was very similar to that faced in East Timor in that the Serbs filled most of the official functions prior to the war and left a vacuum of trained personnel when they left. Even so, the administration of justice in Kosovo prior to NATO deployment once again left a great deal to be desired.

When NATO troops arrived it very quickly became apparent that a key centre of gravity was establishing a fundamental underpinning for the rule of law and the building of an acquiescent environment. There was no prior planning, however, or any consideration as to how this would be done and what legal basis would be used. The result was that each military contingent adopted its own approach to the issue in a widely varying manner. Eventually, all were forced to come up with a rudimentary pre-trial process that was similar in scope and operation to the DMU concept adopted in East Timor. This 'interim period' lasted many months before the international community and the United Nations were able to get local capabilities under development.[16]

The lessons that the United States has started to learn in relation to this common dimension of contemporary operations have been lessons the ADF has been stressing for some time. The US awakening came following a project launched by the US National Defence University which resulted in the publication of a volume entitled 'Policing the New World Disorder'.[17] This work generated much interest and has lead to a more informed debate at higher levels in the US administration. The ultimate result of this debate was the production of Presidential Decision Directive 71 (PDD71) entitled 'Strengthening Criminal Justice Systems in Support of Peace Operations and Other Complex Emergencies'. At a conference at the US Army War College in Carlisle Pennsylvania, recommendations were formulated for submission to the Chairman of the Joint Chiefs of Staff to enable the US military to meet the obligations placed upon it by PDD71.

PDD71 concluded that the issue of re-establishing the rule of law is of the highest priority in a peace operation and will result in the earliest opportunity for the ramping down of military involvement. It will also lay the firm foundation for the economic and political progress that must be the vital 'peace dividend'. To meet this objective, PDD71 directed a substantial commitment to an inter-agency effort to address all aspects of the problem including the judiciary, police and prisons. The Directive also set out the areas of responsibility for the military in supporting law and order activities and the restoration of the rule of law. For example, in relation to the support of the civilian police (CIVPOL) element of a peace operations it stated that:

> The first source for CIVPOL communications and logistics support should be from commercial sources; however, since the military component of a peacekeeping operation is more likely to have effective communication systems, logistic support systems and intelligence or information structures throughout the area of operations, the military commander should consider providing the CIVPOL component access to and mutual use of these capabilities when feasible and allowable by law and when it will not interfere with execution of the mission of the military component . . .
>
> In some instances, military support to the CIVPOL component has proven essential to successful accomplishment of the overall mission. Such support may take the form of technical assistance resident in the civil affairs, psychological operations, military intelligence or military police elements of armed forces.

The Directive ventured further than the provision of this technical assistance. The document recognized that situations would arise in which police would be incapable of handling certain kinds and levels of threat, that there may be delays in their deployment, and that their disparate background may prejudice operational success. Consequently, it may be appropriate for the military to perform robust 'constabulary' functions in the interim as CIVPOL elements 'do not have the unit cohesion, training, or equipment' for such a difficult environment. The preference would be for paramilitary units to deal with such threatening situations, such as those within the Caribinieri or Gendarmarie, but where such units were not available, 'US military forces shall maintain the capability to support constabulary functions abroad, and if necessary carry out constabulary functions under limited conditions for a limited period of time'. The Directive sought to limit the role of the military as far as possible but acknowledged that the military component has 'a vital role to play in the overall recovery of criminal justice capacities'. Its conclusion in this respect was that:

> Unless basic public safety is provided, the civilian organizations will be unable to conduct their tasks. If public safety is not maintained, the social fabric will not be ready for the assistance to be provided by civilian agencies.

The Directive, however, was silent on the legal framework that would be relied on to take this more proactive stance. This contrasts with the approach the ADF has taken to clarify this sort of uncertainty. It was recognized at Carlisle that some work is being undertaken in Europe to look at developing a new framework which would draw on elements of both international humanitarian and human rights law.[18] This fell out of the Brahimi recommendations but there has been skepticism as to whether such a code would be useful or possible.[19] Regrettably, the subsequent G.W. Bush administration was quick to shelve PDD71 but was forced to take on all the same issues and come up with many of the same answers when confronted with the realties of operations in Iraq in 2003.

In East Timor, the problem for the PKF was the generally poor standard and low numbers of the UN police capability. This forced the PKF to fill many gaps in that capability for a long period of time. The balance that had to be achieved involved merging military security concerns and intelligence needs with the human rights standards inherent in the mandated role of UNHCR in handling the returnee issue and the normal criminal processes for detainees, and in wishing to promote the right concept of the role of the military in democratic society for the Timorese looking on. This was achieved through a careful process of producing agreements and guidelines in close consultation that were effectively communicated and trained through normal military processes.[20]

The situation in Iraq in 2003 was a problem of a wholly different order of magnitude. There the 'law of occupation' came into play in a *de jure* sense without argument for the first time since World War II. Soon, the role of the military in not providing immediate public security became highly controversial. After all the care that had been taken in the targeting process in fighting the campaign, much of this was undone by the looting and sabotage that occurred in the vacuum that followed the collapse of the regime. These matters were discussed prior to the operation and concepts such as 'Joint Stability Brigades' were formulated, creating valuable mixtures of Military Police, Intelligence and Civil Affairs personnel. But these ideas were not made operational. Subsequently, it was the military that was in any event forced to fill the void and recover lost ground for a substantial period following the conclusion of the main combat phase. The role of military legal officers at every level in helping to manage this was extensive and extremely valuable. The lesson, though, is that there is simply no excuse for not being prepared for this line of operation in light of such extensive and well-publicized experience.[21]

Defending against global terrorism and the 'eco warrior' role

An evolving aspect of the engagement of the ADF in promoting the globalization of the rule of law has been in the enforcement of environmental regulation. This has occurred under legislation giving effect to Australia's international obligations with respect to protection of the marine environment and our domestic customs regime designed to protect native flora and fauna. The main burden in this area has fallen on the Navy which have undertaken difficult operations in the southern oceans to prevent degradation of the Bluefin Tuna and Patagonian Toothfish populations. They are also engaged on a daily basis in protecting the waters stretching from the northern arc of the continent. ADF personnel and assets have also been heavily involved in the prevention of international drug-trafficking into Australia.

Another area of close ADF involvement is the struggle against global terrorism. The ADF cooperates with international partners to make this a more effective struggle and is equipped and prepared to meet the threat if it materializes on our own shores. This struggle brings home the nature of what is known as the 'asymmetric threat'. This means that the threat is not a conventional military one but has aspects that are best dealt with by a military capability. For example, a terrorist group may be armed with sophisticated military pattern weapons, ordnance or explosives that civil police simply cannot cope with. It has also become increasingly important to be prepared to deal with Weapons of Mass Destruction (WMD) that pose a chemical, biological or radiological threat as these are now within the reach of terrorist organizations. This was illustrated by the Sarin gas episode in Tokyo, which had connections here in Australia, and the right wing terrorist groups in the USA where bubonic plague samples were acquired in one case. The war on terror that was initiated following the September 11, 2001 attack in New York has made this a primary focus for Coalition Forces engaged in this struggle.

It is the military that is best equipped to deal with this type of threat and is trained on a larger scale to operate in such environments and to provide decontamination facilities. The challenge is to have a proper democratic and legal framework to define military input in domestic environments and the recent effective amendments to the Australian Defence Act are good examples of this.[22]

The battle against global terrorism and other non-State armed groups requires close cooperation amongst all law enforcement and intelligence agencies and the military both at home and internationally. This includes the effective separation of such groups from their sources of income. Such sources have included everything from 'legitimate' business interests to the proceeds from the international drug trade or the illegal exploitation of primary resources where States are unable to prevent this plunder. Some examples of the latter include the diamond resources of the Congo, Angola and Sierra Leone during the recent internal conflicts there,[23] and the forests and gems of Cambodia during the Khmer Rouge period of control of the border regions.[24]

The evolution of doctrine, force structure and capability

One important reason for the intensified involvement of the United States in peace operations is that nation's highly developed capability in civil affairs. This capability includes administrative specialists, judges, lawyers, prison officials and police.[25] In addition, there are the related capabilities that have proven very useful when engaged in peacekeeping tasks in the areas of psychological operations, intelligence, special forces, communications, supply, engineering and medicine. The ADF does not have resources in these areas on the US scale but certainly has significant expertise and experience in many of them enabling our contribution to be in the 'high end' aspect of these activities providing direction or training or specialized intervention. Our ability to keep abreast of developments in this area have been enhanced by the establishment of an ADF Civil Military Cooperation (CIMIC) Unit supporting the Deployable Joint Force Headquarters. The first Strategic and Operational level course for CIMIC in Australia was run by the APCML in Sydney in April 2003 and brings together many government, NGO, police, military and regional personnel.

Along with the recognition of the critical importance of these military capabilities and the need to enhance or increase their availability, there has been a transition in the development of military doctrine and training. Where once it was anathema to say that peace operations should drive doctrine and training , there has in fact been a recent recognition that aspects of peace operations form part of 'lines of operation' that may be encountered in any context from conventional through to asymmetric and it is merely a question of priority as to which strategy will be adopted at which time. As such, peace operations cannot be ignored or put at the bottom of the capability list. Given the frequency of their occurrence it is vital that appropriate attention be given to the relevant issues, particularly in training.

In the ADF this has been recognized in the development of the foundation doctrine publication 'The Fundamentals of Land Warfare'.[26] This is a forward-thinking document that acknowledges that rule of law issues are present across the spectrum of operations and are given the designation 'security operations'. Tasks in this area would include aid to the civil authorities in supplementary law enforcement either at home or abroad, the conduct of vehicle checkpoints, cordon and search operations and the issue of population protection and control. Along with this doctrinal basis has come the issue of the equipment and training of the soldier. This has led to a greater emphasis on providing the soldier with the ability to make decisions on the appropriate level of force to apply in any given threat situation. The greatest difference in this respect is the need to consider the application of non-lethal force and stricter guidelines on the application of different types of lethal force in rules of engagement such as prohibition of or tight control on the use of indirect or area weapons.

To provide soldiers with the ability to apply non-lethal force many modern military forces are in the process of acquiring and developing non-lethal weapons and equipment. A proportion of soldier training in a number of developed countries is now spent on the use of these options and also non-lethal techniques before resorting to the lethal weapons and equipment. Effort is also put into focusing on the decision making process in the application of lethal force by putting soldiers through scenario-based training. Soldiers need to know, for example, whether and how they can respond effectively to lethal threats from women and children, as was often the case in Somalia.

The ADF has also recognized the great utility of military police. The role military police can play in restoring the rule of law includes assisting in the development of a local police capability, running temporary detention facilities, advising force commanders and infantry units on training techniques and options for low force level threat environments and communal policing issues and the preservation and gathering of evidence to support tribunals and investigators in the area of war crimes, crimes against humanity and serious crimes of violence during the interim period of peace operations. The ADF has now created a military police battalion that will deliver these skill sets. Uniformed legal officers have also played a significant role in these matters as lessons learned in Somalia, Haiti, Bosnia, East Timor, Kosovo and most recently in Iraq have all shown.

Clearly as a readily deployable asset with relevant skill sets and essential physical capabilities, military forces like the ADF have a role to play in the globalization of the rule of law. They also have a role to play in promoting the rule of law through all forms of engagement with forces from other nations. This challenge is becoming particularly acute as the military is increasingly being called upon to respond to intra-state crises in circumstances where liberty, democracy and the rule of law seem remote and unattainable objectives. In these environments, the military is often the 'last, best hope'.

Notes

1 Van Doren, C. *Benjamin Franklin*, New York: The Viking Press, 1938, p. 773.

2 See: the Comprehensive Review of the Whole Question of Peacekeeping Operations in all Their Aspects 'the Brahimi Report' UN Document A/55/305, S/2000/809 of 17 August 2000, paragraphs 13, 14, 39, 40, 41, 47, 76, 79, 81, 82, 83, 224, 225.

3 The General Framework Agreement for Peace in Bosnia and Herzegovina, 21 November 1995, executed in Paris 14 December 1995 or 'Dayton Agreement' focused on human rights with great particularity beginning with a new Constitution for the country. The Preamble of the document set out clearly that it was inspired by the key international human rights instruments and went on in Article II to entrench the commitment to human rights and fundamental freedoms. Particularly noteworthy was paragraph 8 of Article II which provided for cooperation with and unrestricted access to 'any international human rights monitoring mechanisms established for Bosnia and Herzegovina' as well as the supervisory agencies to be established by the Agreement and 'any other organisation authorized by the United Nations Security Council with a mandate concerning human rights or humanitarian law'. Annex 6 went into some detail to provide the substance and mechanisms by which this agenda was to be implemented. The primary reference was to be the European Convention for the Protection of Human Rights and Fundamental Freedoms though the Parties were also required to secure the rights and freedoms enshrined in another 16 international conventions listed in the Appendix to the Annex. The mechanisms established to ensure compliance with these instruments included a Commission on Human Rights which was to consist of an Ombudsman's Office and Human Rights Chamber. (Chapter 2, Part A, Article II). The Ombudsman was to be appointed by the OSCE and was responsible for choosing his or her own staff. The Ombudsman was not to be a citizen of Bosnia and Herzegovina, or any neighboring state, until the transfer of responsibility for the appointment to the President of Bosnia and Herzegovina after five years (Chapter 2, Part B, Article IV).

The Human Rights Chamber while composed of 14 members was to have only four of these appointed by the Federation of Bosnia and Herzegovina and two from the Republika Srpska, the remainder were to be nominated by the Committee of Ministers of the Council of Europe and were also not to be citizens of Bosnia and Herzegovina or a neighboring state. The Committee of Ministers was to nominate one of its appointees as the President of the Chamber. (Chapter 2, Part C, Article VII). The Ombudsman was given the power to investigate on his or her own initiative or in response to allegations by any Party, person, NGO or group of individuals or complaints on behalf of alleged victims. The Ombudsman could initiate proceedings before the Human Rights Chamber and intervene in any proceedings. He or she was also to have access all official documents, including classified ones, judicial and administrative files. The Ombudsman could also require any person, including government officials to cooperate in providing this material and could enter and inspect any place where persons deprived of their liberty were confined or working. (Chapter 2, Part B, Articles V and VI). A finding that a Party had breached its obligations under the Agreement could lead to corrective action by IFOR while the Chamber was also empowered to order other remedies (Chapter 2, Part B, Article XI).

Under Chapter Three, Article XIII the Parties undertook to promote and encourage the activities of human rights organizations, including an invitation for various agencies and NGOs to establish offices, observers, and rapporteurs. These bodies were to be afforded full and effective access, unhindered and with the full cooperation of the Parties.

4 Agreement on a Comprehensive Political Settlement of the Cambodia Conflict, Agreement concerning the Sovereignty, Independence, Territorial Integrity and Inviolability, Neutrality and National Unity of Cambodia, 23 October 1991, *Australian Treaty Series*, 1991, no. 40. Under Article 16 the United Nations Transitional Authority in Cambodia (UNTAC) was given responsibility for fostering an environment of respect

for human rights, also governed by the provisions of annex. 1. Annex. 1, Section A, paragraph 1 assigned to UNTAC the powers necessary to ensure the implementation of the Agreement. Paragraph 2 put in place a mechanism for resolving issues by requiring UNTAC to comply with the advice of the SNC, provided there was a consensus in the SNC and the advice was consistent with the objectives of the Agreement. If there was no consensus then SNC President Norodom Sihanouk was empowered to make the decision on what advice should be offered UNTAC which it was bound to follow, once again, only if it was consistent with the objectives of the Agreement. If the President was not in a position to make such a decision then the power transferred to the Special Representative of the Secretary-General (SRSG). The determination of whether the advice of the SNC or President was consistent with the Agreement was a matter for the SRSG to determine.

Section B of annex. 1 dealt with civil administration and through paragraph 1 placed under the direct control of UNTAC 'all administrative agencies, bodies and offices acting in the field of foreign affairs, national defence, finance, public security and information'. More specifically, paragraph 4 gave the SRSG the power to:

(a) Install in administrative agencies, bodies and offices of all the Cambodian Parties, United Nations personnel who will have unrestricted access to all administrative operations and information.
(b) Require the reassignment or removal of any personnel of such administrative agencies, bodies and offices.

Paragraph 5 went on to grant the SRSG the authority to determine, in consultation with the Cambodian Parties, the civil police necessary to perform law enforcement. In this respect it was provided that:

> All civil police will operate under UNTAC supervision or control, in order to ensure that law and order are maintained effectively and impartially, and that human rights and fundamental freedoms are fully protected. In consultation with the SNC, UNTAC will supervise other law enforcement and judicial processes throughout Cambodia to the extent necessary to ensure the attainment of these objectives (paragraph 5 (b)).

Under Section D, UNTAC was empowered to organize and conduct the election and to establish a system of laws, procedures and administrative measures for this purpose. (Paragraphs 1, 3(a)).

UNTAC was also tasked to make provisions for the investigation of human rights complaints, and, where appropriate, corrective action. (Section E). Cambodia was obliged to adopt an array of human rights instruments in much the same way as Bosnia was to be under the Dayton Agreement.

5 Roberts, A. and Kingsbury, B. 'The UN's Roles in International Society Since 1945', in A. Roberts and B. Kingsbury (eds) *United Nations, Divided World*, 2nd edn, Oxford: Clarendon Press, 1993, p. 61; Singh, N. 'The UN and the Development of International Law', in Roberts and Kingsbury ibid., pp. 391–411; SG Report on Work of the Org; 2 September 1994, paragraphs 93–5, 321–2, 355–60, 379–80, 383; Cordy-Simpson, R. 'UN Operations in Bosnia-Herzegovina', in H. Smith (ed.) *International Peacekeeping: Building on the Cambodia Experience*, Canberra: Australian Defence Studies Centre, 1994, p. 104; Harris, I., National Director CARE Australia, 'Testimony to Defence Sub-Committee on Peacekeeping', 9 November 1993, p. 279; SG Addendum to '*An Agenda for Peace*', 3 January 1995, paragraphs 89–96; Interim Army Field Manual vol. 5, Operations Other Than War, Part 2, Wider Peacekeeping, 1994, paragraph 42; Helman, G.B. and Ratner, S.R. 'Saving Failed States', *Foreign Policy*, no. 89, Winter 1992, pp. 4–19; Report of Security Council Mission of 10–11 February 1995, dated 28 February 95, paragraphs 6, 14–18, 21–4; Shiner, C. 'The Authority

Vacuum', *Africa Report*, vol. 39, no. 6, November–December 1994, pp. 23–4; Twelfth Progress Report of Secretary General on UNOMIL, 9 September 1995, paragraph 19, 38, 42; UNSCR 1014, 15 September 1995. UNSCR 688; Weiss, T.G. and Campbell, K.M. 'Military Humanitarianism', *Survival*, September–October 1991, vol. xxxiii, no. 5, pp. 451–65, p. 456; UNSCR 724, UNSCR 752, UNSCR 770, UNSCR 771, UNSCR 781. UNSCR 780, UNSCR 827. UNSCR 745, UNSCR 783, Paris Accords of 23 October 1991; Heininger, J.E. '*Peacekeeping in Transition – The United Nations in Cambodia*', Twentieth Century Fund Project, New York, 1994, pp. 31–3, 34, 39, 41, 72, 75–8, 79–82, 88–9, 96–9, 121–2, 124, 127, 131; Eaton, C. 'The Role of Police in Institution Building', in Smith, *Building on Cambodia*, pp. 61–2; McAulay, P. 'Civilian Police and Peacekeeping: Challenges in the 1990s', in Smith ibid., p. 24; McLean, L. 'Civil Administration in Transition: public information and the neutral political/electoral environment', in Smith ibid., pp. 49, 52, 55–8; Bowers, C. 'Submission to Defence Sub-Committee on Peacekeeping', no. 37, vol. 4, p. 1; World Vision, 'Submission to Defence Sub-Committee on Peacekeeping', no. 36, vol. 4, p. 25; Sanderson, 'Testimony to Defence Sub–Committee on Peacekeeping', 8 April 1994, p. 507; UNSCR 918; UNSCR 925; UNSCR 929; UNSCR 935; UNSCR 955; UNSCR 965; Report of SG, 2 September 1994, paragraph 643; Preliminary Report of Commission of Experts, paragraphs 44–78; Final Report, released on 9 December 1994. Report of SG on Situation in Rwanda, 3 August 1994, paragraph 7; Report of SG, 2 September 1994, paragraphs 646–7; Progress Report of Secretary General on UNAMIR, 6 October 1994, paragraphs 39–40; UNSCR 977; UNSCR 977; Report of SG, 3 August 1994, paragraph 3; Progress Report of Secretary General on UNAMIR, 6 February 1994, paragraphs 2, 7, 9; Report of Security Council Mission to Rwanda on 12, 13 February 1995, dated 28 February 1995, paragraphs 8, 25; Progress Report of Secretary General on UNAMIR, 8 August 1995, paragraph 26; Letter from Secretary General to President of the Security Council, 31 August 1995; Report of Security Council Mission to Rwanda on 12, 13 February 1995, dated 28 February 1995, paragraphs 14–20, 24–6. UNSCR 1007; Report of the SG on the Work of the Org., 3 January 1995, paragraph 86 (e); Report of SG on Work of Org., 2 September 94, paragraphs 529–540; Report of the Secretary General on Haiti, 17 January 1995, paragraphs 11, 15, 20, 30–34, 48–49, 50, 64, 66, 86; Sixth Report of the Multinational Force in Haiti (UNMIH Rep) to the Security Council, 5 December 1994; Fourth UNMIH Rep, 7 November 1994; Seventh UNMIH Rep, 19 December 94; Eighth UNMIH Rep, 9 January 95; Eleventh UNMIH Rep, 21 February 1995, paragraphs 8, 5, 14; Twelfth UNMIH Rep, 6 March 1995, paragraphs 4, 7, 9, 13–14. and Thirteenth and Final UNMIH Rep, 20 March 1995, paragraphs 9, 4; Letter From the Contributing Countries to the President of the Security Council, 19 January 1995, Annex II; Ninth UNMIH Rep, 23 January 1995, paragraph 6; Tenth UNMIH Rep, 6 February 1995, paragraphs 6, 8, 14–15; Report of the Secretary General on UNMIH, 13 April 1995, paragraph 7. UNSCR 782 of 13 October 92, 797 of 16 December 92, 818 of 14 Apr 93 and 850 of 9 July 1993; UNSCR 916 of 5 May 1994; UNSCR 957 of 15 November 1994; SG Report on Work of the Org, 2 September 1994, paragraph 593; J. Rixon, 'The Role of Australian Police in Peace Support Operations', in Smith, '*Building on Cambodia*', pp. 121–3; Ingram, J.C. 'The Politics of Human Suffering', *The National Interest*, issue 33, Fall 1993, p. 64; Mwakawago, D. 'Statement to Security Council, Security Council Press Release', 8 February 1995; SG Report on Work of the Org., 2 September 94, paragraphs 447, 449–58, 462–3; E. Leopold, 'UN Proposes 7,500 Strong Angolan Force', *The Australian*, 4–5 February 1995, p. 19; De Moura, V. Statement to the Security Council, Security Council Press Release, 8 February 1995; Albright, M. Statement to the Security Council, Security Council Press Release, 8 February 1995.

6 Rosenau, J.N. 'Sovereignty in a Turbulent World', in G.M. Lyons and M. Mastanduno (eds) *Beyond Westphalia?: state sovereignty and international intervention*, Johns Hopkins University Press, 1995, pp. 191–2; Kostakos, G., Groom, A.J.R., Morphet, S. and

Taylor, P. 'Britain and the New UN Agenda: Towards global riot control', *Review of International Studies*, 17, January 1991, pp. 95–105; Chopra, J. and Weiss, T.G. 'Sovereignty is No Longer Sacrosanct: codifying humanitarian intervention', *Ethics and International Affairs*, vol. 6, 1992, pp. 101–4.

7 *Improving but . . . : Australia's regional dialogue on human rights,* Report of the Joint Standing Committee on Foreign Affairs, Defence and Trade, June 1998 published by the Commonwealth of Australia 1998, p. xvi. See also recommendation 14 'The Australian government review the human rights implications of Australia's defence co-operation with other countries and establish guidelines which prohibit any defence co-operation which could contribute to the recipient forces internal security function'. And recommendation 16 'The Australian government consider evaluating the capacity of ASEAN and ARF (ASEAN Regional Forum) to play a role in the promotion of human rights in the region, and where appropriate, advocate the assumption of such a role by those institutions'.

8 *Law and Military Operations in the Balkans: lessons learned for Judge advocates,* Centre for Law and Military Operations, The Judge Advocate General's School US Army, 1998.

9 *Prosecutor v. Tadic,* Case No. IT-94-1-T, Opinion and Judgement, 7 May 1997 at paragraphs 535–539. See also: the discussion on 'common purpose' in *Prosecutor v. Tadic,* Case No. IT-94-1-A, A. Chapter 15, July 1999 at paragraphs 185–229. See also: the discussion on general principles and the applicability of national laws of evidence in Boas, G. 'Admissibility of Evidence under the Rules of Procedure and Evidence of the ICTY: Development of the 'Flexibility Principle', in R. May, D. Tolbert, J. Hocking, K. Roberts, B.B. Jia, D. Mundis and G. Oosthuizen (eds) *Essays on ICTY Procedure and Evidence,* Kluwer Law International, 2001, pp. 266–9.

10 'These provisions . . . were drafted with a system in mind and are derived from the distinctive legal traditions of the world's major criminal law systems . . . . These agreed-upon fundamental criminal laws and procedures constitute therefore the first true international criminal justice system in codified treaty form . . . . The eleven general principles of criminal law delineate the outer limits of the competence of the Court and cover principles from *ne bis in idem* and *nullum crimen sine lege* to minimum age and individual criminal responsibility; from command responsibility and superior orders to non-retroactivity and non-applicability of statutory limitations; from *nulla poena sine lege* to grounds for excluding criminal responsibility. While these principles themselves may be basic and common to all legal systems, the elaboration of the agreed contents of these principles is a great achievement . . .. The Statute's international criminal justice system represents the successful product of harmonization of the distinctive principles, rules and procedures derived from the world's major judicial systems'. Lee, R. S. 'The Rome Conference and Its Contribution to International Law', in R.S. Lee (ed.) *The International Criminal Court: the making of the Rome statute,* Kluwer Law International, 1999, pp. 32 and 38. 'Because of the definitions and general principles it enshrines, the Rome Statute is of great importance even before it enters into effect. Its provisions serve to reflect prevailing law and at the same time they can be used as examples to help States implement the Rome Statute in their own national legislation'. Bos, A. 'The International Criminal Court: a perspective', in Lee, *The International Criminal Court,* pp. 468–9. See also: Saland, P. 'International Criminal Law Principle', in ibid., pp. 189–216 and Fernandez de Gurmendi S.A. 'International Criminal Procedures', in ibid., pp. 217–304.

11 Plunkett, M. 'The Establishment of the Rule of law in Post-Conflict Peacekeeping', in Smith, *International Peace* Keeping, pp. 65–78.

12 Geneva Convention Relative to the Protection of Civilian Persons in Time of War of August 12, 1949. The Convention is used here as short hand to refer to all of the law of occupation which can also be found in Additional Protocol I to the Geneva Conventions, the Hague Regulations of 1907, the Hague Cultural Property Convention of 1954 and in customary law.

13 Kelly, M.J. *Restoring and Maintaining Order in Complex Peace Operations: the search for a legal framework*, Kluwer Law International, 1999, pp. 33–63.
14 Kelly, M.J., McCormack, T.L., Muggleton, H.P. and Oswald, B.M. 'Legal Aspects of Australia's Involvement in the International Force for East Timor', in *International Review of the Red Cross*, no. 841, March 2001, available at: http://www.icrc.org/Web/eng/siteeng0.nsf/iwpList182/FEC1B40BA2DF7C5FC1256B66005F9DDF (accessed 25 March 2004).
15 *SFOR Lessons Learned: in creating a secure environment with respect for the rule of law based on a study of Bosnia*, unpublished report provided to author by US Armed Forces, (May 2000).
16 Smith, J. 'NATO Forces Stretched to Limit', *Sydney Morning Herald*, 26 June 1999, p. 27. See also: the UN news web site on Kosovo at: www.un.org/peace/kosovo/news/kosovo2.htm (accessed 27 February 2004) and, OSCE Rule of Law Division Report 2 – *The Development of the Kosovo Judicial System* (10 June–15 December 1999).
17 Oakley, R.B., Dziedzic, M.J. and Goldberg E.M. (ed.) *Policing the New World Disorder: peace operations and public security*, National Defence University Press, 1998.
18 Lord, C. *Prague Project on Emergency Criminal Justice Principles: advisory note for Stimson centre/Brahimi commission*, unpublished paper by the Institute of International Relations Prague, 2000.
19 See: *Conference on National Security Law in a Changing World: the tenth annual review of the field* 'The Role of the United Nations in Peacekeeping – recent developments from a legal Perspective', Keynote Address by Mr Hans Corell, Under-Secretary-General for Legal Affairs, The Legal Counsel of the United Nations Washington, 1 December 2000, available at: www.un.org/law/counsel/english/washingtonDec00.pdf (accessed 27 February 2004).

> The Secretary-General basically supported the recommendations, to which I have made specific reference. However, with respect to the recommendation to develop an interim criminal code, the conclusions were somewhat different. The Secretary-General established a working group comprised of experts at Headquarters and legal and judicial experts in UNMIK and UNTAET. This group doubted whether it would be practical, or even desirable given the diversity of countries' specific legal traditions, for the Secretariat to try to elaborate a model criminal code, whether worldwide, regional or civil or common law based, for use by future transitional administration missions.
>
> (pp. 8–9)

Note however that this has in effect been done for the International Criminal Court as described earlier.
20 Experience and observations of the author as Chief Legal Adviser to the UNTAET Peacekeeping Force Commander from 2001–2002.
21 Experience and observations of the author as J06 (legal adviser to Headquarters Australian Theatre) from January–May 2003 and as a member of the Office of General Counsel in the Coalition Provisional Authority in Iraq from 18 May 2003 to November 2003.
22 The Defence Legislation Amendment (Aid to Civilian Authorities) Bill 2000 which added a new Part IIIAAA to the Defence Act 1903. This amendment provided far stricter terms for the situations in which the ADF could be called out and subjected such call outs to a regime of democratic control in the shape of three key Ministers including the Prime Minister, the Attorney General and the Defence Minister and Parliamentary oversight. The legislation ensured that, while ADF members could be utilized where the collective policing resources of the States and Commonwealth were inadequate, the tasks the ADF would be permitted to perform were defined and there was no derogation from the normal provisions governing *habeus corpus* and due process. This legislative framework is reinforced by the training and ethos imbibed by the members who have built a strong tradition and understanding of the place the military in a democracy.

23 See: *Conflict Diamonds: sanctions and war*, Published by the United Nations Department of Public Information in cooperation with the Sanctions Branch, Security Council Affairs Division, Department of Political Affairs, Updated 21 March 2001, available at: www.un.org/peace/africa/Diamond.html (accessed 27 February 2004).

24 Heininger, J.E. *Peacekeeping in Transition – The United Nations in Cambodia*, Twentieth Century Fund Project, 1994, pp. 2–3, 10, 25, 62–3; Jennar, R.M. 'UNTAC: "international triumph" in Cambodia?', *Security Dialogue*, vol. 25, issue 2, 1994, pp. 146 & 150; Shawcross, W. *Cambodia's New Deal*, Washington: Carnegie Endowment, 1994, pp. 16–17, 38, 44–51.

25 *Joint Doctrine for Civil Affairs*, Joint Publication 3–57.1 (US). *Civil Affairs Operations*, Field Manual 41-10 (US Army).

26 *Land Warfare Doctrine 1: The Fundamentals of Land Warfare*, published by Doctrine Wing, Combined Arms Training and Doctrine Centre, Commonwealth of Australia, 1998.

Bibliography

Abegglo, J.C. *Sea Change: Pacific Asia as the new world industrial center*, New York; Sydney: Free Press, 1994.

Aksu, J. and Camilleri, J. (eds) *Democratizing Global Governance*, Basingstoke: Palgrave MacMillan, 2002.

Alexander, L. (ed.) *Constitutionalism: political foundations*, Cambridge: Cambridge University Press, 1998.

Alexander, M. and Mohanty, C. (eds) *Feminist Genealogies, Colonial Legacies, Democratic Futures*, New York: Routledge, 1997.

Allen, T.R.S. *Law, Liberty and Justice*, Oxford: Clarendon Press, 1993.

Alston, P. *The UN and Human Rights*, Oxford: Clarendon Press, 1992.

Alston, P. (ed.) *The EU and Human Rights*, Oxford, England; New York: Oxford University Press, 1995.

Alston, P. 'The Myopia of the Handmaidens: international lawyers and globalization', *European Journal of International Law*, vol. 8, no. 3, 1997, pp. 435–47.

Alston, P. (ed.) *Promoting Human Rights Through Bills of Rights: comparative perspectives*, Oxford: Oxford University Press, 1999.

Alston, P. (ed.) *Peoples' Rights*, Oxford; New York: Oxford University Press, 2001.

Alston, P. and Crawford, J. (eds) *The Future of the UN Human Rights Treaty Monitoring*, Cambridge: Cambridge University Press, 2000.

Alston, P. and Steiner, M. *International Human Rights in Context*, 2nd edn, Oxford: Oxford University Press, 2000.

An-Na'im, A.A. 'Toward an Islamic Reformation: civil liberties', *Human Rights and International Law*, 1990, pp. 162–70.

Archibugi, D., Held, D. and Kohler, M. (eds) *Re-imagining Political Community*, Cambridge: Polity Press, 1998.

Ariyoshi, A., Habermeier, K., Laurens, B., Otker-Robe, I., Canales-Kriljenko J.I. and Kirilenko, A. *Country Experiences with the Use and Liberalization of Capital Controls*, IMF Paper, January 2000, available at: http://www.imf.org/external/pubs/ft/op/op190/ (accessed 26 February 2004).

Arup, C. *The New World Trade Organization Agreements: globalizing law through services and intellectual property*, Cambridge: Cambridge University Press, 2000.

Askin, K. and Koenig, D. (eds) *Women and International Human Rights Law*, vol. 1, Ardsley, NY: Transnational Publishers, 1999.

Australian Law Reform Commission, *Equality Before the Law*, Sydney: Australian Government Publishing Service, 1994.

Ayres, I. and Braithwaite, J. *Responsive Regulation: transcending the deregulation debate*, Oxford: New York, 1992.

Ayuso, J. and Blanco, R. *Has Financial Market Integration Increased During the 1990s?* Paper presented at International Financial Markets and the Implications for Monetary and Financial Stability, a conference of the Bank for International Settlements, 25–26 October 1999, available at: http://www.bis.org/publ/confer08.htm (accessed 26 February 2004).

Baratta, R. 'Should Invalid Reservations to Human Rights Treaties be Disregarded?' *European Journal of International Law*, vol. 11, issue 2, 2000, pp. 413–25.

Barker, E. *Social Contract: essays by Locke, Hume and Rousseau*, London: Oxford University Press, 1947.

Bauer, J. and Bell, D. *The East Asian Challenge for Human Rights*, Cambridge: Cambridge University Press, 1999.

Baxi, U. *Membrino's Helmet? human rights for a changing world*, New Delhi: Har-Anand Publications, 1994.

Bayefsky, A. *The UN Human Rights Treaty System: universality at the crossroads*, 2001, available at: http://www.bayefsky.com (accessed 24 February 2004).

Baylis, J. and Smith, S. (eds) *The Globalization of World Politics: an introduction to international relations*, Oxford, UK: Oxford University Press 1997.

Beck, U. *What is Globalization?* Cambridge: Polity Press, 2000.

Bertrand, M. 'The UN as an Organization: a critique of its functioning', *European Journal of International Law*, vol. 6, no. 3, 1995, pp. 349–59.

Binion, G. 'Human Rights: a feminist perspective', *Human Rights Quarterly*, vol. 17, issue 3, 1995, pp. 509–26.

Blackett, A. 'Whither the Social Clause? human rights, trade theory and treaty interpretation', *Columbian Human Rights Law Review*, vol. 31, 1999, pp. 1–80.

Blackshield, T. and Williams, G. *Australian Constitutional Law and Theory*, 2nd edn, Sydney: The Federation Press, 1998.

Blinder, A.S. 'Eight Steps to a New Financial Order', *Foreign Affairs*, vol. 78, issue 5, September–October 1999, pp. 50–63.

Bobbio, N. *The Age of Rights*, Cambridge: Polity Press, 1996.

Bolt, R. *A Man For All Seasons*, London: Heinemann, 1960.

Bottomley, S. and Kinley, D. (eds) *Commercial Law and Human Rights*, Aldershot: Ashgate, 2002.

Boutros-Ghali, B. *An Agenda for Democratization*, New York: The United Nations, 1996.

Bouwhuis, J. 'International Law by the Back Door?' *Australian Law Journal*, vol. 72, no. 10, October 1998, pp. 794–98.

Bowett, D., Crawford, J., Sinclair, I. and Watts, A. 'The International Court of Justice: efficiency of procedures and working methods', *International and Comparative Law Quarterly Supp.*, vol. 45, 1996, s1–s35.

Braithwaite, J. and Drahos, P. *Global Business Regulation*, Cambridge: Cambridge University Press, 2000.

Brownlie, I. *Principles of Public International Law*, 4th edn, Oxford: Oxford University Press, 1990.

Brownlie, I. *The Rule of Law in International Affairs*, The Hague: Martinus Nijhoff, 1998.

Brysk, A. (ed.) *Globalization and Human Rights*, Berkeley: University of California Press, 2002.

Buchheit, L.C. and Mitu Gulati, G. 'Sovereign Bonds and the Collective Will', *Emory Law Journal*, vol. 51, no. 4, Fall 2002, pp. 1317–64.

Buckley, R.P. 'Now We Have Come to the "ICSID" Party: are its awards final and enforceable?', *Sydney Law Review*, vol. 14, 1992, pp. 358–72.

Buckley, R.P. 'The Role of Capital Controls in International Financial Crises', *Bond Law Review*, vol. 11, no. 2, December 1999, pp. 231–44.

Buckley, R.P. *Emerging Markets Debt*, London: Kluwer Law International, 1999.

Buckley, R.P. 'The Essential Flaw in the Globalisation of Capital Markets: its impact on human rights in developing countries', *California Western International Law Journal*, vol. 32, no. 1, Fall 2001, pp. 119–31.

Buckley, R.P. 'Do Cry for the Argentines: an analysis of their crisis', *Banking and Finance Law Review*, vol. 17, 2003, pp. 373–93.

Buergenthal, T. 'Modern Constitutions and Human Rights Treaties', *Columbia Journal of Transnational Law*, vol. 36, 1997, pp. 211–23.

Buiter W. and Sibert A. *UDROP: a small contribution to the international financial architecture 1999*, Discussion Paper 0425, available at: http://cep.lse.ac.uk/papers/discussion/table.html (accessed 26 February 2004).

Bustelo, P., Garcia, C. and Olivié, I. *Global and Domestic Factors of Financial Crises in Emerging Economies: lessons from the East Asian episodes (1997–1999)*, ICEI Working Paper No. 16, Instituto Complutense De Estudios Internacionales, Madrid, 1999.

Byers, M. (ed.) *The Role of Law in International Politics*, Oxford: Oxford University Press, 2002.

Byrnes, A., Connors, J. and Bik, L. (eds) *Advancing the Human Rights of Women*, London: Commonwealth Secretariat, 1997.

Camilleri, J. and Falk, J. *The End of Sovereignty? the politics of a shrinking and fragmenting world*, Hants: Edward Elgar, 1992.

Campbell, T. (ed.) *Human Rights: from rhetoric to reality*, New York, NY; Oxford, UK: Blackwell, 1986.

Cass, R.A. 'Judging: the norms and incentives of retrospective decision-making', *Boston University Law Review*, vol. 75, 1995.

Cassese, A. *International Law in a Divided World*, Oxford: Oxford University Press, 1986.

Cassese, A. *Human Right in a Changing World*, Cambridge: Polity Press, 1990.

Cassese, A. *International Law*, Oxford: Oxford University Press, 2001.

Castells, M. *The Information Age: the rise of the network society*, vol. 1, Oxford: Blackwells, 1996.

Charlesworth, H. 'Dangerous Liaisons: globalization and Australian public law', *Adelaide Law Review*, vol. 20, no. 1, 1998, pp. 57–72.

Charlesworth, H. and Chinkin, C. *The Boundaries of International Law: a feminist analysis*, Manchester: Manchester University Press, 2000.

Childers, E. and Urquart, B. *Towards a More Effective United Nations*, Uppsala: Dag Hammarskjold Foundation, 1992.

Childers, E. and Urquart, B. *Renewing the United Nations System*, Uppsala: Dag Hammarskjold Foundation, 1994.

Chinkin, C. and Wright, S. 'The Hunger Trap: women, food and development', *Michigan Journal of International Law*, vol. 14, no. 2, Winter 1993, pp. 262–321.

Commission on Global Governance, *Our Global Neighbourhood*, Oxford: Oxford University Press, 1995.

Cook, R. (ed.) *Human Rights of Women: national and international perspectives*, Philadelphia: University of Pennsylvania Press, 1994.

Cotterrell, R. *The Politics of Jurisprudence: a critical introduction to legal philosophy*, London: Butterworths, 1989.

Craig, P. 'Formal and Substantive Conceptions of the Rule of Law: an analytical framework', *Public Law*, 1997, pp. 467–87.

Craven, G. 'The High Court of Australia: a study in the abuse of power', Alfred Deakin Lecture Trust, Melbourne, 1997.

Craven, M.C.R. *The International Covenant on Economic, Social and Cultural Rights: a perspective on its development*, Oxford: New York: Clarendon Press; Oxford University Press, 1995.

Crawford, J. (ed.) *The Rights of Peoples*, Oxford: Clarendon Press, 1992.

Crawford, J. *Democracy in International Law*, Inaugural Lecture, Cambridge: Cambridge University Press, 1994.

Darrow, M. *Between Shadow and Light: the world bank, the international monetary fund and international human rights law*, Oxford; Portland, Or.: Hart, 2003.

Das, C. and Chandra, K. (eds) *Judges and Judicial Accountability*, Commonwealth Law Association, 2003.

Davey, W. 'The WTO Dispute Settlement System', *Journal of International Economic Law*, vol. 3, issue 1, March 2000, pp. 15–18.

'Development in the Laws, International Criminal Law: corporate liability for violations of international human rights law', *Harvard Law Review*, vol. 114, pp. 2025–48.

Dicey, A.V. *An Introduction to the Study of the Law of the Constitution*, 10th edn, London: MacMillan, 1959.

Dicken, P. *Global Shift: transforming the world economy*, 3rd edn, London: Paul Chapman, 1998.

Dijk, P. van and Hoof, G.J.H. Van, *Theory and Practice of the European Convention on Human Rights*, 3rd edn, The Hague; Boston: Kluwer Law International, 1998.

Dixon, M. and McCorquodale, R. *Cases and Materials on International Law*, London: Blackstone Press, 1991.

Dommen, C. 'Raising Human Rights Concerns in the World Trade Organization: actors, processes and possible strategies', *Human Rights Quarterly*, vol. 24, issue 1, February 2002, pp. 1–50.

Dorn, J.A. *A New Global Financial Architecture*, Center for Trade Policy Studies, available at: http://www.freetrade.org/pubs/articles/jd–11–04–98.html (accessed 5 March 2004).

Drèze, J. and Sen, A. *Hunger and Public Action*, Oxford: Oxford University Press, 1999.

Dworkin, R. *Taking Rights Seriously*, London: Duckworth, 1977.

Dworkin, R. *A Matter of Principle*, Cambridge: Harvard University Press, 1985.

Dworkin, R. *Law's Empire*, London: Fontana Press, 1986.

Edwards, M. and Gaventa, J. (eds) *Global Citizen Action*, London: Earthscan Publications, 2001.

Edwards, S. *How Effective Are Capital Controls?* NBER Working Paper No. W7413, November 1999, available at: http://www.nber.org/papers/w7413 (accessed 25 February 2004).

Ehrlich, E. *Fundamental Principles of the Sociology of Law*, Russell & Russell, New York, 1962.

Eichengreen, B. 'Bailing in the Private Sector: burden sharing in international financial crisis management', *The Fletcher Forum of World Affairs*, vol. 23, Winter–Spring 1999, pp. 57–76.

Eichengreen, B. *Toward A New International Financial Architecture: a practical post-Asia agenda*, Washington DC: Institute for International Economics, 1999.

Eide, A., Krause, C. and Rosas, A. (eds) *Economic, Social and Cultural Rights: a textbook*, 2nd edn, Boston: Martinus Nijhoff, 2001.

Ely, J.H. *Democracy and Distrust: a theory of judicial review*, Cambridge: Harvard University Press, 1980.

Espinosa-Vega, M.A., Smith, B.D. and Yip, C.K. *Barriers to International Capital Flows: who should erect them and how big should they be?* Federal Reserve Bank of Atlanta Working Paper, July 1999.

Evans, T. (ed.) *Human Rights Fifty Years On: a reappraisal*, Manchester: Manchester University Press, 1998.

Falk, R. 'Appraising the UN at 50: the looming challenge', *Journal of International Affairs*, vol. 48, no. 2, Winter 1995, pp. 625–46.

Falk, R. *On Humane Governance: toward a new global politics*, Cambridge: Polity Press, 1995.

Falk, R. *Human Rights Horizons: the pursuit of justice in a globalizing world*, London: Routledge, 2000.

Falk, R. and Strauss, A. 'Toward Global Parliament', *Foreign Affairs*, vol. 80, issue 1, January–February 2001, pp. 212–20.

Feldstein, M. 'A Self-Help Guide for Emerging Markets', *Foreign Affairs*, vol. 78, issue 2, March–April 1999, pp. 93–110.

Felice, M. *Taking Suffering Seriously: the importance of collective human rights*, Albany: State University of New York Press, 1996.

Finn, P. (ed.) *Essays on Law and Government*, vol. 1, Sydney: Law Book Co., 1995.

Finnis, J. *Natural Law and Natural Rights*, Oxford: Oxford University Press, 1980.

Forsyth, C. (ed.) *Judicial Review and the Constitution*, Oxford: Hart Publishing, 2000.

Forsythe, D.P. *The Internationalization of Human Rights*, Lexington, MA: Lexington Books, 1991.

Franck, T. *Judging the World Court*, New York: Priority Press, 1986.

Franck, T. 'The Emerging Right to Democratic Governance', *American Journal of International Law*, vol. 86, no. 1, 1992, pp. 46–91.

Franck, T. *Fairness in International Law and Institutions*, Oxford: Oxford University Press, 1995.

Frank, J. *Law and the Modern Mind*, London: Stevens, 1949.

Friedman, T.L. *The Lexus and the Olive Tree*, New York: Anchor Books, 2000.

Fukuyama, F. *The End of History and the Last Man*, New York; London: Avon Books; Penguin, 1992.

Fuller, L.L. *The Morality of Law*, New Haven; London: Yale University Press, 1964, 1969.

Gallagher, A. 'Ending the Marginalisation: strategies for incorporating women into the United Nations human rights system', *Human Rights Quarterly*, vol. 19, issue 2, 1997, pp. 283–333.

Galligan, B. and Sampford, C. (eds) *Rethinking Human Rights*, Sydney: Federation Press, 1997.

Gardner, J.P. (ed) *Human Rights as General Norms and a State's Right to Opt Out: reservations and objections to human rights conventions*, British Institute of International and Comparative Law, London, 1997.

Garten J.E. 'Lessons for the Next Financial Crisis', *Foreign Affairs*, vol. 78, issue 2, March–April 1999, pp. 76–92.

Ghai, Y. 'Human Rights and Asian Values', *Public Law Review*, vol. 9, 1998, pp. 168–82.

Giddens, A. *The Consequences of Modernity*, Cambridge, UK: Polity Press in association with Basil Blackwell, Oxford, UK, 1990.

Giddens, A. and Hutton, W. (eds) *On the Edge: living with global capitalism*, London: Vintage, 2001.

Gills, B. (ed.) *Globalization and the Politics of Resistance*, London: MacMillan, 2000.

Gilpin, R. *The Challenge of Global Capitalism: the world economy in the 21st century*, Princeton, NJ: Princeton University Press, 2000.

Goldstein, M. 'The Future of the International Financial Architecture: a council on foreign relations taskforce', *Foreign Affairs*, vol. 78, issue 6, November–December, 1999, pp. 169–84.

Gowlland-Debbas, V. 'The Relationship between the International Court of Justice and the Security Council in the Light of the Lockerbie Case', *American Journal of International Law*, vol. 88, 1994, pp. 643–77.

Gray, J. *False Dawn: the delusions of global capitalism*, New York: New Press: Distributed by W.W. Norton, 1998.

Guest, A.G. (ed.) *Oxford Essays in Jurisprudence: a collaborative work*, London: Oxford University Press, 1961.

Habermas, J. *Between Facts and Norms*, Cambridge: Polity Press, 1996.

Harden, I. and Lewis, N. *The Noble Lie: the British constitution and the rule of law*, London: Hutchinson, 1986.

Harrington, J. *The Commonwealth of Oceana and A system of Politics*, Cambridge: Cambridge University Press, 1992.

Harris, D.J. *Cases and Materials on International Law*, 4th edn, London: Sweet & Maxwell, 1991.

Harris, D.J. and Livingstone, S. (eds) *The Inter-American System of Human Rights*, Aldershot, UK; Brookfield, VT: Ashgate Publishing Company, 1997.

Hart, H.L.A. *The Concept of Law*, Oxford, Clarendon Press, 1961.

Hart, M. 'The WTO and the Political Economy of Globalization', *Journal of World Trade*, vol. 31, no. 5, 1997, pp. 75–94.

Hayek, F.A. *The Constitution of Liberty*, London: Routledge, 1960.

Hayek, F.A. *The Road to Serfdom*, Chicago: University of Chicago Press, 1944, 1976.

Hayek, F.A. *Law, Legislation and Liberty: a new statement of the liberal principles of justice and political economy*, London; Melbourne: Routledge & Kegan Paul, 1982.

Heininger, J.E. *Peacekeeping in Transition – the United Nations in Cambodia*, Twentieth Century Fund Project, 1994.

Held, D. and McGrew, A. *The Global Transformations Reader*, Cambridge: Polity Press, 2000.

Held, D., McGrew, A., Golblatt, D. and Perraton, J. *Global Transformations: politics, economics and culture*, Cambridge: Polity Press, 1999.

Held, D. *Democracy and the Global Order: from the modern state to cosmopolitan governance*, Cambridge: Polity Press, 1995.

Held, D. and Koenig–Archibugi, M. (eds) *Taming Global Globalization: frontiers of global governance*, Cambridge: Polity, 2003.

Helman, G.B. and Ratner, S.R. 'Saving Failed States', *Foreign Policy*, no. 89, Winter 1992, pp. 3–20.

Henkin, L. and Hargrove, J. (eds) *Human Rights: an agenda for the next century*, Washington, D.C.: American Society of International Law, 1994.

Higgins, R. *Problems and Process: international law and how we use it*, Oxford: Clarendon Press, 1994.

Higgins, R. 'International Law in a Changing International System', *The Cambridge Law Journal*, vol. 58, issue 1, March 1999, pp. 78–95.

Hobbes, T. *Leviathan*, Cambridge: Cambridge University Press, 1991.

Horwitz, M.J. 'The Rule of Law: an unqualified human good?' *Yale Law Journal*, vol. 86, 1977, pp. 561–6.

Hunt, P. *Reclaiming Social Rights: international and comparative perspectives*, Aldershot; Brookfield, Vt.: Dartmouth, 1996.

Hunter, I. *The Westphalian Peace and the Desacralisation of Politics*. Paper presented at the Symposium: thinking peace, making peace: marking the United Nations' International Year for the Culture of Peace, 6 November 2000.

Hutchinson, A.C. and Monahan, P. (eds) *The Rule of Law: ideal or ideology*, Toronto: Carswell, 1987.

Hutchinson, A.C. and Monahan, P.J. 'Law, Politics and the Critical Legal Scholars: the unfolding drama of American legal thought', *Stanford Law Review*, vol. 36, 1983–84, pp. 199–245.

Hutton, W. and Giddens, A. (eds) *On the Edge: living with global capitalism*, London: Johnathan Cape, 2000.

Ignatieff, M. *Whose Universal Values? the crisis in human rights*, The Hague: Foundation Horizon, 1999.

Ignatieff, M. *Human Rights as Politics and Idolatry*, Princeton: Princeton University Press, 2001.

IMF, *Proposals for a Sovereign Debt Restructuring Mechanism (SDRM) A Factsheet*, January 2003, D.5, available at: http://www.imf.org/external/np/exr/facts/sdrm.htm (accessed 26 February 2004).

Ingram, J.C. 'The Politics of Human Suffering', *The National Interest*, issue 33, Fall 1993, pp. 59–67.

International Commission on Intervention and State Sovereignty, *The Responsibility to Protect*, Government of Canada, 2000.

Jayasuriya, K. 'Globalization, Law and the Transformation of Sovereignty: the emergence of global regulatory governance', *Indiana Journal of Global Legal Studies*, vol. 6, issue 2, Spring 1999, pp. 425–55.

Jennar, R.M. 'UNTAC: "International Triumph" in Cambodia?' *Security Dialogue*, vol. 25, issue 2, 1994, pp. 145–56.

Joffe, J. *Gulliver Unbound: can America rule the world?*, The Twentieth Annual John Bonython Lecture, Sydney, 5 August 2003, available at: www.aicgs.org/c/csi.pdf (accessed 24 February 2004).

Jones, R.J.B. *The World Turned Upside Down?: globalization and the future of the state*, Manchester, UK; New York: Manchester University Press, 2000.

Joseph, S. *Transnational Human Rights Litigation against Corporations* (forthcoming, Hart Publications, Oxford, 2004).

Joseph, S., Schultz, J. and Castan M. *The International Covenant on Civil and Political Rights: cases, materials and commentary*, Oxford; New York: Oxford University Press, 2000.

Jowell, J. and Oliver, D. (eds) *The Changing Constitution*, 3rd edn, Oxford: Oxford University Press, 1994.

Kahler, M. (ed.) *Capital Flows and Financial Crises*, Ithaca, NY: Cornell University Press, 1998.

Kamminga, M.T. and Zia-Zarifi, S. (eds) *Liability of Multinational Corporations Under International Law*, The Hague: Kluwer Law International, 2000.

Kaufman, H. 'Protecting Against the Next Financial Crisis: the need to reform global financial oversight, the IMF, and monetary policy goals', *Business Economics*, July 1999, available at: http://www.findarticles.com/m1094/3_34/issue.jhtml (accessed 16 March 2004).

Kelly, M.J. *Restoring and Maintaining Order in Complex Peace Operations: the search for a legal framework*, London: Kluwer Law International, 1999.

Kelly, M.J., McCormack, T.L., Muggleton, H. P. and Oswald, B.M. 'Legal Aspects of Australia's Involvement in the International Force for East Timor' in *International Review of the Red Cross*, no. 841, March 2001, available at: http://www.icrc.org/Web/eng/siteeng0.nsf/iwpList182/FEC1B40BA2DF7C5FC1256B66005F9DDF (accessed 25 March 2004).

Kelsey, J. 'Globalization, State and Law: towards a multi-perspectival polity', *Law In Context*, vol. 14, 1996, pp. 31–51.

Kelsey, J. 'Global Economic Policy-Making: a new constitutionalism?' *Otago Law Review*, vol. 9, no. 3, 1999, pp. 535–55.

Kennedy, D. 'The International Human Rights Movement: part of the problem?' *European Human Rights Law Review*, vol. 6, issue 3, 2001, pp. 245–67.

King, R.G. and Levine, R. 'Finance and Growth: Schumpeter might be right', *The Quarterly Journal of Economics*, vol. 108, issue 3, August 1993, pp. 717–38.

King, R.G. and Levine, R. 'Finance, Entrepreneurship and Growth', *Journal of Monetary Economics*, vol. 32, issue 3, December 1993, pp. 513–42.

Kingsbury, B. 'Sovereignty and Inequality', *European Journal of International Law*, vol. 9, issue 4, 1998, pp. 599–625.

Kinley, D. 'Constitutional Brokerage in Australia: constitutions and the doctrines of parliamentary supremacy and the rule of law', *Federal Law Review*, vol. 22, no. 1, 1994, pp. 194–204.

Kinley, D. (ed.) *Human Rights in Australian Law: principles, practice and potential*, Leichardt, NSW: The Federation Press, 1998.

Kinley, D. and Tadaki, J. 'From Talk to Walk: the emergence of human rights responsibilities for corporations at international law', *Virginia Journal of International Law*, vol. 44, issue 4, (2003–04; forthcoming).

Kirby, M.D. 'The Australian Use of International Human Rights Norms: from Bangalore to Balliol, a view from the Antipodes', *University of New South Wales Law Journal*, vol. 16, no. 2, 1993, pp. 363–93.

Kirby, M.D. 'Constitutional Interpretation and Original Intent: a form of ancestor worship?' *Melbourne University Law Review*, vol. 24, issue 1, April 2000, pp. 1–14.

Kirby, M.D. *Through the World's Eye*, Annandale, NSW: Federation Press, 2000.

Koh, H.H. 'International Law as Part of Our Law', *American Journal of International Law*, vol. 98, issue 1, 2004, pp. 43–57.

Krasno, J. (ed.) *The United Nations: confronting the challenges of a global society*, Boulder: Lynne Reinner, 2004.

Koskenniemi, M. 'The Police in the Temple: order, justice and the United Nations: a dialectical view', *European Journal of International Law*, vol. 6, no. 3, 1995, pp. 325–48.

Kriegel, B. *The State Under the Rule of Law*, Princeton: Princeton University Press, 1995.

Krueger, A. *A New Approach to Sovereign Debt Restructuring*, 2002, available at: http://www.imf.org/external/pubs/ft/exrp/sdrm/eng/index.htm (accessed 26 February 2004).

Krygier, M. *Transitional Questions About the Rule of Law: why, what and how?* East Central Europe/L'Europe du Centre Est. Eine wissenschaftliche Zeitschrift, vol. 28, part 1 (2001).

Krygier, M. and Czarnota A. (eds) *The Rule of Law after Communism*, Brookfield, VT: Ashgate/Dartmouth Publishing Co., 1999.

Kurth, J. *The Protestant Deformation and American Foreign Policy.* Paper presented to The Philadelphia Society, 37th National Meeting (22 April 2001), available at: http://www.townhall.com/phillysoc/Kurth%20Speech.htm (accessed 24 February 2004).

Lauterpacht, H. *International Law and Human Rights*, London: Stevens & Sons, 1950.

Laws, J. 'Is the High Court the Guardian of Fundamental Constitutional Rights?' *Public Law*, 1993, pp. 59–79.

Laws, J. 'Law and Democracy', *Public Law*, 1995, pp. 72–93.

Laws, J. 'The Constitution: morals and rights', *Public Law*, Winter 1996, pp. 622–35.

Lee, R.S. (ed.) *The International Criminal Court: the making of the Rome Statute*, London: Kluwer Law International, 1999.

Leipziger, D. *The Corporate Responsibility Code Book*, Sheffield: Greenleaf, 2003.

Leiser, B.M. and Campbell, T.D. (eds) *Human Rights in Philosophy and Practice*, Dartmouth, UK: Ashgate, 2001.

Leslie, C.R. 'Creating Criminals: the injuries inflicted by "unenforced" sodomy laws', *Harvard Civil Rights, Civil Liberties Law Review*, vol. 35, Winter 2000, pp. 103–15.

Levine, R. and Zervos, S. 'Stock Markets, Banks, and Economic Growth', *The American Economic Review*, vol. 88, issue 1, June 1998, pp. 537–59.

Lewis, C.S. *That Hideous Strength: a modern fairy-tale for Grown-ups*, London: Bodley Head, 1946.

Linehan, J. (2002) 'Women in Public International Litigation', available at: http://www.pict–pcti.org/activities/meetings/London_07_01/Women1.pdf (accessed 25 February 2004).

Lubman, S. (ed.) *China's Legal Reforms,* Oxford; New York: Oxford University Press, 1996.

McBeth, A. *A Look at Corporate Code of Conduct Legislation,* Common Law World Review (2004; forthcoming).

Makin, C. 'Doesn't Anybody Remember Risk?' *Institutional Investor*, April 1994, pp. 41–6.

Maley, W., Sampford, C. and Thakur, R. (eds) *From Civil Strife to Civil Society: civil and military responsibilities in disrupted states*, Tokyo: United Nations University Press, 2003.

Mandel, M. *The Charter of Rights and the Legalisation of Politics in Canada*, Toronto: Wall & Thompson, 1989.

Mandelbaum, M. 'A Perfect Failure: NATO's war against Yugoslavia', *Foreign Affairs*, vol. 78, issue 5, September–October 1999, available at: http://www.foreignpolicy2000.org/library/issuebriefs/readingnotes/fa_mandelbaum.html (accessed 18 March 2004).

Marichal, C.A. *Century of Debt Crises in Latin America: from independence to the great depression 1820–1930*, Princeton, NJ: Princeton University Press, 1989.

Mathew, P. 'International Law and the Protection of Human Rights in Australia: recent trends', *Sydney Law Review*, vol. 17, no. 2, June 1995, pp. 177–203.

May, R., Tolbert, D., Hocking, J., Roberts, K., Jia, B.B., Mundis, D. and Oosthuizen, G. (eds) *Essays on ICTY Procedure and Evidence*, London: Kluwer Law International, 2001.

Meyer, L.H. *Lessons from the Asian Crisis: a central banker's perspective*, Levy Economics Institute Working Paper No. 276, 1999.

Milsom, S.F.C. *Historical Foundations of the Common Law*, London: Butterworths, 1981.

Mittelman, J. *The Globalization Syndrome: transformation and resistance*, Princeton: Princeton University Press, 2000.

Monbiot, G. *The Age of Consent: a manifesto for a new world order*, London: Flamingo, 2003.

Morgan, W. 'Sexuality and Human Rights: the first communication by an Australian to the Human Rights Committee under the optional protocol to the International Covenant on Civil and Political Rights', *Australian Yearbook of International Law*, vol. 14, 1993, pp. 277–92.

Morgan, W. 'Identifying Evil for What it is: Tasmania, sexual perversity and the United Nations', *Melbourne University Law Review*, vol. 19, no. 3, June 1994, pp. 740–57.

Muchlinski, P. *Multinational Enterprises and the Law*, Oxford; Cambridge, MA: Blackwell Publishers, 1999.

Muller, A.S., Raic, D. and Thuránszky, J.M. (eds) *The International Court of Justice: its future role after fifty years*, The Hague: Kluwer, 1997.

Nicholas, B. 'The Vienna Convention', *Law Quarterly Review*, vol. 105, April 1989, pp. 201–43.

Nowrot, K. 'Legal Consequences of Globalization: the status of non-governmental organizations under international law', *Indiana Journal of Global Legal Studies*, vol. 6, issue 2, 1999, pp. 579–645.

Nussbaum, M. 'Capabilities and Human Rights', *Fordham Law Review*, vol. 66, 1997, pp. 273–300.

Nussbaum, M. and Sen, A. (eds) *The Quality of Life*, Oxford: Clarendon Press; New York: Oxford University Press, 1993.

Oakley, R.B., Dziedzic, M.J. and Goldberg E.M. (eds) *Policing the New World Disorder: peace operations and public security*, Washington: National Defence University Press, 1998.

O'Donovan, K. 'Engendering Justice: women's perspectives and the rule of law', *University of Toronto Law Journal*, vol. 39, 1989, pp. 127–48.

OECD, *Guidelines on the Protection of Privacy and Transborder Flows of Personal Data*, Paris, 1980.

Paarlberg, R. 'The Global Food Fight', *Foreign Affairs*, vol. 79, issue 3, May–June 2000, pp. 24–38.

Palmer, K.E. (ed.) *Constitutional Amendments – 1789 to the present*, Gale Group, 1999.

Palmeter, D. and Navrodis, P. 'The WTO Legal System: sources of law', *American Journal of International Law*, vol. 92, 1998, pp. 398–413.

Paolini, A., Jarvis, A. and Reus-Smit, C. *Between Sovereignty and Global Governance: the United Nations, the state and civil society*, London: MacMillan, 1998.

Parker, G. *The Military Revolution: military innovation and the rise of the West 1500–1800*, 2nd edn, Cambridge; Melbourne: Cambridge University Press, 1996.

Patterson, D. 'Langdell's Legacy', *Northwestern University Law Review*, vol. 90, no. 1, 1995, pp. 196–203.

Perry, A. 'An Ideal Legal System for Attracting Foreign Direct Investment? Some Theory and Reality', *American University International Law Review*, vol. 15, no. 6, October 2000, pp. 1627–57.

Peters, J. and Wolper, A. (eds) *Women's Rights Human Rights: international feminist perspectives*, New York; London: Routledge, 1995.

Petersmann, E.-U. 'How to Constitutionalize International Law and Foreign Policy for the Benefit of Civil Society', *Michigan Journal of International Law*, vol. 20, no. 1, Fall 1998, pp. 1–30.

Pettifor, A. 'Resolving International Debt Crises – the Jubilee Framework for International Insolvency', January 2002, available at: www.jubileeplus.org/analysis/reports/jubilee_framework.html (accessed 26 February 2004).

Pocock, J.G.A. (ed.) *The Political Work of James Harrington*, Cambridge: Cambridge University Press, 1977.

Polden, M. 'The Law, the Environment and the Mosquito', *Amicus Curiae*, issue 28, June 2000.

Pollis, A, and Schwab, P. *Human Rights: a Western construct with limited applicability*, Pennsylvania: Pennsylvania State University Press, 1980.

Pound, R. *Philosophy of Law*, New Haven, Conn.: Yale University Press, 1954.

Qureshi, A. *The World Trade Organisation: implementing international trade norms*, Manchester: Manchester University Press, 1996.

Radin, M.J. 'Reconsidering the Rule of Law', *Boston University Law Review*, vol. 69, 1989, p. 791.

Raffer, K. 'Applying Chapter 9 Insolvency to International Debts: an economically efficient solution with a human face', *World Development*, vol. 18, issue 2, February 1990, pp. 301–11.

Raffer, K. 'Solving Sovereign Debt Overhang by Internationalising Chapter 9 Procedures' *Studien von Zeitfragen*, 2002, available at: http://www.jahrbuch2002.studien-von-zeitfragen.net/Weltfinanz/RAFFER_1/raffer_1.HTM (accessed 5 March 2004).

Raffer, K. *To Stay or Not to Stay – a short note on differing versions of the SDRM*, January 31, 2003, available at: http://www.jubilee2000uk.org/latest/raffer310103.htm (accessed 26 February 2004).

Rasche, P.W. 'Argentina: test case for a new approach to insolvency?' *Studien von Zeitfragen*, January 5, 2002.

Ratner, S.B. 'Corporations and Human Rights: a theory of legal responsibility', *Yale Law Journal*, vol. 111, issue 3, December 2001, pp. 435–537.

Rawls, J. *A Theory of Justice*, MA: Harvard University Press, 1971.

Rawls, J. *Justice as Fairness: a restatement*, Cambridge, MA: Harvard University Press, 2001.

Raz, J. 'The Rule of Law and its Virtue', *Law Quarterly Review*, vol. 93, 1977, pp. 195–211.

Raz, J. *The Authority of Law: essays on law and morality*, Oxford: Clarendon Press, 1979.

Raz, J. *Ethics in the Public Domain: essays in the morality of law and politics*, Oxford: Oxford University Press, 1995.

Roberts, A. and Kingsbury, B. (eds) *United Nations, Divided World*, 2nd edn, Oxford: Clarendon Press, 1993.

Robertson, A. and Merrills, J. *Human Rights in the World*, 4th edn, Manchester: Manchester University Press, 1989.

Robertson, G. *Crimes Against Humanity: the struggle for global justice*, London: Allen Lane, The Penguin Press, 1999.

Rogge, M.J. 'Towards Transnational Corporate Accountability in the Global Economy: challenging the doctrine of forum non conveniens, in re: union carbide, Alfaro, Sequihua and Aguinda', *Texas International Law Journal*, vol. 36, issue 2, Spring 2001, pp. 299–318.

Rogoff, K. *International Institutions for Reducing Global Financial Instability*, NBER Working Paper No. W7265, 1999, available at: http://www.nber.org/papers/w7265 (accessed 26 February 2004).

Rogoff, K. and Zettelmeyer, J. 'Early Ideas on Sovereign Bankruptcy Reorganization: a survey', IMF Working Paper WP/02/57, 2002, available at: http://www.imf.org/external/pubs/ft/wp/2002/wp0257.pdf (accessed 5 March 2004).

Rose, D. (ed.) *Lewis Australian Bankruptcy Law*, Sydney: Law Book Co., 1994.

Rothbard, M. 'Death of a State', *Reason*, July 1975, pp. 31–2.

Rousseau, P.L. and Sylla, R. *Emerging Financial Markets and Early U.S. Growth*, Cambridge, MA: National Bureau of Economic Research, 1999.

Runciman, D. 'A Bear Armed with a Gun', *London Review of Books*, vol. 25, no. 7, 3 April 2003, available at: http://www.1rb.co.uk/v25/n07/runc01_.html (accessed 10 March 2004)

Rung, C.F. and Senauer, B. 'A Removable Feast', *Foreign Affairs*, vol. 79, issue 3, May–June 2000, pp. 39–51.

Safeguarding Prosperity in a Global Financial System: the future international financial architecture, Report of an Independent Task Force Sponsored by the Council on Foreign Relations, September 1999.

Sajó, A. (ed.) *In and Out of Authoritarian Law*, The Hague: Kluwer Law International, 2002.

Sampford, C. *Democratic and Global Challenges to the Concepts of 'Sovereignty' and 'Intervention'*. Paper presented at the 19th World Congress on Philosophy of Law and Social Philosophy, New York, June 1999.

Sampford, C. (ed.) *Asia Pacific Governance 2000: from crisis to reform*, Aldershot: Ashgate, 2002.

Sampford, C., Condlln, S., Palmer, M. and Round, T. (eds) *Asia Pacific Governance: from crisis to reform*, London: Ashgate, 2002.

Santos, B. de Sousa, *Toward a New Common Sense: law, science and politics in the paradigmatic transition*, New York: Routledge, 1995.

Saunders, C. and Le Roy, K. (eds) *The Rule of Law*, Annandale, NSW: Federation Press, 2003.

Scholte, J., O'Brien, R. and Williams, M. 'The WTO and Civil Society', *Journal of World Trade*, vol. 33, no. 1, 1999, pp. 107–24.

Scott, C. 'Reaching Beyond (Without Abandoning) the Category of 'Economic, Social and Cultural Rights', *Human Rights Quarterly*, vol. 21, issue 3, 1999, pp. 633–60.

Sellers, M. (ed.) *Sovereignty, Human Rights and the Self-Determination of Peoples*, Oxford: Berg, 1996.

Selznick, P. 'Sociology and Natural Law', *Natural Law Forum*, vol. 6, 1961, pp. 83–108.

Selznick, P. *The Moral Commonwealth: social theory and the promise of community*, Berkeley: University of California Press, 1992.

Sen, A. 'Freedoms and Needs', *New Republic*, 10 & 17 January 1994, pp. 31–8.

Shapiro, I. (ed.) *The Rule of Law*, New York: New York University Press, 1994.

Shawcross, W. *Cambodia's New Deal*, Washington: Carnegie Endowment, 1994.

Shearer, I. *Starke's International Law*, 11th edn, London: Butterworths, 1994.

Shelton, D. 'International Law and Relative Normativity', in Evans, M. (ed.) *International Law*, Oxford: Oxford University Press, 2003, chapter 5.

Shklar, J. *Political Thought and Political Thinkers*, Chicago: University of Chicago Press, 1998.

Shihata, I.F.I. *The World Bank Inspection Panel: in practice*, 2nd edn, Oxford: Oxford University Press, 2000.

Shiner, C. 'The Authority Vacuum', *Africa Report*, vol. 39, no. 6, November–December 1994, pp. 22–5.

Shiva, V. *Women, Ecology and Economic Globalization: searching for an alternative vision*, Indian Association of Women's Studies, 1995.

Singer, H.W. and Sharma, S. (eds) *Economic Development and World Debt*, London: Macmillan, 1989.

Singer, P. *One World: the ethics of globalisation*, Melbourne: Text Publishing, 2002.

Singh, K. 'Restructuring the International Financial Architecture', *Asia–Europe Dialogue Articles*, 1999, available at: http://www.ased.org (accessed 5 March 2004).

Skubik, D.W. *At the Intersection of Legality and Morality: Hartian law as natural law*, New York: Peter Lang, 1990.

Slaughter, A. 'The Real New World Order', *Foreign Affairs*, vol. 76, issue 5, September–October 1997, pp. 183–97.

Smith, H. (ed.) *International Peacekeeping: building on the Cambodia experience*, Canberra: Australian Defence Studies Centre, 1994.

Soros, G. *The Crisis of Global Capitalism*, London: Little Brown, 1998.

Steiner, H.J. and Alston, P. *International Human Rights in Context: law, politics, morals: text and materials*, Oxford: New York: Clarendon Press; Oxford University Press, 1996, 2000.

Stiglitz, J. *Globalization and its Discontents*, London: Allen Lane, The Penguin Press, 2002.

Sullivan, R (ed.) *Business and Human Rights: dilemmas and solutions*, Sheffield: Greenleaf, 2003.

Summers, R. 'A Formal Theory of the Rule of Law', *Ratio Juris*, vol. 6, no. 2, July 1993, pp. 124–42.

Sur, S. 'The State Between Fragmentation and Globalization', *European Journal of International Law*, vol. 8, no. 3, 1997, pp. 421–34.

Sutherland, P. *Managing the International Economy in an Age of Globalization*, The 1998 Per Jacobsson Lecture, the annual meeting of the IMF and the World Bank.

Tay, A. Erh-Soon 'The New Century, Globalisation and Human Rights', *Asia Pacific Law Review*, 8, 2000, pp. 139–52.

Teitel, R. 'Transitional Jurisprudence: the role of law in political transformation', *Yale Law Journal*, vol. 106, issue 7, May 1997, pp. 2011–72.

Teubner, G. (ed.) *Global Law Without a State*, Aldershot: Dartmouth, 1997.

Thirlway, H. 'The International Court of Justice' in Evans, M. (ed.) *International Law*, Oxford: Oxford University Press, 2003.

Thomas, J.C. and Tereposky, G.A. 'The Evolving Relationship Between Trade and Environmental Regulation', *Journal of World Trade*, vol. 27, no. 4, 1993, pp. 23–45.

Thomson, E.P. *Whigs and Hunters: the origin of the black act*, London: Penguin, 1990.

Toohey, J. 'A Government of Laws, and Not of Men?' *Public Law Review*, vol. 4, no. 3, 1993, pp. 158–74.

Tripley, D. 'Safe Trade and the WTO', *Amicus Curiae*, issue 28, June 2000.

Tushnet, M.V. 'Critical Legal Studies: a political history', *Yale Law Journal*, vol. 100, 1991, pp. 1515–44.

Twining, W. *Globalisation and Legal Theory*, Evanston, Ill.: Northwestern University Press, 2000.

United Nations, *The United Nations and Human Rights (1945–1995)*, Blue Book Series, vol. VII, New York: UN Publications.

United Nations Development Programme, *Human Development Report*, New York: Oxford University Press, 1995.

Van Doren, C. *Benjamin Franklin*, New York: The Viking Press, 1938.

Van Ness, P. (ed.) *Debating Human Rights: critical essays from the United States and Asia*, London: Routledge, 1999.

Viscio, I. 'The Recent Experience with Capital Flows to Emerging Market Economies', *OECD Economic Outlook*, vol. 65, June 1999, pp. 177–95.

Waltz, S. 'Universalizing Human Rights: the role of small states in the construction of the universal declaration of human rights', *Human Rights Quarterly*, vol. 23, issue 1, February 2001, pp. 44–72.

Ward, C. 'A v Minister for Immigration and Ethnic Affairs: principles of interpretation applicable to legislation adopting treaties', *Federal Law Review*, vol. 26, no. 1, 1998, pp. 207–18.

Waring, M. *Counting for Nothing: what men value and what women are worth*, North Sydney; Wellington, NZ: Allen & Unwin, 1988.

Weber, M. *Wirtschaft und Gesellschaft: Grundriss der verstehenden Soziologie*, Tübingen: Mohr, 1976.

Weeramantry, C. *Armageddon or Brave New World?: reflections on the hostilities in Iraq*, Ratmalana: Vishva Lekha, 2003.

Weerasooria, W. (ed.) *Perspectives on Banking, Finance & Credit Law*, St Leonards, NSW: Prospect Media, 1999.

White, M., 'Sovereigns in Distress: do they need bankruptcy?', *Brookings Paper on Economic Activity*, Spring 2002, pp. 287–320.

Williams, P. *The Alchemy of Race and Rights*, Cambridge, MA: Harvard University Press, 1991.

World Bank, *Global Development Finance 1998*, vol. 1, World Bank, 1998.

World Bank, *2002 World Development Indicators*, available at: www.worldbank.org/data/wdi2002/economy.pdf (accessed 26 February 2004).

Yoo, J.C. 'Globalism and the Constitution: treaties, non self-execution and the original understanding', *Columbia Law Review*, vol. 99, no. 8, December 1999, pp. 1955–2094.

Young, K. 'The Implementation of International Law in the Domestic Laws of Germany and Australia: federal and parliamentary comparisons' *Adelaide Law Review*, vol. 21, no. 2, 1999, pp. 177–208.

Yourow, H.C. *The Margin of Appreciation Doctrine in the Dynamics of European Human Rights Jurisprudence*, London, New York, The Hague: Martinus Nijhoff Publishers, Kluwer Press, 1995.

Zifcak, S. *The New Internationalism: Australia and the United Nations human rights treaty system*, The Australia Institute, Discussion Paper 54, April 2003.

Index